DATE DUE

MR 24 '97			
NV 29 97			
AP 2 0 10			

DEMCO 38-296

Bureaucracy and Self-Government

Interpreting American Politics

Michael Nelson, Series Editor

Brian J. Cook

Bureaucracy and Self-Government

Reconsidering the Role
of Public Administration
in American Politics

The Johns Hopkins
University Press

Baltimore & London

© 1996 The Johns Hopkins University Press
All rights reserved. Published 1996
Printed in the United States of America on recycled
acid-free paper

06 05 04 03 02 01 00 99 98 97 96   5 4 3 2 1

The Johns Hopkins University Press
2715 North Charles Street
Baltimore, Maryland 21218-4319
The Johns Hopkins Press Ltd., London

ISBN 0-8018-5409-1
ISBN 0-8018-5410-5 (pbk.)

Library of Congress Cataloging-in-Publication Data
will be found at the end of this book.

A catalog record for this book is available from the
British Library.

To Meredith and Lauren

The essence of obedience consists in the fact that a person comes to view himself as the instrument for carrying out another person's wishes, and he therefore no longer regards himself as responsible for his actions. STANLEY MILGRAM

Democracy is for friends and citizens, not masters and slaves.
WILSON CAREY MCWILLIAMS

Contents

Series Editor's Foreword

In the view of most Americans, the proper role of public administration in a democracy is that of a tool—"a hammer or a saw," in Herbert Kaufman's famous formulation—to be used by elected officials for the sole purpose of carrying out popularly ordained public policies. But such a narrow, *instrumental* view of administration is naïve, according to Brian J. Cook. Even simple tools are more than instruments; they have *constitutive*, or formative, effects on those who use them. "With a hammer in one's hand," the maxim goes, "the world looks surprisingly like a nail." Or, in Montesquieu's more ominous observation, "At the birth of societies, the rulers establish institutions; and afterwards, the institutions mold the rulers."

Americans' narrowly and naïvely instrumental view of public administration has deep roots in both theory and history, Cook argues. Theoretically, to confront the constitutive influence of unelected bureaucrats would render the deep cultural commitment to popular sovereignty problematic. It also is difficult to reconcile the power of administration with a constitution that devotes separate articles to Congress, the presidency, and the judiciary but scarcely mentions, much less empowers, the bureaucracy.

Historically, Americans have spent more than two centuries establishing and trying to breathe life into their instrumental conception of bureaucracy. The framers of the Constitution were, of necessity, inexperienced at administration—during colonial times, the legislature was their domain and administrators were appointees of the British crown. At the convention, the framers naturally inclined to a view of administration as purely instrumental, rejecting the idea, for example, that department heads, like judges, should serve "during good behavior."

As Cook shows, the instrumental approach to administration has been strengthened by every subsequent wave of bureaucratic reform: Andrew Jackson's spoils system and administrative reorganization, the sharp distinction Woodrow Wilson drew between politics and administration, Franklin D. Roosevelt's alphabet agencies to combat the Depression, and so on. The efforts of President Bill Clinton and Vice President Al Gore to "reinvent government" have been grounded in an image of administration scarcely less naïve than hammers and saws: on the ship of state, suggest David Osborne and Ted Gaebler, the leading theorists of the Clinton-Gore reforms, political officers "steer" and administrators "row."

The history of bureaucratic reform has not been the history of bureaucracy, however. Indeed, administrative power had grown in the face of every effort to domesticate it. The primary reason it has done so is that the tasks of government have grown dramatically more extensive and complex, forcing elected officials both to rely on administrators for advice in policy making and to allow them considerable discretion in policy implementation.

As the gap has grown between instrumental theory and constitutive reality, Cook notes despairingly, the American people have grown increasingly angry at and disenchanted with bureaucracy. Just as, in Richard Fenno's classic statement, modern candidates run *for* Congress by running *against* Congress, so do presidential candidates run for chief executive by running against the executive branch.

Cook has little doubt about what the political system needs to do to resolve its bureaucracy problem: acknowledge that public administration has powerful constitutive effects, and work to make those effects beneficial. He is equally emphatic in his advice to those who teach public administration, namely, strive to develop Aristotle's *phronesis,* or practical wisdom, in their students. "To conjoin knowledge of principles of right with considerations of what is suitable" is no small aspiration for the public administration profession.

Michael Nelson

Preface

Specialists in Soviet politics had a devil of a time in the early 1990s coming to grips with their slide toward irrelevance. The political, economic, social, and cultural system at the core of their scholarly careers had disintegrated in the historical equivalent of a blink of an eye. Their search for new and securely relevant research and teaching specialties looked much like the academic version of a mad scramble. A departmental colleague of mine, of Ukrainian heritage, successfully maneuvered through these dangerous straits by transforming herself into a specialist in Ukrainian politics. What she observed in the midst of that difficult scholarly transition, during a journey to a conference in the western Ukrainian city of L'viv, was quite illuminating.

As striking as what had changed since the crumbling of the Soviet system was what had stayed the same. And what had remained the same most emphatically was the essential character of the old Soviet bureaucracy. Upon arriving in L'viv on a plane from Warsaw, the passengers disembarked to face one-and-a-half hours of tortuous passport control. Two officials were available for processing 150 people. No information was offered regarding where the proper forms could be found or how they should be filled out. Nor did it seem absurd to these two officials that all these people, with all their luggage, were to get through a set of double doors, one side of which was closed and locked, to reach them. The bus trip from the airport to the hotel was just as bad, turning into a three-hour nightmare of official processing, bargaining about routes and stops, and unplanned side trips.

Confirmed were my colleague's long-held suspicions that the most notable features of the old Soviet bureaucratic system, often perceived as the result of incompetence and bureaucratic pathology, were intentional. They served to subjugate and demean citizens and visitors, forcing them into submission and dependence. The bureaucrats were the masters, and all others who entered their sphere of officialdom were subjects to be controlled.

For the better part of the twentieth century, Western democracies, and the United States in particular, have expended tremendous effort to avoid the totalitarian bureaucratic nightmare. My neighbors in Worcester may insist, only half-jokingly, that a visit to the Massachusetts Registry of Motor Vehicles for new license plates is not much different from a trip to L'viv. In truth, however, Americans have been wildly successful at keeping public or "state" bureaucracy under control. Formal and informal restraints abound, and American political culture is suffused with messages reminding public administrators of their proper place: the people are the masters, and bureaucrats are, quite literally, the servants.

Despite this triumph, the American people are at best ambivalent and apprehensive about public bureaucracy, reflecting a tradition that reaches to the very taproot of American political culture. At worst, evidence from recent public opinion polls and popular culture outlets suggests that segments of the public have become truly antigovernment. They are angered by the behavior of the federal government in particular, including federal administrative officials. For these citizens, the threats that officialdom poses to the American way of life are evident on a daily basis.

Michael Sandel has observed that all this anger and apprehension directed toward government signals "the fear that we are losing control of the forces that govern our lives" (McWilliams 1995, 197). This sense of loss of control, I would argue, reflects in part the loss of genuine aspirations to self-government. Public bureaucracy is implicated in this loss to the extent that, in the eyes of many Americans, it is not subject to citizen control. Many citizens may sense that, quite the opposite, they are subject to the control of bureaucrats, who answer only to politically powerful groups or to other bureaucrats. To them, public bureaucracy is deeply and permanently involved in structuring relations between groups of citizens and in shaping public purposes. Thus, public bureaucracy, when seen as master rather than servant, represents the central impediment to the full realization of popular self-rule.

Moreover, this range of citizen reaction to government bureaucracy, from ambivalence to angry rejection, indicates that the idea of public administration and its status as a political institution are in extreme flux.

The time is ripe, then, for a thorough reconsideration of the role of public administration in American government and politics. In my attempt at such a reconsideration, I tapped into several intellectual movements in the study of government and politics in the United States.

The first of these movements has emerged from the conclusion reached by a considerable number of political scientists that their discipline has become nearly ahistorical. To counteract this, they have sought to stress in their work the importance of historical context in explaining currently prominent features of the American political landscape. In doing so, they have closely investigated the possibility that the basis for many current problems and controversies can be found in the major ideas and forces that have shaped American political development.

Scholars leading the second movement have raised serious questions about the capacity of liberal democratic regimes to sustain themselves in their current form. They have tackled anew the core question of what constitutes a good society. In the process, they have returned to the early intellectual foundations of a political science oriented toward finding the combination of elements that could produce more capable, more resilient democratic polities.

Finally, a third movement has engaged in a searching reappraisal of the status of public administration in the American constitutional system. Spurred by increasingly strident assaults on public bureaucracy, specialists in public administration have been in the vanguard of this endeavor. They have produced scholarship of considerable intellectual richness and originality, the conclusions of which have, however, not been embraced by all.

Drawing upon all three of these intellectual currents, I argue that public bureaucracy is deeply and permanently involved in structuring relations between groups of citizens and in shaping public purposes. This is an inevitable fact of life in a modern liberal democratic regime. It will always have both positive and negative consequences, but which predominates will be a function of how well citizens and political leaders understand and deal with the basic fact.

Conceptions of public administration and its place in the American constitutional system, it turns out, have been a important motif in the public discourse and political action that have propelled American political development. Unfortunately, the rhetoric and ideology that have emerged, and the public expectations about popular control of bureaucracy that have accumulated across time as a result, have increasingly deviated from the basic fact of public administration's formative role in the regime. The consequence has actually been less popular influence on bureaucracy. Worse, it has produced untoward limitations on the capacity of public administration to contribute, within its proper sphere, to the maintenance and enhancement of American self-government.

I present my argument in the form of an extended essay, or perhaps more accurately, in the form of a proposition or hypothesis. My principal concerns are the development of ideas about public administration across the course of American political development, the discontent with government and public bureaucracy that has arisen, and how past ideas and current theory can contribute to an appropriate response. The conceptual core of my argument is the distinction between the instrumental and constitutive qualities of political institutions, including public administration.

I begin by establishing the contemporary context of the problem and proceed then to explore the differences between instrumental and constitutive reasoning. All of this unfolds in chapter 1. I try to show in particular how the two kinds of reason can, considered separately and together, contribute to our understanding of politics and political institutions, including public administration.

I apply this conceptual frame in an analysis of the ideas about public administration that were given voice in public debates that epitomized the political struggles of major eras in the development of the United States. In chapter 2, for example, I examine in detail the original debates sparked by Congress's creation of the first executive departments and the question of the president's power to remove from office department heads and other executive officers. I conclude that the character of this debate—the depth of the insights and the crystallization of distinctive conceptions of administration's place under the Constitution—as well as the outcome, set the principal boundaries for most of the subsequent confrontations over the status of administrative power in the constitutional system. The seeds of the divergence between public belief and administrative reality were planted there.

In chapters 3, 4, and 5, I follow the progression of that divergence, manifested as an increasingly narrow and intense commitment to a strictly instrumental conception of public administration in American public affairs. I examine, in particular, the confrontation between Andrew Jackson and Senate Whigs over the president's removal power, the debates spawned by civil service reform and regulation of interstate commerce, the efforts of the progressives to redefine executive power, and the New Deal struggle over executive reorganization.

In the final two chapters, I consider the prospects for rejuvenating the idea of public administration in American politics. I begin by considering the implications of a predominantly instrumental conception of public administration in American politics. This is prelude to an appraisal of the benefits of resuscitating and invigorating the constitutive dimension of public administration and to a delineation of what needs to be considered, and accomplished, to realize those benefits. I conclude by renewing the call for a constitutional theory of public administration. I discuss the basic principles, centered on fostering responsible administrative discretion, on which such a theory might be established.

No one should expect, of course, that a precise delineation of the scope and meaning of public administration in American government will ever be realized. It will remain forever subject to political contention and debate. Understanding systemic and institutional fundamentals and their implications can, however, inform the debate. Hence, the theory building I advocate is crucial intellectual work if we are ever again to see a time when thoughtful citizens, and men and women in public life, regard public administration as a vital part of a distinctively American capacity for self-government.

Acknowledgments

I have many people to thank, and much to be thankful for, as I reach a new milestone with the publication of this book. Sid Milkis of Brandeis University regarded my ideas, and the scholarly endeavor I envisioned, with respect and seriousness from the very beginning. He provided superb guidance on early chapter drafts, and his own work stood as a model of scholarly craftsmanship while providing the foundation for key portions of my analysis. Steve Elkin of the University of Maryland remains the central source of intellectual substance for much of my work. He read parts of the manuscript at various stages of development, offering strategic direction and helping me polish various dimensions of the argument.

Larry Terry, Rick Green, Martha Derthick, Theodore Lowi, Drew McCoy, and the anonymous reader for the Johns Hopkins University Press read all or part of the manuscript and provided helpful criticism that improved the final product. They also offered words of support that increased my confidence that I indeed have said something worth saying. Series editor Michael Nelson provided reasoned advice and oversight and enthusiastic support for the project from the very beginning. I hope in the end that I met his expectations. Henry Tom, executive editor for Johns Hopkins University Press, proved to be a pillar of patience and flexibility when I missed several deadlines. He also made easy the path through final review, approval, and production. Anne Whitmore edited the manuscript. She rescued me from many of the worst idiosyncrasies in my writing style. I thank her for her skill, her hard work, and her generous encouragement.

Clark University Librarian Sue Baughman and reference librarians Mary Hartman and Ed McDermott furnished me with a spare yet cozy and quiet space to work, friendly greetings on oh so many 8:00 a.m. arrivals in the library, and expert, efficient service in finding vital material.

My thanks also to the many other public administration scholars and political scientists from whom I have learned so much. They just keep generating new and exciting ideas, leaving me busy and content to follow in their wake.

My warmest and most affectionate thanks I reserve for my wife, Ruth, and my daughters, Meredith and Lauren. Their unqualified love, support, concern, and curiosity granted me the power and inspiration to keep going and provided me refuge from the pressures of trying to complete a book manuscript and chair a political science department at the same time. They know there will be other projects to follow, but we will also take time to relax, reflect, and have some fun.

Bureaucracy and Self-Government

1

Public Administration as Instrument and Institution

During the 1995 debate on the budget for federal regulatory programs, Representative Thomas Delay, a Republican from Texas,
called the U.S. Environmental Protection Agency "the Gestapo of government." He characterized the agency as "one of the major claw hooks"
clutching at American business and the American people (Associated
Press 1995, A4). If Mr. Delay's rhetoric seems excessive, perhaps he
would claim in his own defense that revolutionary times require blunt
speech about the administration of government. After all, Thomas Jefferson included in the Declaration of Independence the accusation that
George III had "erected a multitude of new offices, and sent hither
swarms of officers to harass our people and eat out their substance."

As this similarity of rhetoric suggests, the administration of government is a prime target for forces agitating for change in the American
polity. Indeed, the question of how the Republic can best administer its affairs has been at the center of nearly every political conflict that has
marked a new stage in the nation's development. Yet this question of administration is now as critical as it has ever been, because the searching
examination and spirited debate about the meaning of American self-
government now under way, and the crescendo of proposals for administrative reform or dissolution following in its train, seem to have left the
American people as ambivalent and confused as *they* have ever been about
the place that public administration should occupy in the politics of the
nation. The situation requires a conceptual and factual reconnoitering.

It is currently the view of some elected officials, political commentators, and citizens that government agencies and the officials who manage them exert considerable influence on people's lives but that these officials are often poorly controlled and unresponsive. To some, the actions of government bureaucrats may even pose an imminent threat to life and liberty (see Zinsmeister 1995b, 16). The bulk of opinion data indicates, however, that although the public is dubious about government performance generally, citizens are considerably more positive when it comes to specifics.

For more than twenty years, majorities of people surveyed have expressed a lack of confidence in government, especially the federal government ("Opinion Roundup" 1987; Public Opinion and Demographic Report 1993, 89–90; Flanigan and Zingale 1994, 8–11; Roper 1994, 3). More pertinent to the question of administration, fairly large majorities have come to conclude over the past two decades that the federal government is wasteful and inefficient ("Opinion Roundup" 1987, 27; Public Opinion and Demographic Report 1993, 90; Zinsmeister 1995a, 16). By a more recent assessment, only 43 percent held a high or fairly good opinion of federal agency officials, ranking them, among professionals, below even lawyers—but above members of Congress and politicians generally (Roper 1994, 5). In contrast, Charles Goodsell concludes from his review of survey data that clients of public bureaucracy "are satisfied most of the time with what happens to them, and often very satisfied. Bureaucrats are seen as usually helpful, honest, responsive, adaptable, efficient, dependable, fair, friendly, respectful, considerate, courteous. This is true on all levels of government and even in difficult, low reputation fields such as law enforcement, public welfare, and the Postal Service" (Goodsell 1994, 46).

George and David Frederickson explain the contradiction between general opinion survey results and specific performance assessments as the result of the "paradox of distance" and the "lack of role differentiation." In the paradox of distance, "people trust and even revere those government officials who are near at hand," while they "believe that government officials who are far away are lazy, incompetent, and probably dishonest" (Frederickson and Frederickson 1995, 167). Lack of role differentiation refers to the public's tendency "not to distinguish between persons elected to legislative bodies, persons elected as executives, persons politically appointed, and permanent civil servants" (165). Because of this lack of differentiation, inept and corrupt behavior by elected and appointed officials taints the public's perceptions of the competence and integrity of all officials.

I would argue, however, that the incongruity between the general and the specific in public perceptions of government and public administration goes to the heart of the current debate about defining the nature of American self-government and the contributions that regulation and bureaucratic administration make to that definition. The paradox of distance implies that public perceptions of government administration generated by a distant, broad, and general perspective are more abstract, less real, while perceptions created through close, narrow, and specific interactions are more concrete and grounded in reality. But both perspectives, and the perceptions they generate, are equally valid and real. It is only the latter perspective that matches public expectations about the role of public administration in American public life, however. Thus, when government bureaucrats function as the instrumentalities of individual welfare, serving people's wants and needs, as is usually the case in close, specific, client-oriented encounters, public administration wins positive public judgments. When viewing administrative agencies from a broad, general, distant perspective, however, people more readily see the impact they have on public policy, especially on the general pattern of interactions among citizens. That reality violates basic expectations, so public reactions are then almost wholly negative.

These expectations for a wholly instrumental, service-oriented public administration have been built up over the long American struggle with one of the most enduring dilemmas in liberal democratic politics and government: how can a long-range, stable, even permanent exercise of governmental authority be reconciled with a regime of popular sovereignty? The answer that has dominated public thinking and political rhetoric in the United States is that public agencies are best understood, and treated, as subordinate instruments or servants of the public will. But as a broad, distant perspective on government administration reveals to many citizens, the picture is much more subtle and complex than this. Administrative agencies, in their multiple and varied forms, are engaged in more than achieving goals already designated for them. They shape public purposes and order the relations among important groups of citizens in American society in intricate and far-reaching ways.

In the public experience if not in the expectations of many American citizens, then, public administrators and their organizations not only help to serve the goals, wants, and needs of the people; they also help to determine those goals, wants, and needs, in complex and sometimes worrisome ways. This is the fundamental reality that must be examined and understood if the nation is to profitably reassess the place of public bureaucracy in its political and governmental life. That reassessment can best begin with a consideration of distinctive kinds of reasoning, and such a consideration can in turn serve as an effective device for developing in more detail a multidimensional understanding of political institutions, and of public administration in particular.

Instrumental and Constitutive Reasoning

Consider a common household tool—the claw hammer. It may be used to drive a nail but also to prop open a window or smash open a piggy bank. In every one of these cases, nevertheless, the hammer is merely the means to an end designated by the user. Another way of stating this is to say that the hammer has no *intrinsic* significance. It has no "essential nature," because its identity is determined by its use. All tools or instruments—the power drill, the automobile, the computer—are similar means, simple or complex, for achieving some purpose defined externally to them by some human user. They do not define ends and are not ends themselves.

This way of speaking and thinking about the world and its objects is *instrumental*, or *means-end*, rationality. It is also called economic rationality, or *economizing*, because it is the epistomological foundation of economics, and of the social institution called the market economy, in which everything in society is conceived of as the means to an ultimate end: human want satisfaction (Diesing 1962, ch. 2; Elkin 1985, 253–56). Instrumentalism is a particularly powerful form of reason, and in many ways it is the defining form of rationality in Western culture, underlying as it does the market economy's advancing reach. "The increasing scope of the economy forces people to make an increasing number of allocation decisions, in which means are allocated to alternative ends. Hence people come to think of decisions in terms of means and ends; they come to believe ... that all practical questions are questions of means and ends" (Diesing 1962, 36).

The reach of instrumentalism, or economizing, has extended, quite easily in fact, to policy making and political institutions. Before appraising that, however, it is important to see that instrumentalism is not the only form of reason. "The efficient achievement of predetermined goals is a special kind of effectiveness. If there are other kinds of value besides goal values then there are presumably also other kinds of effectiveness or rationality" (Diesing 1962, 3). So, consider again the hammer, and the adage that "with a hammer in one's hand, the world looks surprisingly like a nail." Informally codified as the Law of the Hammer (Stone 1988, 144), this apothegm expresses the idea that a tool, or more expansively a technology, can have a "profoundly formative influence" (Tribe 1973, 652).

Most people, adults anyway, are able to control the influence that their use of a simple tool has on their psyche and world view. This may be less true for more complex technologies. Think of the many stories in the popular press about children, and even some adults, whose lives have come to be defined by the games and other activities available on their personal computers. The choice and use of even a simple tool, and certainly of more sophisticated technologies, can therefore have at least some perceptible impact on the end toward which one is using it. "For virtually every human action . . . is at once both operational (or 'instrumental') *and* self-forming (or 'constitutive') (Tribe 1973, 635, emphasis in original). One can take this a step further and note that the hammer or computer may not only shape the end but may *become* the end. One's purpose in life becomes to hammer or work or play on the computer (to compute). What were once simply tools devoid of meaning except through use become intrinsically significant.

In contrast to instrumental rationality, *constitutive* rationality is reasoning about forms and purposes. Constitutive rationality refers to individuals, or even societies, making sense of the composition of something, reasoning about how to make something into what they wish it to be, or even deciding what it is they desire in the first place. The effects of a public policy and the institutions that undergird it, for instance, can be judged not only on the basis of whether specifically designated objectives are achieved but also against broader standards that members of a society hold for the form or composition of the social fabric. Society's members may consider whether the policy alters the relations between particular classes of citizens in ways that do not accord with the conception of their society that they hold and seek to maintain. Hence, constitutive rationality can inform policy evaluation, because it encompasses value other than that of means meeting ends and therefore is about another kind of effectiveness.

Consider the relatively familiar activity of painting a picture. One can speak of it quite readily in instrumental terms by stating that painting a picture makes one feel good. Painting is the means to an end—personal pleasure. To address why an artist has painted a particular canvas in a particular way becomes difficult for instrumental reasoning, however. The artist may say she has painted the sky in a landscape a particular color or positioned trees in a particular way because that is her preference. It is the means to her preference satisfaction. She may argue that she chose that color or placement of trees to achieve an intended effect. But the question of why that intended effect and not another cannot be answered instrumentally. Instrumental rationality, involving as it does the search for and matching of appropriate means to *given* ends, can say little about how the ends are chosen, except that "the specification of goals, values, or ends must ultimately rest on logically arbitrary . . . expressions of will and desire as opposed to acts of reason and understanding" (Tribe 1973, 636; also see MacIntyre 1981, 84–102; White 1990, 134–37).

However, if one can cite reasons for choosing the end, such as affinity with a moral system, code of ethics, or, in the case of the artist, a particular school or period in landscape art, one is being rational rather than arbitrary. Just as important, in choosing ends and being able to articulate reasons for doing so beyond arbitrary will or preference, one is shaping one's character or identity. Through her painting, the artist gives expression to the kind of landscape artist she is; and with a particular painting, she further shapes, or *constitutes,* herself as a landscape artist. Painting is thus an end in itself—it has intrinsic significance—and it is formative.

These several facets of constitutive rationality apply with equal if not greater force to whole societies. Take the case of war. At the height of the Persian Gulf War in 1991, much of the public discussion centered on the nature of the ultimate goals of the U.S.-led allied forces. Many observers noted that the conduct of the war was itself having a determinative effect on American objectives. Columnist George Will, for example, contended that "American policy is to inflict from the air sufficient attrition on Iraq's defenses to achieve American war aims—*whatever they eventually will be*—without crossing the crucial threshold to intolerable casualties" (Will 1991, emphasis added).

In the aftermath of the war, agreement was widespread, if not unanimous, that the war had in fact exerted a transformative influence on the nation, a consequence that George Bush in particular emphasized. Much the same has been said about nearly every other war, but little attention has been paid to how remarkable such a notion really is. It says in effect that war, which must be regarded as the ultimate instrumentality employed by a nation-state to achieve its goals and protect its interests, cannot be judged solely on the basis of whether goals were in fact successfully achieved and interests successfully protected. It is precisely this noninstrumental dimension of war that Studs Terkel (1984) explored in his oral history of World War II, and it is reflected in the title of his book: *The Good War.* The dark side of this phenomenon is the devastating, long-run, and clearly transformative social impact of the Vietnam War.

Tools and technologies, then, have "the effect of significantly altering the ends—and indeed the basic character—of the individuals [or] societies that choose them" (Tribe 1973, 642). The import of this phenomenon is that "social choices serve not merely to implement 'given' systems of values, but also to define and sometimes to reshape the values—indeed the very identity—of the choosing . . . community" (634; also see Leiss 1990). A society may even seek to define its identity in terms of particular artifacts or technologies. One can think of the cargo cults of Melanesia, or even the United States during the several decades of this century when it appeared that the nation's chief if not sole purpose was to be a nuclear superpower. And it is certainly not unreasonable to speak of war as becoming, for some individuals, groups, or whole societies, an end in itself.

If tools and technologies can at least in part be understood as constitutive of individuals and societies, as contributive to making individuals or societies what they are, then that effect must apply *a fortiori* to the institutions of society. As the example of the Gulf War strongly implies, this is particularly so for the institutions of politics and government, because they are the very building blocks, the basic organizing units, of polities. It is particularly important to recognize that too heavy a reliance on instrumental reasoning and an instrumental understanding of public affairs can leave a nation blind to formative consequences. The added cost of failing to embrace a constitutive understanding of public action, it turns out, is a negated politics, a degenerative political science, and an impaired day-to-day management of public life.

Neutralizing Politics and Administration

Because of the predominance of instrumental reason in contemporary American life, the conception and use of social structures—the market or marketlike arrangements, or public agencies—as problem-solving tools seems altogether sensible. To employ them as means to relatively narrowly specified objectives can be labeled "programmatic" economizing, and it is already ubiquitous. Surely no reader was surprised by the logo accompanying a series of articles on economic incentives for pollution control in the May–June 1992 issue of the *EPA Journal:* an open toolbox.

A grander version of economizing is also prevalent in public affairs and modern theories of democratic politics and constitutional government. In this grander version, political institutions, and politics in general, are the instruments for achieving some ultimate social goal or the vehicles for reaching some ideal social end-state. In Harold Lasswell's well-known formulation (1936), for example, politics involves principally "who gets what, when, where, and why." That is, politics serves to distribute social goods (and bads). In a somewhat different formulation, David Truman (1971) concluded his exhaustive study of group organization and political involvement by arguing that "the total pattern of government over a period of time ... presents a protean complex of crisscrossing relationships that change in strength and direction with alterations in the power and standing of interests, organized and unorganized." In E. E. Schattschneider's influential description (1960), a governmental institution, or government as a whole, is an "arena of conflict," in which relatively advantaged or disadvantaged interests seek, respectively, to limit or expand the scope of conflict, in an effort to advance their chosen ends. The central notion in all these conceptions of politics was perhaps most succinctly put by Arthur Bentley: "We are forcibly reminded that the governing body has no value in itself, except as one aspect of the process, and cannot even be adequately described except in terms of the deep-lying interests which function through it" (Easton 1971, 149).

Whether in the micro or the macro sense, then, politics and political institutions are empty of meaning if not used in some way by segments of society outside of them. They are either instruments to which society gives meaning only when they are employed to achieve some externally defined end or they are mere stages or backdrops upon which a complex calculus, like preference aggregation, is practiced or great political dramas, like interest-group conflict, are played out.

Public administration is particularly susceptible to being conceived of as an instrument. Policy makers and the public at large generally understand regulation and regulatory agencies, for example, as the primary mechanisms for informing, guiding, manipulating, or even coercing citizens to behave in ways that will allow the community as a whole to achieve its objectives. "The boundaries of the 'public administration' problem have leapt far beyond the question of how to effectively organize and run a public institution and now encompass the far more vexing question of how to change some aspect of the behavior of a whole society" (Schultze 1977, 12). The reason for attempting such behavioral change is to reach some grand social goal, be it "prosperity and price stability," or "equitable income distribution" (1).

In fact, most public organizations are not even privileged enough to be seen as engaging in such a grand social endeavor. Instead, they are stuck in a programmatic economizing world, understandable, for example, as a "system of administration viewed as industry structures ... composed of diverse, independent agencies, collaborating in supplying and arranging for the availability of different bundles of collective goods and services.... Once one begins to think in this way, one can imagine the possibility of an education industry, a police industry, a fire-protection industry, a trash and garbage disposal industry, a welfare industry, a health-services industry, and many other public-service industries that would appropriately characterize ... public administration" (Ostrom 1987, 204).

This way of thinking, not only about government agencies, but about all large social and political institutions, is already so prevalent in public consciousness that it has prompted Theodore Lowi to proclaim the existence of a Republic of Service Delivery (1985, 96). "Thus, firmly embedded in the public mind is the relatively new idea that institutions, including government, are to be trusted and accorded legitimacy not in terms of the effort they make or in terms of the amount and character of the representation they provide but in terms of service delivery" (94). It is important not to construe Lowi's Republic of Service Delivery as simply a consequence of economists invading the public realm, although the increasing influence of economic thinking and economic advice in public affairs after World War II is one strand in the story. An instrumental conception of politics and public institutions has a number of deep roots.

First, the cornerstone of this conception is liberalism. As Benjamin Barber argues, "liberals . . . regard political community as an instrumental rather than intrinsic good" (1984, 7). In his extensive dissection of liberal democracy in *Strong Democracy,* Barber repeatedly stresses that it is liberalism that treats political institutions, indeed all of politics, as an instrument for the achievement of largely private wants, and he especially notes the instrumentalism inherent in the "peculiar logic" of social-contract theory (67).

Furthermore, liberalism is, of course, the philosophical anchor for economic thought. Hence instrumentalism, or the "means-ends schema," is a central element in "the value system developed by economic progress" (Diesing 1962, 36). And the effects of economic progress, and thus of liberalism, have been substantial. "One cultural element after another has been absorbed into the ever-widening economy, subjected to the test of economic rationality, rationalized, and turned into a commodity or factor of production. So pervasive has this process been that it now seems that anything can be thought of as a commodity and its value measured by a price, and that all values can be thought of as utilities" (24).

The increasing influence of economists in public affairs may be regarded as a particular effect of the general trend of economic progress. Although the effect of economic progress has not yet been to transform or "rationalize" political institutions into commodities with prices attached, it has had the effect of "neutralizing" them (Diesing 1962, 25); that is, they have increasingly come to be regarded as neutral, interchangeable devices for attaining whatever society deems most important. As Barber states it, "politics is prudence in the service of *homo economicus*—the solitary seeker of material happiness and bodily security" (Barber 1984, 20).

This is especially so for public administration. In particular, the privatization thrust of the past decade and a half is an extension of the logic of economizing, wherein public agencies become interchangeable with private entities in the pursuit of some program objective or, much less often, some grand social goal (see Savas 1987; Kettl 1988, 1993; Salamon 1989; Goodsell 1994, 84–89).

Second, quite distinct but not wholly separate from economic progress is the influence of *democratic* progress. Democracy—as a theory of government and a way of life, at least in the form Barber labels "unitary" (1984, 149)—has the effect of subjugating and instrumentalizing public institutions. Alexis de Tocqueville observed the several dimensions of this characteristic of democracy and considered its consequences throughout *Democracy in America* (1988). Democratic progress can be linked with economic progress in that economic progress provides for greater equality in economic conditions. Democracy, however, is concerned with the equality of *all* social conditions. As a society moves closer to the equality of social conditions, popular pressures increase and the mass of the people press the institutions of government, and the officials that staff them, into service to satisfy society's wants. "Democratization opened up the possibility that citizens might now use government for their own benefit, rather than simply watching government being used for the benefit of others. . . . Once citizens perceived that government could operate in response to their demands, [they] became increasingly willing to support the expansion of government" (Lowi and Ginsberg 1990, 23).

Third, political science has played a small but significant role in promoting an instrumental conception of politics and public institutions by assuming a neutral orientation toward them. Whereas American political science in its original conception scrutinized the practice of government with an eye toward the "maintenance and improvement of the liberal democratic experiment" (Anderson 1990, 195), since the 1950s and the so-called "behavioralist revolution," the discipline has for the most part approached politics and political institutions as phenomena, to be examined with the value-neutral tools of scientific method.

The effect has been to cut loose political institutions from the context of the regime that gives them meaning. They become simply arenas in which individual actors do battle in a civilized form of combat called politics. Conceived thus, the institutions are valueless, as Bentley asserted, and can be pressed into service in the cause of any ideology, of which liberal democracy is only one (again, see Anderson 1990, 195). The consequence of the "revolution" in political science was particularly pronounced with respect to the discipline's treatment of public administration. For a time, political scientists seemed to regard public bureaucracies as nonentities, that is, as having no intrinsic political value worthy of study (see Hill 1992, 33–36). The more general point, however, is that the education of several generations of American public officials in American universities has reinforced the more widespread effect from economic progress: conceptualizing political institutions as instruments, amenable to (instrumentally) rational, objective or value-neutral analysis of their effectiveness in achieving ends defined externally to them.

Finally, quite apart from and in addition to a grounding in liberalism, the Constitution and the mythology that has grown up around it have had their own impact on public thinking about politics and government. The Constitution has come to be regarded as the profound and singular constitutive act of the American people. In his treatise on the constitutional legitimacy of the administrative state, for instance, John Rohr argues that the Constitution has a special "moral vitality," because it is "the great work of the founding period of the Republic" (1986, 8). In turn, the nation's founding and the Constitution it produced are unique because they represent the decisive acts "of the sovereign" (80). Hence, to paraphrase Woodrow Wilson (and the title of Rohr's book), everything that has come after the founding has been about *running* the Constitution, filling in the details, striving to achieve its purposes.

Indeed, nearly every new goal or purpose the American people have defined for themselves over 220 years has been anchored in the Constitution, or at least in constitutional rhetoric. That has proven vital to the survival and stability of the nation, but it has also made everything else that has come after seem merely instrumental in character. The ideal end-state, presumed to be readable between the lines of the Constitution's text, is a perpetually receding horizon. The American people are ceaseless in their pursuit of that horizon, rarely pausing to reflect on how they may have changed in their relationships with one another as citizens during the pursuit or how their perception of what stands on that horizon may have changed as well.

A wholly instrumental conception of American politics and government, and thus of public administration as well, is likely to be not only inadequate but ultimately debilitating. Understanding more fully how constitutive rationality applies to political institutions, and to public bureaucracy specifically, is essential to realizing other possibilities.

Politics: The Shape and Substance of Public Life

The idea that societal institutions, especially political and governmental institutions, can shape the manner in which individuals behave, as well as the ends toward which they strive collectively, is hardly new. The eighteenth-century French philosopher Montesquieu remarked, "At the birth of societies, the rulers establish institutions; and afterwards, the institutions mould the rulers" (Rohr 1986, 5). The American founders were quite cognizant of the formative quality of political institutions. In advocating the peculiar arrangement of republican institutions and practices embodied in the Constitution, Alexander Hamilton, for example, saw not only a greater general prosperity accruing to the American people but also that this "commercial republic" he sought would form a particular kind of citizenry, with attachments to and preferences for particular institutions.

In *The Federalist* No. 10, James Madison offered an especially powerful example of constitutive reasoning in his comparative analysis of democratic and republican government. In one of the most famous passages in the *Federalist* papers, Madison argued that the effect of representation, a distinguishing feature of republican government, "is, on the one hand, to refine and enlarge the public views by passing them through the medium of a chosen body of citizens, whose wisdom may best discern the true interest of their country and whose patriotism and love of justice will be least likely to sacrifice it to temporary or partial considerations." The second half of Madison's point is less well known, but it adds considerable force by virtue of the negative images it conjures up: "On the other hand, the effect may be inverted. Men of factious tempers, of local prejudices, or of sinister designs, may, by intrigue, by corruption, or by other means, first obtain the suffrages, and then betray the interests of the people." In neither case does it make sense to think about the conditions that Madison described only as ends for which representation is the means. Instead, representation is the end as well as the means. It is the state of political existence to which liberal democrats aspire. Moreover, it embodies particular features and imparts certain qualities on, or constitutes, public opinion, depending on whether another condition is present or absent, namely size, as in the extended republic.

Constitutions and constitution making are, not surprisingly then, rich sources of constitutive thinking about politics and government. As Benjamin Barber observes, constitutions make a people by creating the framework that will condition what they know or do not know: "In designing our political institutions we are sculpting our knowledge. In founding a constitution, we are determining the shape and character of our political epistemology" (Barber 1984, 170). Russell Hardin argues that a constitution "regulates a long-term pattern of interactions. It establishes conventions . . . that make it easier for us to cooperate and to coordinate in particular moments" (1989, 101). And in discussing the U.S. Constitution as "stimulator and shaper," Peter Nardulli argues that, "although the Constitution reflects Lockean values, it also has affected their evolution and extension. This effect is clear with respect to the political liberties which are defined in the Constitution but which have also evolved within the constitutional framework." Hence, the "Constitution's significance . . . , is not limited to generating issues that at times dominate American politics. It also shapes how groups define the issues they raise" (1992, 15).

Constitutive reasoning is not restricted to foundings, however, nor are constitutions the only political constructs that exert a formative influence on a polity. The greatest observer of and commentator on the formative effects of social, economic, and political institutions on the American polity, or more precisely on how these institutions have made the American polity what it is, remains Alexis de Tocqueville. *Democracy in America* is a bountiful source of material about how political parties, interest groups, judicial power, and town government go into the mix that is the distinctive regime called the United States. Tocqueville concluded, for example, that "the strength of free peoples resides in the local community. Local institutions are to liberty what primary schools are to science; they put it within the people's reach; they teach the people to appreciate its peaceful enjoyment and accustom them to make use of it. Without local institutions a nation may give itself a free government, but it has not got the spirit of liberty" (1988, 62–63). The Henry Reeve translation is even clearer on the central point: "municipal institutions *constitute* the strength of free nations," that is, they are what we mean by a free nation; they impart the qualities that define a nation as free (Tocqueville 1945, 63, emphasis added).

It is with his brief but penetrating study of the comparative effects of slavery, however, that Tocqueville captured all the subtleties of the constitutiveness of an institution that is at once social, economic, and political.

> On the left bank of the Ohio work is connected with the idea of slavery, but on the right with well-being and progress; on the one side it is degrading, but on the other honorable; on the left bank no white laborers are to be found, for they would be afraid of being like the slaves; for work people must rely on the Negroes; but one will never see a man of leisure on the right bank: the white man's intelligent activity is used for work of every sort. . . .
>
> The American on the left bank scorns not only work itself but also enterprises in which work is necessary to success; living in idle ease, he has the tastes of idle men; money has lost some of its value in his eyes; he is less interested in wealth than in excitement and pleasure and expends in that direction the energy which his neighbor puts to other use; he is passionately fond of hunting and war; he enjoys all the most strenuous forms

of bodily exercise; he is accustomed to the use of weapons and from child-hood has been ready to risk his life in single combat. Slavery therefore not only prevents the white men from making their fortunes but even diverts them from wishing to do so. (Tocqueville 1988, 346–48)

As these commentaries reveal, the constitutiveness of political institu-tions, like constitutive reasoning more generally, can be understood along several dimensions. First, political institutions are constitutive in the sense that they are among the fundamental elements, or constituent parts, of the whole system of government and politics created by a con-stitution—what is commonly called a regime. In other words, they are institutions in the core meaning of a "custom, practice, relationship, or behavioral pattern of importance in the life of a community or society" (*The American Heritage Dictionary*, 3rd ed., 1992, s.v. "institution").

It is simply incomplete thinking, then, to regard the American regime as consisting of the Constitution and the American people, with the in-stitutions of government and the people who populate them merely de-vices or tools for achieving the people's ends. Indeed, a distinctive Amer-ican political regime does not exist absent a peculiar arrangement of institutions and cadre of public officials. From this perspective, the re-publicanism of the Constitution holds that the people, who are the ulti-mate sovereigns, and the institutions and officers of government in their representative and governing capacities, *together* constitute the regime. That is what the Constitution stands for.

Carrying this line of reasoning one step further, one may even con-tend that an identifiable American people could not exist if there were no political institutions to give them a distinctive identity. Or, as Stephen Elkin has put it, political institutions "say who the people are by defining their way of life, by creating a body of activities which helps to define their purposes. We may call this political way of life the 'regime,' and po-litical institutions are fundamental to defining it" (1985, 264).

This second dimension of the constitutiveness of political institutions is their "formative bearing" (Elkin 1987, 104). It has two dimensions of its own (107). For the psychological and educational, or tutelary, compo-nent, the effect is principally on individual attributes and character. The individual citizen comes to define himself, his political identity, and his relationships with others partly through the formative influence of polit-ical institutions. Reflecting on just such an influence exerted by pluralis-tic institutional arrangements, Robert Dahl has written that "structures and consciousness are loosely coupled. . . . Nevertheless, social structures and civic consciousness do influence one another. To what extent, then, must democratic pluralism necessarily weaken civic virtue by fostering egoism and political conflict?" (1982, 138). Thus, concepts common to political science—personal and political efficacy, for example—have no operative meaning without some reference to the manner in which political institutions shape the political identities of citizens.

Dahl's reference to civic virtue further reinforces the tutelary effect of political institutions, because it brings to mind the American Antifederalists, concerned as they were with the promotion of civic virtue, which they saw as achievable through the "educative function" of the "whole organization of the polity" (Storing 1981, 21). This concern reflected the civic republican roots of Antifederalist thought. The focus in civic republicanism is on political deliberation and its "transformational power" (Seidenfeld 1992, 1529), particularly through education. "By informing citizens about others' conceptions of the public interest and by revealing to them how their own conceptions might harm others, the deliberative process can help educate citizens and unmask self-delusions" (1537; also see Barber 1984, chs. 8, 9).

Beyond the individual psychological and educative impacts, however, the formative bearing of political institutions also exerts its influence at a collective level, on the whole polity, providing the citizenry "an organized existence" (Elkin 1985, 262). Political institutions have this effect because they operate like constitutive rules (see Elkin 1987, 108 and sources cited therein). Consider a game, like baseball, with a complex set of rules. To talk of the game of baseball apart from the rules makes no sense. The rules of the game literally *are* the game. Without reference to the rules, all the central actions of the game—pitching, hitting, running bases, fielding, balls, strikes, outs, runs—would appear unconnected and meaningless. But when the rules for the game are codified, as they most assuredly are in baseball, they define the actions that are crucial to the play of the game. Thus, the game itself is created, the players are defined, and the purposes of what they do are also created and defined. Moreover, the actual play of the game gives further meaning and refinement to the rules that make the game.

Similarly, the creation of the basic rules for politics and government in a constitution is simultaneously the creation of the institutional superstructure for the practice of politics and government. The institutions are the expression of the basic rules and thus the central shapers of the actual "play" of the "game" of politics and government. As with the constitutive rules of a game, moreover, by creating political institutions, a polity defines the meaning of citizenship and of what the collectivity is by creating purposes—"political institutions are purpose- or end-creating activities" (Elkin 1985, 262)—and the means to achieve them. It is only in this context, in fact, that the connection between specific institutional or programmatic means and general societal ends makes any sense. One might argue, then, that instrumental reasoning is subordinate to constitutive reasoning when the composition and ongoing activity or life of the society is the object of the reasoning.

The individual psychological and collective components of the formative bearing of political institutions do overlap. The "teaching" function of political institutions is in fact critical to understanding the proper forms of activity and the relations between citizens that take place within those institutions vital to the regime, and to understanding the place of these activities and relations in the way of life of the polity. So, political institutions teach individuals about the nature of the regime of which they are a part and about how that regime may be maintained. "Democratic political institutions must be judged, therefore, at least in part on the extent to which they pose policy questions in civic as opposed to self-interested terms. It is through the deliberative discussions of such questions that citizens develop, discover, and clarify their own understanding of their mutual rights and responsibilities" (Landy, Roberts, and Thomas 1990, 280).

Political institutions are not means to externally defined ends. The whole notion that the goals a community of individuals seeks to achieve could somehow come from outside that community and the structures that order its active public life is a fiction. Political institutions embody both political means and political ends. They help to create, to express, and to realize a nation's public purposes, principally by defining the types of relations and forms of activity occurring among the individuals who regard themselves as citizens of that political community.

Different institutions define different relationships and forms of activity. What people come to expect of themselves and others in one institutional context may, however, carry over to other contexts (Elkin 1987, 109), tying together different forms of political activity and understandings of citizenship in that overall political way of life, or regime. The intrinsic significance of a political institution thus is tied to the particularities of a given regime. "Unlike economizing, which promises to be a universal abstract science, political rationality is in great part particularistic, because it focuses on a *specific* regime" (Elkin 1985, 268, emphasis in original). This emphasizes further the appropriateness of questioning a "neutral" political science.

Political institutions are therefore central to the ongoing process of constituting a regime. They give operative meaning and formal organization to a political way of life identifiable in the aspirations of members of a polity. A political community that aspires to be just, for example, cannot conceive of the value of justice separate from its system of justice—

its courts, law enforcement, and legal representation. Moreover, across time, judicial and law enforcement institutions continue to shape the meaning of justice in a regime, that is, how citizens relate to one another in just or unjust ways.

An ongoing refinement of purposes, of the character of institutions, and thus of the meaning, purposes, and basic rules of the regime, emerges from actual political practice. This is readily evident in the more than 200 years of American political development. The institutions established by the founders in accord with their aspirations to republican government, especially the principle of popular sovereignty, spawned and have subsequently been shaped by increasingly populist aspirations (also see Herson 1984, chs. 10, 11; Adams et al. 1990, 220–27). Indeed, this interactive quality of political institutions provides citizens their primary opportunity to rethink and reform the purposes of the regime and, by definition, the principal political institutions.

Public Administration as a Political Institution

Do all such characteristics of the constitutiveness of political institutions apply to public administration as manifested in public bureaucracies? Are administrative agencies not simply the basic organizational tools modern societies use to educate children, protect life, limb, and property, and stabilize currency markets, among many other things? Isn't that what is meant by the idea of a public or civil *service*?

The Political Effects of Administration

Among the institutions to receive his special scrutiny Tocqueville included public administration. Perhaps his most widely known observations in this regard pertain to the extremely decentralized character of public administration in the United States, a degree of decentralization that Tocqueville concluded made for an extremely unstable, underdeveloped, even "stateless" administration (Stillman 1991, chs. 1, 2). Yet Tocqueville's observations about public administration are also quite revealing about the formative effects administrative arrangements can exert on individuals, their interactions, and the character of the whole society. Tocqueville noted, for example, "A vast number of people make a good thing for themselves out of the [fragmented] power of the community and are interested in administration for selfish reasons" (Tocqueville 1988, 69). He surmised that "peoples who make use of elections to fill the secondary grades in their government are bound greatly to rely on judicial punishments as a weapon of administration" (75). It is in his comparative analysis of centralized and decentralized administration, however, that Tocqueville offers his most important conclusions about public administration as a shaper of individuals and societies.

He admitted that a certain degree of administrative centralization was desirable, to keep "the spirit of innovation in bounds" (Tocqueville 1988, 130). Stability was thus maintained, avoiding the abrupt substitution of one set of administrative principles with another. Nevertheless, Tocqueville contended that "administrative centralization only serves to enervate the peoples that submit to it, because it constantly tends to diminish their civic spirit" (88). The administrative consequences of extreme decentralization could also be undesirable: "Useful undertakings requiring continuous care and rigorous exactitude for success are often abandoned in the end, for . . . the people proceed by sudden impulses and momentary exertions" (92). Ultimately, Tocqueville admired principally the "political effects" of administrative decentralization, which were to teach the "multitude" to use liberty well in "small matters," thus preserving it in "great matters" as well (96). The result was that the great potential for despotism in democracy, by the majority, could be broken, or at least diminished.

Building and Teaching Society

Although later observers have largely not drawn from Tocqueville's remarkable insights, the twentieth century has seen several bursts of intellectual energy and attention directed at public administration and questions about its character and its status in a democratic polity. The cumulative result has been to illuminate aspects of administration's constitutiveness along both the individual and collective dimensions.

Writing as one of the premiere voices for progressivism, Herbert Croly characterized the "democratic administrator" as "more of a probation officer than a policeman," and "more of a counsellor and instructor than a probation officer. He is the agent not of a merely disciplinary policy, but one of social enlightenment and upbuilding" (Croly 1914, 354). Croly's characterization is somewhat ambiguous, reflecting the acute struggle of the Progressives to reconcile competing conceptions of administration (a point to which I return in chapter 4). His statement can, however, be read as capturing both an educative and a reconstitutive role for public administration.

Slightly more than twenty years later, Marshall Dimock offered a clearer statement, calling public administration "more than a lifeless pawn. It plans, it contrives, it philosophizes, it educates, it builds for the community as a whole" (Dimock 1936; and quoted in Denhardt 1993, 12). Similarly, Norton Long rejected "the view of bureaucracy as instrument and Caliban" (Long 1952, 810) and promoted public bureaucracy as critical to the "working" constitution precisely because it was not a neutral instrument but a representative institution that also gave added meaning to—helped constitute—the "division of power in government" (817).

With the work of Arthur Maass and Lawrence Radway (1959) as prelude, scholars of the New Public Administration movement (e.g., Marini 1971) pushed hard for the realization that public agencies could not simply function as helots to the powerful. Instead, agencies and administrators could and should work to alter the structure and distribution of power relations in American society. Similarly, beginning with Paul Appleby (1952), the now vast literature on administrative ethics (see Meier 1993, 193–98) at least implies that the actions of administrative officials have substantial effects—formative and transformative—on society and therefore need to be guided by strong ethical principles.

Finally, the late 1980s and early 1990s brought a broad, rich, and sustained scholarly examination of the nature of public administration and its role in a liberal democracy. In his eloquent defense of the legitimacy of the modern administrative state, John Rohr has argued that it "offers millions of employees the opportunity to fulfill the aspirations of citizenship—to rule and be ruled. Of these millions, thousands have the opportunity to instruct millions of nongovernmental employees in the ways of citizenship. Thus the administrative state has the capacity to increase and multiply public spiritedness and thereby infuse the regime with active citizens" (1986, 53). Richard Green, Lawrence Keller, and Gary Wamsley argue that "public administration constantly presents people with political and moral choices that define and redefine good living. It contributes to the formation of habits and character" (Green, Keller, and Wamsley 1993, 519). And Robert Denhardt contends that at "the root of every act of every public official, whether in the development or execution of public policy, there is a moral or ethical question" (1993, 263). This echoes Stephen Elkin's conclusion that political institutions are constitutive because they "concern the morality of a people—or, perhaps it is best to say, their mores" (1987, 109).

Constitutional Design, Societal Values, and Public Goals

What one can read out of this whole body of scholarship, particularly that of the past two decades, is a fairly consistent message: like legislatures, courts, political parties, and other political institutions that are created by constitutions or emerge within constitutional frameworks, public administration exhibits constitutive qualities. For at least three reasons, administration must be considered a fundamental political institution in its own right.

Public administration is, first of all, a unique, constitutionally recognized component of the regime. It singularly fulfills critical elements of constitutional design (Long 1952; Rohr 1986; Cook 1992; but see Lowi 1993b). Most apparent, it is responsible for organizing, if not always directly undertaking and completing, public tasks, particularly the collective endeavors, whether modest or great in scope, without which no liberal democracy could long survive and prosper. As a result, some public bureaucracies perform fundamental social functions, and they work to conserve the basic values associated with those functions (Terry 1990). Second, public administration as a whole gives concrete, institutional embodiment to values critical to defining and sustaining the regime. These values include stability and continuity in public policy, a reliance at least in part on special knowledge and expertise in public decision making, and perhaps most important, the need to balance reasoning about means and ends, that is, practical reason. Third, even when tightly controlled in their decisions and actions, public agencies independently influence the ideas and interactions of citizens by, among other actions, shaping the public goals they, the agencies, will be instructed to pursue. They thereby give form to public life in both efficacious and deleterious ways.

It is relatively easy—too easy—to personify these multidimensional political qualities of administration. The likes of Gifford Pinchot, Robert Moses, David Lilienthal, and Hyman Rickover, in their capacities as administrators and by virtue of their personal talents and energies, unquestionably shaped the character and direction of the nation for both good and ill. It is much more difficult to demonstrate the independent effect of public administration on regimes from an institutional perspective, because the work of officials and their agencies is so tightly intertwined with the actions of legislatures, elected executives, and organized interests. This is in part what gives credence to the iron triangle, or policy network, concept. More important, it is precisely the point about public administration's political nature, and thus its constitutiveness. Considering two brief examples, each of which captures in its own distinctive way something of the integral and formative impact of public bureaucracies on the regime, may be instructive.

The U.S. Customs Service is one of the oldest federal agencies. In fact, its establishment in July 1789 predated the founding of its current organizational superior, the Treasury Department. In the early years of the Republic, the Customs Service was "perhaps the most important body of federal agents dealing directly with citizens" (White 1951, 148), and its impact on the formative development of the constitutional regime was substantial.

Collectors of customs operated "under instructions that were designed to reduce discretion to a minimum, but still with a large degree of autonomy" (White 1951, 157). Under these conditions, customs officers shaped commercial relations and business-government interactions in the early republic by striking "a delicate balance between convenience to . . . importers and protection of the revenue" (148). Customs collectors thus gave concrete meaning to the founders' idea of a commercial republic. The operation of the Customs Service under both the Federalists and the Jeffersonians also substantially shaped early public images of civil service and the trustworthiness of executive power in a republic (White 1948, 515; 1951, 157, 413–14). In their interactions with administrative and political superiors, customs officers contributed mightily to the conceptions of administrative discretion and control that developed in the early republic (White 1948, 204–5). During Jefferson's embargo against trade with Britain and France in 1807–8, the performance of customs officers gave credibility to the increased concentration of executive power Jefferson had initiated (White 1951, chs. 29–30). Finally, the Customs Service influenced the lives of many Americans, not the least of whom were the people employed in the customs houses. Nathaniel Hawthorne wrote personally and vividly about this influence in the "Introductory" to *The Scarlet Letter.*

A second case in point is the National Park Service. In 1916, when it was established, Americans made approximately 168,000 visits to the magnificent western jewels of the national park system: Glacier, Mount Ranier, Rocky Mountain, Sequoia, Yellowstone, and Yosemite. In 1994, these same six parks hosted nearly 15 million visits. The National Park Service has had a profound effect on how visitors to any of its many sites think of recreation, how they see their relationship to the natural world, and how they conceive of the meaning of collective responsibility to future generations, all of which come bundled with a distinctive image of the Park Service that is "part naturalist, part policeman, part resource manager, and even part educator" (Foresta 1984, 1).

Through fire management policy, for example, the National Park Service has shaped, more than once, the very physical experience of natural, scenic areas. During the California gold rush, before the establishment of the first western parks, those who had crossed the Sierra Nevada reported seeing "wide-spaced columns of mature trees that grew on the lower western slope in gigantic magnificence. The ground was a grass parkland, in springtime carpeted with wildflowers." By virtue of an absolute fire suppression policy that lasted into the late 1960s, however, the areas under park service supervision had become impenetrable thickets where "wildflowers [were] sparse, and to some at least the vegetative tangle [was] depressing, not uplifting" (Leopold et al. 1963, and quoted in van Wagtendonk 1991, 12). After implementation of a prescribed natural fire management policy, visitors could again see such areas as Yosemite and Sequoia in their more "natural" states. Moreover, the devastating fires in the greater Yellowstone area in 1988 and the scrutiny of park service fire policy that followed influenced how Americans thought and talked about nature and human attempts to manage wilderness and wild forces.

Certainly, both the U.S. Customs Service and the National Park Service have been buffeted by powerful social, economic, and political forces. We have, after all, intended them to be instruments for achieving some of our collective objectives in the vital areas of international commerce and natural resource preservation, so they are purposely vulnerable to influence and control. But these agencies have also been critical to developing and refining our understanding of commerce and natural resource preservation and what we want to achieve as a polity in these areas. In subtle yet deep and lasting ways, they have had an influence on the character of the regime.

Conclusion

Comprehending public organizations like the Customs Service and the National Park Service, and public administration more generally, from a constitutive perspective opens up a whole world of possibilities closed off by an exclusively instrumental conception of public action. These possibilities include the improvement of the conduct of the public's business, or "public management" in contemporary lexicon. The possibilities also include the resuscitation of the American people's understanding of and energetic engagement in self-government.

What has yet been missing from the substantial scholarly treatment of public administration, however, is an explicit recognition and systematic assessment of its constitutiveness in *combination* with its obvious instrumental qualities. It is an appreciation for the combination of the instrumental and the constitutive that lies at the heart of a political understanding of public administration.

Again, this is the basic fact on which progress in any debate about public bureaucracy's role in the American system of self-government must be built. That basic fact, moreover, can only be fully appraised in historical context, for the way our effort to comprehend and address public administration has unfolded has had a profound effect on the authority, competence, and legitimacy it has come to possess in the regime. That effort to comprehend has encompassed how much emphasis to place on an instrumental conception of public administration versus a constitutive conception and how well political leaders have grappled with the tensions between the instrumental and constitutive qualities that administration embodies. The outcome has, to a considerable extent, determined whether public administration now essentially undermines or gives sustenance to aspirations to self-government.

2

Preserving the Chain of Dependence

The Ideas of the Founding and Early Republic

On May 19, 1789, Representative Elias Boudinot of New Jersey introduced a resolution on the floor of the U.S. House of Representatives to establish a department of finance. "If we take up the present Constitution," he declared, "we shall find it contemplates departments of an Executive nature in aid of the President; it then remains for us to carry this intention into effect, which I take it will be best done by settling principles for organizing them in this place" (*Annals of the Congress of the United States* 1834, 368; hereafter cited as *Annals*).

In the style of the early Congress, in which much of the legislative drafting occurred first on the floor of the House and Senate, several representatives offered amendments to improve and expand upon Boudinot's resolution. Egbert Benson of New York called for the creation of the three most necessary departments: Foreign Affairs (later State), Treasury, and War. James Madison, representing Virginia, "took charge of the question" (Elkins and McKitrick 1993, 51) and proposed just such an all-encompassing substitute. He then moved to begin work first on the Department of Foreign Affairs, to be headed by a secretary, to be "appointed by the President, by and with the advice and consent of the Senate, and to be removable by the President" (*Annals,* 370–71).

When the House, in Committee of the Whole, began debate on the mode of appointment for the secretary of foreign affairs, William Smith of South Carolina objected to Madison's language, particularly the provision that the President alone would have the power of removal. On the heels of Smith's objection, Richard Bland Lee of Virginia argued that the secretary should be considered an inferior officer. The president was the "great and responsible officer of the Government," (*Annals* 372) and the secretary was only to aid him in performing his executive duties. Smith replied, "This officer is at the head of a department, and one of those who are to advise the President; the inferior officers mentioned in the Constitution are clerks and other subordinates" (372). Smith contended that as the head of a department, a position mentioned explicitly in the Constitution, the secretary could only be removed by constitutionally prescribed means, namely impeachment and conviction.

This brief exchange held the seeds of two competing perspectives on the status of administration under the Constitution. The influence of each view waxed and waned during the six days of debate on the removal power. The first perspective conceived of public administrators, both heads of departments and "inferior officers," as pure agents or instruments of the "political" branches. The function of public administrators in this view was to aid the president and Congress in the performance of their constitutional duties and to undertake any other tasks assigned to them. The second view conceived of department heads, at least, as constitutional officers in their own right and not just as legal or political subordinates. This competing perspective regarded public administration as a distinctive, semiautonomous institution in the constitutional scheme.

The two understandings of administration articulated during the debate on the president's removal power, which led up to what has come to be called the Decision of 1789, reflect to a remarkable extent the instrumental and constitutive conceptions of administration. Through the efforts of a small band of representatives in the First Congress, the two conceptions were contemplated together in a single time and place and under real decision conditions requiring tests of constitutional principles in the crucible of politics and the necessities of governing. This presented the new nation's political leaders the opportunity to sort out the two perspectives and seriously to consider situating and building a public administration within the Constitution's framework in a manner that embraced both qualities.

Notwithstanding its somewhat ambiguous expression in the debate, the instrumental conception decisively prevailed. The Decision of 1789 did not forever foreclose public discussion and contemplation of the constitutive qualities of public administration. However, the character of the decision, and its long-run impact on subsequent generations of political leaders, diminished the possibility that administration, with both its constitutive and its instrumental character, would be fully recognized and consciously embraced as an important component of American politics and government.

In this chapter, I commence my exploration of the origins of, and the development of political responses to, the dilemma public administration poses for American constitutional democracy. My method is to describe how political leaders have thought and spoken about public administration in the practice of politics, through their own words or the interpretations of scholars and commentators. I use as guideposts the most familiar and widely studied stages of American political development and train my attention especially on the responses of political leaders to the instrumental and constitutive qualities embodied in public administration and the consequences of those responses for its public standing and its capacity to contribute to a regime predicated on the idea of self-government.

It is clear from the evidence and scholarly assessments that public administration has had a prominent role, as both means and object, in every major effort at political and governmental reform associated with the political development of the United States. This is not surprising, since the Constitution itself was intended, in part, as a solution to the abundant problems of national administration encountered under the Articles of Confederation. Despite the conscious efforts of founding statesmen, particularly Alexander Hamilton, the design of the Constitution and the political philosophies and traditions from which it emerged left insufficiently reconciled with the principle of self-government an activity and assemblage of organizations that, although primarily understandable as instruments of the people's will, clearly would help define who the people were and what their aspirations would be.

Subsequent reformers, including the Jacksonians, the Progressives, the New Dealers, and the activists of the 1960s and 1970s, animated by the pressure of democratic expansion, had to grapple further with this central dilemma: whether, and if so how, to recognize and legitimate the constitutive qualities of public administration in a regime that privileges the instrumental. Shaped by the founding and the Decision of 1789, the responses of these reform movements have distinctively and cumulatively made the instrumental conception of administration even more prominent in mainstream political thought and political practice. This has had marked consequences for the status, organization, function, and competence of public administration in the United States.

The Procession of Democracy

At the very beginning of *Democracy in America,* Tocqueville explained that what he found most remarkable during his visit to the United States was "the equality of conditions" (1988, 9). He argued that the force behind this was not found only in the United States. He proclaimed a "great democratic revolution . . . taking place in our midst. . . . Everywhere the diverse happenings in the lives of people have turned to democracy's profit" (11). Among the principal features of the "gradual progress of equality" (12) were its universality and its permanency.

Generations of American school children have been told, and as adults have customarily continued to believe, that democratic governance and equality of social conditions are best for society; indeed, that the former should encompass the latter. Tocqueville generally agreed, although most of *Democracy in America* is intended as a warning about the bad endings to which democracy and egalitarianism could lead and the need for particular sentiments, mores, and institutional arrangements to shape and direct the unstoppable democratic tide. This, Ann Stuart Diamond tells us, is exactly what the Constitution's framers, Madison especially, were up to. In explaining the whole context of the constitutional convention debate on the composition of the House of Representatives, for example, she stresses that the "very intensity of the concern about the dangers of the democratic form demonstrates that the framers were determined both to be democratic and to avoid the classic problems of democracies" (1980, 25). Something happened, however, to lead the American experiment in properly chastened democracy to deviate from what Diamond calls the "decent, even though democratic" regime the framers intended. As Jeffrey Tulis has characterized it, "It is the break upon public opinion [in the Constitution] rather than the provision for its influence that causes skepticism today" (1987, 35–36).

Numerous answers to the question of what happened have been forthcoming. Diamond argues that "the modern success of utopianism interposes between us and the American founding a radical theory of democracy" (1980, 18) and that, absent an aristocratic heritage, Americans make the "error of mistaking for an aristocratic manifestation whatever slows the expression of the majority will" (19). Lawrence Herson suggests that "the answer may lie in the nineteenth century's growing push for an expanded suffrage that ties, in turn, to the egalitarian lifestyle and political demands of the western frontier. Or, the answer may lie in the . . . lengthening stability of our political system [that] gradually removed public apprehensions over democracy" (1984, 61).

Quite provocatively, Gordon Wood has argued that the Federalists were themselves to blame. He contends that what the Constitution wrought was closely akin to an "aristocratic system" (1980, 17). To win approval in the campaign for ratification, the Federalists had to usurp "the popular revolutionary language that rightfully belonged to their opponents and, in the process, helped to further the extraordinary changes taking place in the American conception of politics and democracy" (15). No wonder, then, that one finds Alexander Hamilton, the quintessential Federalist, arguing in *The Federalist* No. 22 in favor of "the necessity of laying the foundations of our national government deeper than in the mere sanction of delegated authority. The fabric of American empire ought to rest on the solid basis of THE CONSENT OF THE PEOPLE. The streams of national power ought to flow immediately from that pure, original fountain of all legitimate authority."

Finally, Tocqueville's answer captures elements of the arguments of Diamond, Herson, and Wood, and is, as indicated at the outset, firmly anchored in the idea of the inevitability of democracy and the steady progress of equality. He contended that after the Revolutionary War, the nation was divided by two philosophies with deep and venerable roots in human society. He associated the Federalists with the desire to restrict popular power and the Republicans with the desire to extend popular power indefinitely. Tocqueville concluded that it was inevitable in the United States, as the land of democracy, that doctrines favoring popular power would become dominant. But the moral authority of the minority view of the Federalists, enshrined in the Constitution, allowed the "new republic time to settle down and afterwards to face without ill consequences the rapid development" of democracy (1988, 177).

By the time Tocqueville visited America, the effect of democratic politics and government on public administration was clear and consequential. "The majority, being in absolute command both of lawmaking and of the execution of the laws, and equally controlling both rulers and ruled, regards public functionaries as its passive agents. . . . It treats them as a master might treat his servants if, always seeing them act under his eyes, he could direct or correct them at any moment" (Tocqueville 1988, 253–54).

The arguments about the role of public administration as an institution in American politics and government advanced by statesmen and scholars, at least with respect to the establishment of federal administrative units and a federal civil service, nevertheless experienced substantial elaboration and development before, during, and immediately after the founding. To assess the characteristics of those and subsequent instances of such elaboration and development, a brief review of the structure of American political development is helpful.

A Developmental Sequence

Historians and political scientists have developed a variety of conceptual frames for imposing order on and providing explanations for American political and governmental development. Most of these schemes identify eras defined by a distinctive set of characteristics embracing both the ideology and practice of politics and government. The termination of one era and the inception of another are typically marked by a major crisis that is followed by a response that captures widespread support. Such is the idea of the interlocking concepts of critical elections and partisan realignments (e.g., Burnham 1970). Some of the resulting transformations have been so substantial, in the estimation of some scholars, as to mark the initiation of new regimes, because of the extensive constitutional expansion or reinterpretation they produced (see, for example, Lowi 1979; Tulis 1987). Invariably, both the crisis and the response, and thus the transformation, have been linked to reform efforts energized by a strong drive for democratization in some form (see Morone 1990).

The organization, conduct, and character of the people involved in public administration have been vehicles for and targets of the reform movements implicated in American political development. Scholars have applied a variety of very similar developmental sequences to chart the evolution of American public administration. For example, Leonard White's series of studies in administrative history encompassed what he called the "Federalist," "Jeffersonian," and "Jacksonian" periods and the "Republican Era." Frederick Mosher's treatment of the evolution of civil service concepts identifies six periods: government by gentlemen, by the common man, by the good, by the efficient, by administrators, and by the professional (1968, ch. 3). Michael Nelson (1982) charts four sometimes overlapping periods of public administration development characterized by the distinctive ironies of revolution, Jacksonian democracy, reform, and representation. Herbert Kaufman (1965) identifies three more encompassing periods: "the stable years" (1789–1829), "the rhythm of the spoils system" (1829–83), and "neutralizing the civil service" (1883–1964).

Closest to the structure, subject matter, and central conceptual components of the argument I develop, however, is the approach taken by James Morone (1990, esp. xii, 15–30). Morone examines the impact of populist aspirations on American political development associated with the founding and Jacksonian, progressive, and New Deal politics. His central objective is to explain how the "democratic impulse" shaped the construction of the American administrative state. I tell much the same story but focus on the development of the *idea* of public administration. The democratic proclivity remains as the basso continuo.

The roughly similar demarcation of epochs in administrative and political development employed in these and other works, and the insights gleaned from them by virtue of such a framework, provide firm foundations for investigating the origins and progression of distinctive conceptions of public administration in American politics and government. The outcomes of the struggles, in political thought and in the practice of government, to accommodate such conceptions still reverberate today.

The Founding: Temporary and Dependent Administration

Administration was neither the preference nor the experience of public service for America's revolutionary statesmen. Most American political leaders gained their political training and experience in legislative assemblies, while administration was reserved for royal governors and their underlings. Moreover, most of the dissension and anger of the colonists and their leaders which built up to the Declaration of Independence and the Revolutionary War was directed at the abuse of administrative power (M. Nelson 1982, 750; Elkins and McKitrick 1993, 53). The consequence was that administration as a public activity, and thus as a political and governmental institution, was seriously suspect. It was to be kept subordinate, dependent, and minimized. Three interdependent concerns of the leaders of the Revolution and of the Republic under the Articles of Confederation worked together to produce this characterization of administration in American government.

First, true republican government meant legislative supremacy. In the extreme thinking of Samuel Adams and the "liberative, expulsive, or destructive school" (Sanders 1935, 3; also Short 1923, 51–53, following Wharton 1889), no permanent and distinct executive institution should have been contemplated. Others, less extreme in their thinking, saw "as eminently proper and in keeping with republican notions of government" (Sanders 1935, 4) that administration be merely "adjunct" (i.e., "attached to another in a dependent or subordinate position," *The American Heritage Dictionary*, 3rd ed., 1992, s.v. "adjunct," def. 1). This was the case whether administration was to be by committees composed of legislators, by independent boards or commissions, or by departments led by single executives, which was the developmental progression for American administration before the Constitutional Convention. The heads of the relatively mature executive departments, for instance, were elected by and answerable exclusively to Congress, although they were not members of Congress.

Second, in light of the dominant republican notions of the time, many political leaders regarded administration as a *temporary tool*, born of the necessity of meeting the single and relatively clearly defined objective of winning a war and gaining independence. In fact, the Continental Congress was itself "regarded as a temporary body, assembled for a temporary purpose; and consequently no need for a permanent executive was at first experienced" (Short 1923, 37, quoting Bullock 1895). Even after the necessity of a more permanent governing body became evident during prosecution of the War for Independence and contemplation of what might follow victory, the "most outstanding feature of administrative organization" remained "the total absence of any element of permanency" (Short 1923, 50).

Third, the need for more permanent executive units—again, eventually departments headed by single executives—was driven by the need for "compatibility" with a military campaign (to paraphrase George Washington, as quoted in M. Nelson 1982, 751). Consequently, the extant conception of administration as temporary, subordinate to legislating, and simply a tool was reinforced and extended to its taking a form to suit the hierarchical, and thus demonstrably instrumental, design of military command structure.

Thus was an instrumental conception of administration firmly embedded in the very wellspring of the Republic and directly connected to the republican, that is to say *democratic,* ideology of the Revolution. Nevertheless, hints of a less stringent instrumentalism, if not of a distinctly constitutive conception, emerged in response. Opposed to Sam Adams's "town-meeting ideas" (Sanders 1935, 4) was a "constructive or remedial" school (Short 1923, 51), espousing ideas of "executivism" (Sanders 1935, 5). Alexander Hamilton was its "most outspoken advocate" (Short 1923, 53). Hamilton and the other constructivists were the force behind the move away from administration by committees and boards and toward single-headed executive departments. They conceived of administration as a distinctly important component of sound government, deserving of its own structure, even if the units in that structure remained wholly subordinate to the legislature.

During the decade of governance under the Articles of Confederation, in the Constitutional Convention debates, and in the campaign for ratification of the Constitution, conceptions of public administration and its place in an American system of government and politics were subjected to further development—one might even say further experimentation. A remarkable dimension of this development was the idea that administrators might even be part of the formative (e.g., deliberative) activities of government. In 1785, for example, James Madison remarked, "I have always conceived the several ministerial departments of Congress, to be provisions for *aiding their councils* as well as executing their resolutions, and that consequently whilst they retain the right of rejecting the advice which may come from either of them, they ought not to renounce the opportunity of making use of it" (Short 1923, 60, emphasis added).

More significant were the numerous proposals proffered during the Philadelphia Convention for some form of an executive council as the proper executive structure. In many of these proposals, the heads of the principal executive departments would form the council; and in some versions of this arrangement, the executive council would even *govern with* the president. For example, James Madison, the "first to advocate such a council, . . . before the opening of the convention, suggested . . . the idea of associating the heads of departments with the executive in a 'Council of Revision,' with authority to examine and pass upon all legislative acts" (Short 1923, 82). John Randolph and Charles Pinckney offered similar plans. Suggesting a representative function for the council, Elbridge Gerry asserted "that a Council ought to be the medium through which the feelings of the people ought to be communicated to the Executive" (Short 1923, 83).

On the whole, however, the conception of administration as a tool of the people and the people's representatives remained prominent. By June of 1787, Madison supported a single executive, "aided by a Council, who should have the right to advise and record their proceedings, but not to control his authority" (Short 1923, 83). James Wilson rejected the idea of a multiple executive as threatening to "interrupt the public administration" (White 1948, 14). And, making the status of appointed officials quite clear, Gouverneur Morris stated that, "there must be certain great officers of State; a minister of finance, of war, of foreign affairs, etc. These . . . will exercise their functions in subordination to the Executive" (Short 1923, 81).

The Hamiltonian Solution

The executive council failed to win support for inclusion in the Constitution, except in the clause of Article II, Section 2 stating that the president "may require the Opinion, in writing, of the principal Officer in each of the executive Departments, upon any Subject relating to the Duties of their respective Offices." This, John Rohr concludes, is indication that the founders not only rejected the idea of heads of executive departments giving collective advice to the president but that the chief administrative officers should be subordinate assistants to the president (1986, 142–43). In *The Federalist* No. 72, Hamilton articulated the idea more expansively, arguing that the principal administrative officers "ought to be considered as the assistants or deputies of the Chief Magistrate, and on this account they ought to derive their offices from his appointment, at least his nomination, and ought to be subject to his superintendence."

Hamilton's conception of administrators as subordinate to, dependent upon, and thus simply carrying out the orders of the president should not be read too narrowly, however. It was Hamilton, after all, more than any other member of the founding generation, who engaged in a genuine struggle to think through the effective design and legitimation of a national system of public administration for a liberal democratic regime. And in articulating his ideas, Hamilton recognized and sought to validate peculiarly constitutive qualities in administration, within a system that already accepted administration as distinctly, if not exclusively, instrumental (for a detailed treatment, see Green 1990).

Evidence for Hamilton's more expansive thinking about administration appears in the often quoted opening passage of *The Federalist* No. 72, in which he offers a definition of public administration that, by its very sweep, would appear to encompass not only the identification and development of means but the formation of ends as well. "The administration of government, in its largest sense, comprehends all the operations of the body politic, whether legislative, executive, or judiciary." But Hamilton is perhaps most revealing about his conception of the reach, impact, and status of administration in a rarely quoted but extraordinary passage in *The Federalist* No. 27. It appears in the midst of his argument that obedience to federal law would not require any more extraordinary coercion than the laws of the individual states had required.

> I will, in this place, hazard an observation which will not be the less just because to some it may appear new; which is, that the more the operations of the national authority are intermingled in the ordinary exercise of government, the more the citizens are accustomed to meet with it in common occurrences of their political life, the more it is familiarized to their sight and to their feelings, the further it enters into those objects which touch the most sensible chords and put in motion the most active springs of the human heart, the greater will be the probability that it will conciliate the respect and attachment of the community.

The effect Hamilton describes in this passage, that of public administration's permeating the very foundations of the public life of the citizenry and winning its allegiance to the regime, is really quite extraordinary, given the founders' intentions to create a limited government and thus a large, protected sphere of private activity. But this "administrative" republic (Flaumenhaft 1981, 103) would not come about unless it rested firmly on the foundation of an "efficacious" administration, an argument that Hamilton takes great pains to make clear by advancing it in *The Federalist* No. 17 and again in No. 69, and with Madison's help in No. 46. The consequence of good administration would be a stable, long-lasting regime, the affinity of the people for the regime, and more: their attachment "to civic virtue itself" (Storing 1981, 43). As Storing goes on to argue, government "that can actually accomplish its resolves, that can keep the peace, protect property, and promote the prosperity of the country, will be a government respected and obeyed by its citizens. It will, moreover, promote private and public morality by providing them with effective protection."

Thus, although the Constitution defines certain general goals for the regime, it also sets the framework for the elaboration and extension of those purposes, the creation of new ends, and the promotion of a particular kind of citizenry defined by its public and private morality. It will also be a regime that is "truly popular" because it is founded on a citizenry that will come to prefer "the long-run and long-lasting outcomes of government" rather than "what is immediately popular" (Flaumenhaft 1981, 75). Public administration is integral to all of this, but Hamilton warned that a "principle like this was hard to make immediately clear to the people," a warning that would be borne out by subsequent events.

Despite Hamilton's emphatic acknowledgment of public administration's essential constitutiveness as an integral part of a liberal democracy, helping to shape the character of the citizenry, refine the regime's purposes, and thus guide its development, administration had to fit properly within the well-accepted tripartite structure of the Constitution. For Hamilton, being of strong "executivist" proclivities, the solution was easy. The opening passage of *The Federalist* No. 72 continues, "but in its most usual and perhaps in its most precise signification, [administration] falls peculiarly within the province of the executive department." It also followed logically that administrative officers would be subject to presidential superintendence. With a strong and energetic executive, moreover, this structural arrangement would produce the efficacious administration, with its salutary constitutive effects, that Hamilton envisioned.

But Hamilton's statement of the solution was not as neat and simple as it sounded. John Rohr, from his examinations of the complex treatment of administration in *The Federalist*, concludes that it was conceived as "instrumental for achieving higher political ends, such as winning support for the new government" (1989b, 8). Rohr contends, nevertheless, that it is erroneous to interpret the founders' vision of administration as a "corporate structure, with a president as the chief executive officer of a tightly organized firm whose subordinates are merely the instruments of the president's will" (10). The "model of administration was more political than managerial." The function of the heads of departments "was to assist the president in exercising his constitutional duty to take care that the laws be faithfully executed; they were not simply to do the president's bidding" (10).

At the founding, an instrumental linkage between administration and the will of the people in a hierarchical arrangement was at the center of public thinking about politics and government. Indeed, it was, according to Herbert Storing, what governance under the Constitution was all about. "Government was no longer seen as directing and shaping human existence, but as having the much narrower (though indispensable) function of facilitating the peaceful enjoyment of the private life. In this view, government and the whole public sphere are decisively instrumental; government is reduced to administration" (1980, 97). Hamilton's response to this narrow view was brilliant, because he was able to situate, and legitimate, a constitutive understanding of adminstration within the predominantly instrumental conception. His "political" model of administration, and the assistance but not subjugation to the president provided by administrators within that model, was nevertheless problematic, raising important questions that could not be answered easily.

For example, how much leeway should subordinate administrators be allowed in providing assistance in faithful execution of the laws? This is the longstanding problem of administrative discretion, and Hamilton came down on the side of broad leeway. He was "emphatic about the need to recognize that the business of administration cannot be fully subordinated to rule as some would wish; the machinery cannot work without latitude in interpreting the rules" (Flaumenhaft 1981, 82). The discretion should flow through the president, however, and should be restricted to the highest ranks of administrative officials (White 1948, 449–51). Did presidential superintendence mean that the president had exclusive, constitutionally sanctioned power to remove administrators from office? What hand could Congress have in influencing the assistance administrators rendered in executing the laws? Finally and perhaps most importantly, did the constitutive effect of administration, and the integral role in shaping the character of the regime this implied, require that the authority under which administrators operated be anchored directly and independently in the Constitution rather than indirectly as a derivative of the constitutional authority of the president or of Congress?

These were questions of theory and principle, to be sure, but they were also questions of practical politics and governance. In the first year under the rule of the new Constitution, the Congress had to address such questions, with a result that had significant implications for how subsequent generations of political leaders also thought about and responded to them.

The Decision of 1789: Dependency and Responsibility Affirmed

The debates surrounding the establishment of the first executive departments seem to have achieved universal acclaim as momentous. They are
included in a compilation of material from the *Annals* of the First Congress entitled *A Second Federalist* (Hyneman and Carey 1967). More significantly, Leonard White described the Decision of 1789 as the "first major constitutional debate" to take place in Congress (1948, 20). Charles
Thach went so far as to argue that it was "a constitutional convention, so
far as subject matter is a criterion," with its work "simply a continuation
of that done in Philadelphia two years before" (1922, 141). Students of
the debate have also generally concluded that an instrumental, subordinate status for public administrators was already widely accepted before
commencement of the debate. As Thach stated it, for administrators, the
1789 debate on establishing executive departments and on the president's
power of removal was exclusively about deciding "the fundamental question of whether the legislature or the chief executive was their master"
(141).

Nevertheless, the 1789 debate on the removal power is worthy of further scrutiny, because some of the most articulate representatives who
participated in the debate were not entirely convinced by the proposition
that administrators were simply subordinate to one or both political
branches. Although only a small minority, they resolutely sought an alternative conception of the constitutional status of public administrators
by attempting to define a constitutionally independent role for the heads
of departments mentioned in the Constitution. For anyone interested in
the meaning of public administration, as well as the effectiveness of current public management efforts, the competing conceptions of the place
of public administration in the constitutional system debated in 1789
bear directly on public administration's status, structure, legitimacy, and
contributions to the regime.

The President's Arm and Eye

It is important to keep in mind, in assessing the debate, that the subject
was the president's power to remove specifically the secretary of foreign
affairs (soon thereafter secretary of state). Although the Constitution's
conception of the presidency and executive power is ambiguous (see
Rohr 1989a), in this case the Constitution gives express power over much
of foreign diplomacy to the president. Hence, a secretary of foreign affairs most closely fits the idea of a presidential instrument. This makes all
the more remarkable the alternative conception of administration that
was presented during the debate.

The foundation of the instrumental conception championed in the debate was responsibility, and James Madison proved to be its most lucid and persistent advocate. Here is how Madison rendered that conception at two points in the debate.

> Now, if the heads of the Executive departments are subjected to removal by the President alone, we have in him security for the good behavior of the officer. If he does not conform to the judgment of the President in doing the executive duties of his office, he can be displaced. This makes him responsible for the great Executive power, and makes the President responsible to the public for the conduct of the person he has nominated and appointed to aid him in the administration of his department. . . . (*Annals*, 379)
>
> . . . If the President should possess alone the power of removal from office, those who are employed in the execution of the law will be in their proper situation, and the chain of dependence be preserved; the lowest officers, the middle grade, and the highest, will depend, as they ought, on the President, and the President on the community. The chain of dependence therefore terminates in the supreme body, namely, in the people, who will possess, besides, in aid of their original power, the decisive engine of impeachment. (499)

Distinctions within this instrumental conception are evident in the debate. Some members argued that executive officers were agents purely of the President, as originally insisted by Richard Bland Lee. For example, John Vining of Delaware likened the secretary of foreign affairs to an arm and eye of the president, who "sees and writes his secret dispatches, [and] is an instrument over which the President ought to have complete command" (*Annals,* 511). Similarly, Theodore Sedgwick of Massachusetts perceived the secretary "as much an instrument in the hands of the president, as the pen is the instrument in the hands of the Secretary in corresponding with foreign courts. . . . This officer should be dependent upon him" (522). Most forcefully, Michael Stone of Maryland and Elias Boudinot argued that whatever authority department heads could exercise was derived from the president.

> The power of appointing an officer arises from the power over the subject on which an officer is to act. It arises from the principal who appoints having an interest in and right to conduct business, which he does by means of an agent. Therefore, this officer appears to be nothing more than an agent, appointed for the convenient dispatch of business . . . and the principle will operate from the Minister of State down to the tidewaiter. (*Annals* [Stone], 492)

The President nominates and appoints; he is further expressly authorized to commission all officers. . . . Who vests the officer with authority? Who commissions him? The President does these acts by his sole power, but they are exercised in consequence of the advice of another branch of government. If, therefore, the officer receives his authority and commission from the President, surely the removal follows as coincident. ([Boudinot], 527)

Echoing in some ways the legislative supremacy thinking of the revolutionary period, other members contended that administrators were largely agents of the law and thus of the legislature, under the Constitution's "necessary and proper" clause. Roger Sherman of Connecticut argued, "As the officer is the mere creature of the Legislature, we may form it under such regulations as we please, with such powers and duration as we think good policy requires" (*Annals*, 492). Anticipating arguments advanced by Senate Whigs in their battle with Andrew Jackson forty-five years hence, Elbridge Gerry of Massachusetts warned that if the president had unlimited control over treasury officers, we might "expect to see institutions arising under the control of the revenue, and not of the law" (502).

Out of these two lines of argument from the 1789 debate emerged the view of public administrators as agents of both the president and Congress. As Madison stated it late in the debate, "the powers relative to offices are partly Legislative and partly Executive" (*Annals*, 581). Congress would adopt this doctrine most clearly in its creation of the Treasury Department (see White 1948, 118–19). Madison also later anticipated officials with a mix of legislative and judicial duties (*Annals*, 611–14). Congress and the president, and at times also the courts, have struggled over control of administration ever since, a struggle that intensified as the conception of administration that prevailed in the 1789 debate expanded its reach (see, for example, Corwin 1984, ch. 3; Fisher 1985, 66–98; Aberbach and Rockman 1988).

Independence and Firmness in Administration

An appreciation for the importance of the 1789 debate cannot end here, however, for a number of representatives were clearly uneasy about making an executive officer "the mere State-dependent, the abject slave" of the president (*Annals* [Alexander White], 458), as suggested by the instrumental conception of administration given voice in the debate. Mr. White, of Virginia, later asked,

Who are the heads of departments? We are to have a Secretary of Foreign Affairs, another for War, and another for Treasury; now are not these the principal officers in these departments? . . . But who are their inferior officers? The chief clerks and all others who may depend on them. These, then, are the inferior officers, whose appointments may be vested in the respective heads of departments. . . . The gentlemen who formed the Constitution seem not inclined, at all events, to give to the President the power of appointing even these inferior officers, to which is attached the power of removal. (518)

John Page of Virginia observed, "To the argument [supporting the President's removal power], which is drawn from the necessity of having energy in Government, despatch, secrecy, and decision; I think all these advantages may be had without putting the respectable heads of departments in a situation so humiliating, that I can scarcely suppose a man of true independent spirit, and fit to be in such an office, could submit to" (*Annals*, 549).

It was left to William Smith of South Carolina and James Jackson of Georgia, however, to articulate fully an alternative to the strict subordination of Madison's instrumental conception. Smith opened the June deliberations with some potent ammunition: the opening paragraph from *The Federalist* No. 77, wherein Alexander Hamilton argued that the "consent of that body [the Senate] would be necessary to displace as well as to appoint," a requirement that would contribute to stability in administration. Theodorick Bland of Virginia had made the same argument in May without reference to Hamilton. John Rohr has called Hamilton's "musings" on this point, "merely speculative" (1986, 141), while Harvey Flaumenhaft (1981, 102) has suggested that Hamilton may have taken this position strategically, to advance ratification and make a larger point about stability. In any case, Hamilton apparently later repudiated or at least clarified his position in advice to Washington during the controversy over the Neutrality Proclamation of 1793 (Goldsmith 1974, 181–82; Fisher 1985, 66). William Smith sought to expand on the point, however, by linking stability not with the Senate so much as with executive officers holding office "on a better tenure" (*Annals*, 472).

Smith argued that if the Constitution stated that Congress could vest appointment of inferior officers in heads of departments, that vestiture made department heads "principal" officers, removable only by impeachment. Smith said his opponents on the question considered the head of a department "an inferior officer in aid of the President. This, I think, is going too far; because the Constitution, in the words authorizing the President to call on the heads of departments for their opinions in writing, contemplates several departments. It says, 'the principal officer in each of the Executive departments'" (*Annals*, 459). Smith went on to contend that as advisors to the president, as designated in the Constitution, heads of departments were more than merely the president's subordinates, reflecting some of the thinking from the constitutional convention on the role of heads of departments in an executive council.

Initially, in May, Smith based his position on impeachment as the sole method of removal, on the argument that offices were a form of property. Incumbents of executive offices thus could not be deprived of their property without something approximating a judicial proceeding, a requirement that impeachment satisfied. Many of his colleagues derided this aspect of Smith's argument, along with his more general proposition that impeachment was the only constitutionally prescribed method for removing principal executive officers. John Rohr has argued, however, that Smith's position "has been reborn in recent time as the liberal constitutional doctrine of the 'new property.' Under this doctrine, many classified civil service positions are treated as a form of property. This treatment gives career personnel . . . extensive constitutional protection against unwarranted dismissals and thus sharply curtails the power of their administrative superiors over them" (1989b, 19).

From my reading of the 1789 debate, however, it seems relatively clear that Smith let his property argument fade into the background, while remaining steadfast in his defense of impeachment as the sole means of removal. A statement by Smith made in the middle of the June proceedings compared the tenure of judges, elected officials, and heads of departments and is a better representation, I believe, of his overall position. It shows that his arguments were not isolated or extreme. Although scholarly consensus has relegated Smith to a marginal role in the debate, his ideas were important in shaping the course of the debate and spoke to the question of the proper role for administration within the constitutional system.

> It has been inferred from the clause in the constitution, declaring judges to hold their offices during good behavior, that there are no other officers who hold their offices by this tenure. Now, I apprehend, that this clause was inserted to distinguish them from other officers who hold their offices for a limited period. . . . It was seen to be proper to have them independent; and that could only be secured by such a declaration in the constitution. . . . With respect to the other offices to be established by law, there is nothing to prevent us from limiting their appointment. . . . Let us then limit the duration of the Secretary of Foreign Affairs for as short a period as is thought to be salutary. Here we are not restricted. But I conceive, as the constitution now stands, they cannot be removed in any other way but by impeachment. (*Annals,* 507–8)

James Jackson's principal arguments reinforced Smith's position, and provided perhaps the clearest expression of the view that department heads deserved special constitutional status.

> I appeal to the good sense of the committee to determine whether these officers are not established by the Constitution as heads of departments. How then can they be merely instruments of the President, to conform implicitly to his will? for I deny the principle that they are mere creatures of the law. They have Constitutional rights that they may exercise. If the president alone is the head of the whole Executive Department, and these the mere creatures of the law, where is the necessity of calling them heads of departments in the Constitution? . . . (*Annals,* 530)
>
> . . . I call upon gentlemen to show me, why heads of departments are necessarily dependent upon the President, when the Constitution specifically points them out. I cannot, for my part, admit that any part of the Constitution authorizes the President to exercise an uncontrolled power over them, because I perceive, as a fundamental principle in the Constitution, that the exercise of all power should be properly checked and guarded. (532)

Jackson's arguments quoted here are particularly interesting. He insisted that the highest ranking administrative officials have a constitutionally recognized independent status. As John Rohr has observed, "surely a constitutional provision for a principal officer in each of several executive departments implies that these high officials hold some sort of executive power in their own right" (1989a, 110). Beyond even that, however, Jackson contended that the highest-ranking administrators play a special role that would be fully consistent with a basic constitutional principle—checking the power of the president. Administrators exercising some sort of check on the president is much the same idea as that on which the advocates of an executive council had based their arguments, and it would reappear in later legal and political battles involving administration and governmental and political reform. One might even count it as being among the elements that made for an efficacious administration. Combining the Smith and Jackson arguments, the thrust of their contention seems to be that although administrators are subject to substantial control by statute and presidential command, they nevertheless retain a constitutionally recognized status and function that cannot be altered.

The proponents of the strictly instrumental conception never fully neutralized Jackson's and Smith's constitutional arguments, because they could never provide an explanation for why the framers, a number of whom were participants in the House debate, specifically included department heads in the Constitution if they did not intend them to have special status. Faced wtih a stalemate on the constitutional arguments, the two sides turned the the issue into a question of practical (i.e., instrumental) politics and governance. What purposes would administration best serve?

The utility of granting special constitutional status to department heads and protecting them from arbitrary removal is that executive officers could provide stability in government and in the regime and could act as an additional check upon the president. These may be counted among the "higher political ends" to which Rohr refers. With few exceptions, the parties to the 1789 debate agreed that stability was a critical contribution that administration could make to the new regime created by the Constitution. The disagreement was over how stability through administration would best be achieved and whether administration could serve as an effective constitutional check on the president. Madison argued that the inability to weed out incompetent or corrupt officials because of the lack of a presidential removal power would most likely undermine the stability of administration and thus of the regime. Smith, Jackson, White, and a few others argued that a public administration completely at the mercy of the president would destroy stability because, as Bland contended, every new president would be tempted to turn out "the great officers, . . . and throw the affairs of the Union into disorder" (*Annals*, 381), an argument also advanced by Hamilton in *The Federalist* No. 72.

Madison and others argued against allowing department heads to serve during good behavior (that is, indefinitely unless impeached) precisely because such tenure would provide them with the power to resist presidential commands. Such power would weaken unity and energy in the executive, creating a multiheaded monster that would smash the "great principle" of responsibility. In fact, the imagery employed generated a cascade of references from members regarding how many heads and how monstrous the new government would become. Such references became increasingly derisive in mocking the arguments of Smith and Jackson (see for example, the remarks of Reps. Vining [*Annals*, 511] and Sylvester [560]).

By pointing out that "the Constitution also has confidence in the heads of departments" (*Annals*, 519), by warning of the risks in depriving department heads "of their independency and firmness" (488), and in asserting the benefits of a department head "invulnerable in his integrity," who could serve as "a barrier to your Executive officer" (472), however, a small band of holdouts in the 1789 debate provided the political leaders of the young nation the opportunity to appraise an independent constitutional foundation for administration that might more securely legitimate the constitutive qualities envisioned by Hamilton. Their arguments favoring independence and a distinctive constitutional status for departments heads captured a way of thinking about administration that showed its significance to democratic governance beyond even its service in the achievement of higher political ends.

William Smith, James Jackson, John Page, and perhaps one or two others, argued that administration was a unique institutional component of government under the Constitution and that it had to be recognized as such, because it would, from the very beginning, help to shape the character of the government and the nature of political life in the regime. However, like the Hamiltonian scheme, articulated so well by Madison in the debate, this alternative conception was problematic as well, because it raised the red flag of accountability and control that has remained the central focus of American thinking about public administration to the present day. This demonstrates just how difficult a challenge equilibrating the instrumental and constitutive qualities of administration within a liberal democracy really is.

The Meaning of the Hamiltonian Solution and the Decision of 1789

Two of its features made the Decision of 1789 as distinctive and important as any action affecting administration taken during the Philadelphia Convention or the ratification debates. First, in an open public forum, in the context of making decisions about the actual structure and function of the constitutional scheme, political leaders grappled with the instrumental and constitutive in public administration and the evaluative perspectives associated with each. A considerable majority of the representatives embraced the instrumental conception and argued that administrators ought to be evaluated on how well they served the ends of the Constitution, as those ends might be further shaped and refined exclusively by the people and their elected representatives. The minority contended that administrative officials ought to be understood as a vital influence on the purpose-creating and refining activities of elected representatives, that they would, further, have a hand directly in shaping and refining the aims and purposes of the regime, and thus that they ought to be evaluated on these grounds. This set the pattern for subsequent struggles with the administrative dilemma, although the circumspection of 1789 would never be attained again, and the public expression by practicing politicians of the idea of constitutive administration would become weaker or at least more diffuse.

Assessing the impact of Federalist ratification strategy, Gordon Wood has contended that "the Federalists helped to foreclose the development of an American intellectual tradition in which differing ideas of politics would be intimately and genuinely related to differing social interests." Using "the most popular and democratic rhetoric," Wood maintains that, "the Federalists of 1787 furthered the American disavowal of any sort of aristocratic conception of politics and encouraged the American belief that the ills of democracy can be cured by more democracy" (1980, 17). The Decision of 1789, with its confirmation of executive unity, responsibility, and administrative dependence and subordination, may have been vital to ensuring the governing capacity of the constitutional system, as Leonard White (1948, 25), among others, has concluded. But, as a second distinctive feature of its importance and again because the forum was public and required decisions about putting the Constitution into operation, the Decision of 1789 had consequences much like those Wood attributes to the Federalist ratification effort. It was a decisive reinforcement of the idea of administration as principally if not exclusively an instrument linked to popular rule. In its immediate aftermath, the dominant rhetoric of the debate, if not the legal effect of the decision, forged this link most closely to the presidency through the emphasis on executive unity. Who held the controlling end of Madison's chain of dependence—the president or Congress—would, however, become the source of continuing and sometimes bitter dispute.

In significant ways, the conception of administration advanced by Alexander Hamilton nicely resolved the dilemma posed for liberal democracy by the need for a vigorous, permanent public administration. Hamilton's solution was nevertheless problematic, because it conceived of administration's constitutiveness as derived from an instrumental, subordinate status and from being exercised in a particular way, that is, in response to a unitary, energetic executive. If one accepts public administration as fundamentally a political institution, however, it is by definition constitutive. If true, this was bound to become evident in practice, thus making the indirect linkage of public administration's authority to the Constitution in Hamilton's scheme a potential threat to popular understanding and acceptance of administration's essential contributions to the regime.

The losers in the 1789 debate strove to establish a direct constitutional linkage and insisted that public administration be evaluated not just for how well it filled in the details and achieved policy objectives but also for its overall contribution to the definition, maintenance, and active expression of constitutional principles. This they found difficult to do, because administration appears only in bits and pieces in the Constitution, mostly within Article II. Thus, the most basic feature of the Constitution's design—the tripartite distribution of powers—is at the heart of the problem. Our political leaders, however, must work with what they have, which means locating, designing, and practicing a public administration that best balances its instrumental and constitutive qualities, and so helps maintain and enhance the best qualities of the regime.

As changes in American society occurred and problems surfaced in the practice of politics and government under the Constitution, however, the response of political reformers at successive stages of American political development was not only the addition of more democracy in some form, as Tocqueville had indicated would be inevitable, but also more sharply honed instrumental conceptions of and designs for public administration, tied in most but not all instances to the presidency. These ideas and designs have aggravated the problematic dimension of Hamilton's solution, keeping popular regard for public administration's constitutive character from developing in the manner Hamilton had envisioned, and leaving attentive citizens with little expectation that public administration might be involved in something so fundamental as shaping the ends toward which public resources are employed.

With an irony much like that uncovered by Michael Nelson (1982), in which successive reform efforts aimed at bringing administration under tighter political control have actually increased its political independence, American public administration has suffered an erosion of its public support and its potential for contributing to the healthy development of the regime. This has occurred even though each reform effort has been, in many respects, an attempt through further subordination and control to tie administration more closely to the regime in ways that would preserve increasingly popular aspirations to self-government. Signs that this developmental pattern would emerge appeared quite soon after the Decision of 1789, during the "stable years" of "gentlemanly" administration under the first five presidents.

Administration in Practice and the Political Response

Scholars have generally described early public administration at the federal level as elitist in character, if not downright aristocratic. George Washington's standard of "fitness of character" for appointees, which measured primarily a man's standing in his community and the respect he had gained from his neighbors, often manifested in previous electoral support, would appear to have been the principal influence. Herbert Kaufman describes the first four decades of national administration as years of stability (1965, 12–20) in part because of the skillful efforts of President Washington and the seriousness with which he undertook to build an administration from scratch.

The Hamiltonian solution to the administrative dilemma, given practical force by the Decision of 1789, was the cornerstone of the elitism and stability that characterized administration in the early years of the Republic. In the first months of his presidency, for example, Washington commented that the officers of the "great departments" were to "assist the supreme magistrate in discharging the duties of his trust" (Short 1923, 106). More pointedly, James Flexner has concluded that Washington's ministers, "even the transcendently able Secretaries of State and Treasury, were never actually denied authority, but at the same time they were given no final authority that they could count upon" (Flexner 1969, 403). A decade after he left the presidency, Jefferson remarked that the president could seek the advice of the heads of departments "either separately or all together, and remedy their decisions by adopting or controlling their opinions at his discretion" (Short 1923, 110). Taking a broader sounding, Kaufman has noted that "not one of the first five Presidents ever expressed any concern about the dangers of sabotage of their policies by a hostile public service—an anxiety not all of their successors escaped. They sometimes removed men who had worked for their opponents in elections, but they did so to provide reward for their own followers rather than to ensure obedience in the discharge of public office; the latter was taken for granted" (1965, 19).

Governing experience also began to indicate, however, that the role administration would play under the Constitution could not be as easily confined as the Decision of 1789 had implied. Basing fitness of character in part on previous electoral success brought politicians into administration, guaranteeing that administrators and administration would be regarded, and practiced, as a political undertaking. Indeed, at least until the presidency of Andrew Jackson, cabinet secretaries operated as politicians and statesmen (see Fowler 1943).

The premiere example, of course, was Hamilton himself, who, as Washington's treasury secretary, laid the foundations for a dynamic modern political economy (e.g., Elkins and McKitrick 1993, 114–23, 258–62). Although Hamilton's actions as treasury secretary largely personified his notion that quite broad discretion and independent action could be granted but restricted to heads of departments, many of his deeds as secretary strained the limits of his authority—and the soundness of the Decision of 1789—to the breaking point. Worse, the independent political behavior of some department heads turned out to be merely crass politicking by ambitious politicians seeking the presidency within the congressional caucus nominating system (M. Nelson 1982, 753). If administration was an instrument, after all, then political men could put it to many uses, not all of them necessarily in service of broad public ends. Even Jefferson, who opposed many of Hamilton's policy initiatives as well as his conception of administrative power, had to acknowledge, in the midst of his presidency, the extent to which his administrators engaged in governing.

> For our government although in theory subject to be directed by the unadvised will of the President, is, and from its origin has been, a very different thing in practice. The minor business in each department is done by the head of the department on consultation with the President alone; but all matters of importance or difficulty are submitted to all the heads of departments composing the Cabinet. Sometimes, by the President consulting them separately and successively, as they happen to call on him, but in the gravest cases calling them together, discussing the subject maturely, and finally taking a vote, on which the President counts himself but as one. So that in all important cases the Executive is in fact a directory, which certainly the President might control; but of this there was never an example either in the first or the present administration. (Short 1923, 109–10)

In addition, congressional participation in controlling the administrative instrument, inherent in the Constitution and forcefully defended by many senators and representatives during the 1789 debates, became increasingly assertive after Washington retired to Mount Vernon. Congress pursued increasingly bold efforts to place limits on presidential power, exerting control over administration by granting administrative officers ministerial discretion that was direct rather than derivative from the president, specifying and thus limiting the grounds for removal of officials from office, and building a patronage system involving the federal workforce that was initially enshrined in law by the Tenure of Office Act of 1824.

With respect to the problem of dual presidential and congressional control of administration, Michael Nelson has argued that "agencies, forced to live with the ambiguities of control from both elected branches, set about developing power resources of their own. . . . [They] began to play one branch off against another; if neither president nor Congress was supreme, then law was, and the agencies interpreted and implemented the law" (1982, 755). Nelson sees in this the irony of a system of dual control becoming one of limited control that ultimately enhances the power of bureaucracy. But dual control also illuminates the difficulty inherent in attempting to ignore or suppress the essential governing role administration plays even in a popular regime, and it clarifies the necessity of grounding that role in a legitimate source, namely, the law.

From the perspective of the American democratic ideology, which sees administration, indeed most of politics, as instrumental, these necessities are difficult to understand and accept, and the Hamiltonian solution did not adequately address them. In the "revolution" of 1800, therefore, Jefferson and Madison put an end to what Madison called Hamilton's "wishing . . . to administer the Government into what he thought it ought to be" (Banning 1984, 25). The vehicle they employed to achieve their triumph— the political party—they regarded with unease and hoped that its existence might only be temporary, being representative of the threat that factions still posed to the regime. Under the Jacksonians, however, the party would, working through the president, become a more permanent solution to controlling and subordinating administration to the popular will.

3

Restoring Republican Virtue
The Impact of Jacksonian Ideals

A collision has taken place which I could have most anxiously wished to avoid; but it was not to be shunned. We have not sought this controversy; it has met us, and been forced upon us. In my judgment, the law has been disregarded, and the Constitution transgressed; the fortress of liberty has been assaulted, and circumstances have placed the Senate in the breach; and although we may perish in it, I know we shall not fly from it. . . . We shall hold on, Sir, and hold out, till the people themselves come to its defence.

This melodramatically defiant declaration was made by Daniel Webster near the conclusion of a speech delivered on May 7, 1834, on the floor of the U.S. Senate (see Wiltse and Berolzheimer 1988, 34–71). Webster's speech climaxed three weeks of Senate debate. A Senate resolution had charged that President Andrew Jackson, in his removal of Secretary of the Treasury William J. Duane, had assumed "upon himself authority and power not conferred by the constitution and laws, but in derogation of both" (Richardson 1911, 3:69). On April 15, Jackson had sent to the Senate a message of protest, requesting that it be entered in the Senate's journal. All of this was, in turn, part of the larger battle between Jackson and Senate Whigs over the Second Bank of the United States, national economic policy, and executive patronage, making the nascent federal bureaucracy a major focal point in a contest of competing conceptions of the Republic and its foundations. Public administration, and its political manipulation, was subjected to sustained public scrutiny, which raised serious questions about its structure and status within the regime.

The federal service was a critical component in the efforts of Andrew Jackson and his supporters to restore republican virtues they believed had been lost after the end of the Jefferson administration. The Jacksonians' conception of the administrative structure that would be needed to realize their restoration project changed over time from personal to impersonal organization. More important, their most forceful public rhetoric about what they believed the status of public administration should be departed from, if not openly contradicted, their own expectations for administration connected with their restoration project. Because views of the structure and status of public administration under the Constitution emerged from other quarters as well and generated dynamic tensions and a vigorous interplay of ideas, I examine the commentary of several senators, most of them Whigs. From their arguments emerged a conception of administration based on responsible discretion and fidelity to law.

The ideas and arguments about public administration that surfaced during the Jacksonian era largely amplified the effects of the Decision of 1789. They heightened the tensions between the democratic ideology of subordinate and instrumental administration and the reality, even in a regime of limited government under a written constitution, that appointed officials would be deeply and continuously involved in shaping the aims of the polity and defining the character of the citizenry. The vigorous new assertion of popular control that marked this era thus contributed little to answering questions about how the instrumental and constitutive qualities of administration might be reasonably balanced under the Constitution, leaving politicians and attentive citizens more confused and dismissive about the status of public administration in the regime.

Jacksonian Restoration: Personal and Unitary Administration

By most accounts, great changes were occurring in American society at the time of Andrew Jackson's election. Many of them had a distinctly democratic cast: more concretely structured and active political parties, presidential nominating conventions, expansion of the franchise, and the phenomenal growth of a middle class of craftsmen, shopkeepers, and tradesmen. Many of these democratizing changes have been directly linked to Jackson's election, and even to Jackson himself. Lecturing on the Jacksonian "democratization of the Constitution," William Bennett Munro described Old Hickory as "the product of his military experience and his bucolic surroundings, a democrat with a small 'd.' He was of the common people and understood them" (Munro 1930, 96). Jackson's election, in turn, culminated "a great surge of equalitarian sentiment; the greatest, perhaps, that the country has ever known" (97).

The introduction on the federal level of rotation in office and the spoils system, deeply tied to the democratic sentiment of the time and carrying significant meaning for the form and character of public administration nationally, is the most widely recognized legacy of the Jackson presidency. Yet the "democraticness" of the Jacksonian reform efforts was of a peculiar sort. Making sense of it, and of the role of the spoils system in the reform drive, is central to any appreciation of the Jacksonian contribution to public thinking about, and understanding of, public administration's place in the regime.

As Matthew Crenson has explained, the democratic-reform thrust of the Jacksonians was not class based but idea based and emotion based. What they sought was a "return to the old republican virtues" or the "restoration of republican virtue" (Crenson 1975, 24, 27). Furthermore, the Jacksonians confronted and were deeply affected by the fundamental changes in social institutions occurring at the time (Kohl 1989, 9–10). These changes represented for the Jacksonians and their sympathizers the loss of traditional values and ways of life and thus the loss of the anchors of orderliness in society that traditional values provided (15–16). Facing this loss, the Jacksonians also sought in their reform efforts to stem the tide of, or at least to come to grips with, the moral decay emanating from the upheaval in major social institutions and the resultant loss of authority these institutions suffered. As Crenson points out, the Jackson people were not good at weaving these concerns and efforts into a coherent governing ideology or managerial approach (see Crenson 1975, 27–29). These emblematic considerations of the Jacksonians nevertheless had substantial implications for ideas and actions respecting public administration, including the use of the spoils.

Party Dominance and the Character of the Spoils

The spoils system was certainly a weapon of partisanship in the hands of the Jacksonians. As Crenson states it, "the theory of rotation was recruited to the service of Old Hickory's ambitions and those of the Jacksonian coalition. The president launched his administration in a spirit of lusty partisanship" (1975, 49). Such partisanship was also quite purposeful. The aim of the Jacksonians was to keep tight constraints on government, and thus on administrative power as well. "The first Jacksonian impulse was to deny government power over private interests so that there would be no temptation to abuse it. This struggle to limit power was unending, since there was always a tendency in government to expand its authority" (Kohl 1989, 123). The party, in turn, would be the vehicle for imposing and maintaining the proper constraints. Thus, in the view of Martin Van Buren, principal architect of the Democratic party and Jackson's successor as president, the idea was to "constrain excessive personal or programmatic ambition" and make party principle supreme (Milkis and Nelson 1994, 131).

The effect, not surprisingly, was to reduce public administration to the role of servant of party rule, partisanship being the premiere expression of the democratic spirit during the Jacksonian era. "The executive branch became an auxiliary of the party organization, and the 'art of administration' was absorbed by the art of politics" (Crenson 1975, 168). Looking back upon the era, the Progressive standard-bearer, Herbert Croly, offered a similar assessment.

> It was . . . the very tendency to independence on the part of the Federal Law and government which had been so disconcerting to the Democracy, and which had much to do with the creation of this unofficial partisan government supplementary to the official system. It could not disintegrate this Federal organization, but by heroic efforts and drastic measures it could reduce it to much more effective control. It could elect a Democratic administration and by the power of partisan allegiance keep it after election under tolerable subordination. By virtue of this subordination the administration could be very much weakened. The adoption of the principle of rotation in elective offices and the application of the spoils system to appointive offices did much to injure the independence of the Federal system and to impair its integrity. The local partisan organization named the Federal officials and took care that they served their real rather than their ostensible master. (1914, 70–71)

In Leonard White's (1954) appraisal, the effect of Jacksonian partisanship was largely external and institutional. As Crenson puts it, the impact was to alter "relationships between the federal establishment and other political institutions" (1975, 166).

If partisan democracy subjugated public administration through the spoils system, however, that system hardly effected a clean sweep of appointive offices; it appears to have reached only about 10 percent of federal government personnel put in office under Jackson's predecessors (Crenson 1975, 51). Furthermore, Jackson's replacements did not differ much in socioeconomic and demographic characteristics from the people they succeeded. Therefore, in Crenson's estimation, "where there are differences between the Jacksonian civil service and its predecessors, they are small, and they appear as continuations of a long-standing and very gradual trend toward democratization of the administrative elite" (16).

It might be better, therefore, to think of the spoils system and the dominance of partisanship, more generally, as themselves vehicles to effect the changes in the federal government, including personnel administration, that the Jacksonians sought in order to meet their concerns about restoring republican virtue and stemming the loss of moral authority and the institutional anchors for fundamental values. The change in institutional relationships was nonetheless significant, for it represented a marked departure from the conception of administration's proper place in the regime which had been prominent at the founding and in the early years of the republic.

The new Jacksonian administrative order, at least initially, was a return to simplicity in administrative arrangements, especially to the ideas of personal organization and unity of command (Crenson 1975, 51). That simplicity harkened back to, if it was not consciously grounded in, the allegedly simple and virtuous governance of George Washington's presidency (66–67). Yet Jackson carried the banner of personal organization further and intensified unity of command. Thus, not only were the operations of each department, bureau, and office to depend on personal organization and unity of command, but the entire executive branch must do so as well, with Jackson of course at the helm. In this sense Jackson did adhere to the main thrust of the Decision of 1789, and no where did he give more powerful formal expression to it, then in his protest to the Senate. A harsher instrumental conception of administration and a greater distancing of public administration from constitutional roots can be found in his response.

The Presidential Protest

The Bank of the United States was Alexander Hamilton's idea, integral to his plans to restore the health of the nation's finances under the Constitution and to invigorate the national economy. Hamilton's push to establish the bank contributed substantially to his rift with Jefferson, who argued that it would eventually lead to unrestrained federal power. Hamilton prevailed in the dispute when Washington sided with him in support of a charter for the bank. The bank was rechartered in 1816 and its charter designated for renewal again in 1836.

The Whig party, in many respects the successors of the defunct Federalists, supported the bank. Jackson and the Democrats opposed it, in particular, from Jackson's viewpoint, because the bank and the internal improvements it helped to finance represented an unconstitutional expansion of federal power and intrusion in state affairs that were undermining the republican values—honest toil, thrift, and reward for merit (Crenson 1975, 25)—of the revolution and the founding. The bank was at the center of the bitter presidential contest of 1832, and after he was re-elected, Jackson was more determined than ever to destroy the bank. Amos Kendall, a Treasury official and close friend and advisor to Jackson who would soon become Jackson's Postmaster General, prepared a plan for removing the bank's assets and depositing them in selected state banks, an example itself of a "subordinate" official having substantial influence on the shape and direction of public policy.

The bank's congressional charter, however, gave sole authority for removing deposits to the Secretary of the Treasury. This reflected the uniquely closer relationship to Congress that Treasury enjoyed as a result of its 1789 enabling act, as well as recurring efforts by Congress to vest discretionary authority directly in department heads rather than indirectly through the president. Moving around departmental appointments and ambassadorships in early fall 1833, Jackson appointed William J. Duane to the Treasury post. Duane was known to oppose the bank, but as it turned out, he supported allowing the bank's charter to expire rather than removing the deposits as the way to kill the bank. Duane thus resisted Jackson's order to remove the deposits, and he refused to resign. Jackson then fired Duane, installed his attorney general, Roger Taney, as treasury secretary, and Taney executed the asset transfer plan.

Whig leaders in the Senate, in furious response, pushed through in early spring 1834 the resolution that accused Jackson of assuming power and authority not granted to him by constitutional provision or statute. Jackson responded in turn with his formal message of protest of the Senate resolution. Despite the president's request, the Senate refused to enter the message into the journal of its proceedings. In his protest, prepared with the help of Roger Taney, Amos Kendall, and Attorney General–Designate Benjamin Butler, Jackson challenged the formality of the Senate resolution on constitutional grounds. More importantly, he revisited the Decision of 1789 and found in it an authoritative interpretation of the Constitution in which "the executive power is invested exclusively in the President" (Richardson 1911, 3:71). Jackson repeated this assertion several times and then connected it with the idea of unity of command and the subordination of executive officials.

> Being thus made responsible for the entire action of the executive department, it was but reasonable that the power of appointing, overseeing, and controlling those who execute the laws—a power in its nature executive—should remain in his hands. (79)

> The whole executive power being vested in the President, who is responsible for its exercise, it is a necessary consequence that he should have

a right to employ agents of his own choice to aid him in the performance of his duties, and to discharge them when he is no longer willing to be responsible for their acts. (79–80)

The Secretary of the Treasury being appointed by the President, and being considered as constitutionally removable by him, it appears never to have occurred to anyone in the Congress of 1789, or since until very recently, that he was other than an executive officer, the mere instrument of the Chief Magistrate in the execution of the laws, subject, like all other heads of Departments, to his supervision and control. (81)

Jackson continued throughout the protest to reiterate his conception of the unity of the executive, and toward the conclusion he warned, as Madison did in 1789, of the loss of responsibility without that unity. "The President is the direct representative of the American people, but the Secretaries are not. If the Secretary of the Treasury be independent of the President in the execution of the laws, then is there no direct responsibility to the people in that important branch of this Government to which is committed the care of the national finances" (Richardson 1911, 3:90). The persuasive power in Jackson's protest is precisely the link he makes to responsibility, which grasps at the heart of American worries about controlling officials not chosen through the ballot box: how can a people engage in self-government if some officials can act independently of direct popular influence?

Jackson's conclusion that "it appears never to have occurred to anyone in the Congress of 1789, or since" that administrators were other than mere instruments of the president is, of course, disingenuous, because the historical record is plain that many others thought administrators were more than just implements of the president. What is distinctively absent from the protest, even accepting an exclusively hierarchical line of authority from presidents to administrators, is any idea of a unique contribution administration would make to the regime, like that discernible from Hamilton or the challengers to the Decision of 1789. Executive officials were reduced to a single, indirect link to the Constitution, with no raison d'etre other than what the president bid.

Administration Depersonalized

Even as the contests over the Bank of the United States, the removal power, and the spoils system raged, many of Jackson's closest advisors, some holding important posts in his administration, had come to the realization that the concepts of personal organization and unity of command were inadequate for addressing their concerns about republican virtue and moral decay. Indeed, Jackson stalwarts were concluding that, in many respects, personal organization was *contributing* to the corruption and moral decay within the federal service.

In the institutions from which Jackson, as well as his predecessors, drew most of his appointees—especially law, but also commerce and manufacturing—personal organization predominated. The changes under way in American society had affected these institutions greatly (Crenson 1975, ch. 2). The institutions had lost much of their moral authority, and their practitioners could no longer impress upon men the old republican virtues that had made them trustworthy for federal employ. No longer could Jackson or his principal appointees "assume that their subordinates were fundamentally decent and that field administrators practiced the same standards of conduct which had prevailed for generations in the American legal profession and business community" (103). Whether the "great surge of equalitarian sentiment" and the pursuit of economic gain that Tocqueville linked to it (see, for example, Tocqueville 1988, 551–54) were, at the root, the problem is not altogether clear. But it was undeniable that the trust and expectations of obedience that Herbert Kaufman associated with the administrative orientation of the first five presidents was now naïve, if not debilitating.

Indeed, enough instances of corruption by appointees of both Jackson and his predecessors came to light (in some instances the people implicated had robbed the federal government blind) that something had to be done. The principal response of the Jacksonians, not necessarily in any coordinated fashion, was to begin to separate office from officeholder, in order to depersonalize the functions of the offices, bureaus, and departments of the federal government. In this effort, the spoils system may have been useful as well, for it bore the seeds of bureaucratic structure and of the interchangeability and commensurability associated with economic reasoning. "In this system, individuals could be placed or replaced without upsetting the integrity of the whole. Men were fitted to this system, not it to men. It was the administrative counterpart of the interchangeability of machine parts" (Marshall 1967, 455–56).

Thus, the spoils system could be regarded as "an instrument of bureaucratic depersonalization" (Crenson 1975, 56), and Jackson might "look forward to a time when the personal characteristics of the officeholder would not define the office, when one administrator could be exchanged for another without any disruption of public service" (57). Of course, the purpose for introducing bureaucratic elements into federal administration was not principally the more familiar ones of achieving greater efficiency through division of labor and harnessing specialization and expertise. The object was, instead, to constrain administrative iniquity. "Where the federal government had once relied on good character to assure the successful conduct of public business, it now depended on mechanical checking and balancing devices, arrangements which would make possible an almost automatic supervision of civil servants. Impersonal organization would reduce the government's reliance on 'good character'—so that it could also be freed from the depredations of bad character" (133). It also fit well the party ideal of constraining personal and programmatic ambition in favor of party principle.

In pursuing such internal changes in administrative structure as depersonalization, however, the Jacksonians revealed tensions and discrepancies between their rhetoric and the reality that even they recognized of the influence of public administrators on the character of the polity. Jacksonian rhetoric about public administration, and about politics more generally, was suffused with references to subordinate and dependent agents and instrumentalities. This was most evident in their adherence to the principle of instruction. "Instruction was the right of the people to dictate their views to the elected representatives, and the duty of their representatives to abide by that dictation" (Kohl 1989, 124–25). One logical consequence of the principle was that, "with the people constantly instructing the representative of their will, there was no need for knowledge, wisdom, or discerning judgment" (125). In commenting on attacks in the South against post offices, because of abolitionist pamphlets carried in the mail, Jackson claimed, "But we are the instruments of, and executors of the law, we have no power to prohibit anything from being transported in the mail that is authorized by law" (Crenson 1975, 151).

It comes as a rather jarring inconsistency, then, to discover that Jackson and his supporters had intended for government generally and public administration particularly a more constitutive role, in the formative or tutelary sense. As Crenson concluded, "the moral character of the citizens . . . seems to have caused them considerable worry, and administrative agencies had a role to play in restoring republican virtue to American society. The Jacksonians seem to have held the belief that the character of the nation's civil servants might help to shape the character of its people" (1975, 173). In other words, within the Jacksonian scheme of keeping governmental and administrative power in check, the adjustments in administrative structure and operations were expected to have some salutary effect on the wider society and individual citizens toward whom government's actions were to be kept in check.

As Robert Lane has pointed out, democratic peoples generally find "the thought of governmental shaping of behavior . . . unattractive" (1981, 12). In its most nightmarish form such behavior conjures up visions of government controlling not only citizens' actions but their thoughts and feelings as well. It was the Constitution's framers who sought to place relatively strong constraints on the tendencies of democratic government, in the hands of a passionate majority, to be preoccupied with people's tastes or the purity of their souls (Elkin 1987, 115–16). A reflective citizen of Jackson's time might therefore have asked, "How can public administration be a pure agent and instrument of the people's will if it is to have a hand in shaping that will?" The problem that the Jacksonians created for themselves, and, in a more long-lasting way, for the effectiveness of American public administration, was simply that the people's trust in and support for public administrators and administration as an institution could not be built on such an incongruity. Acknowledging the goal-determining and character-shaping qualities as well as the goal-achieving attributes of administration is necessary.

Michael Nelson has argued that the spoils system democratized the public service, thus helping "to legitimate the national government among the new classes of Jacksonian America and assimilate those that emerged later" (1982, 765). This reflected the fundamental political role of administration, as described here by Matthew Crenson: "The federal establishment was itself an organ of the political order, as much a part of the political struggle as were the party organizations. . . . It was not simply that the executive branch was staffed with party workers but, more important, that the administrative apparatus provided a link between the nation's political authorities and its citizens. In this capacity, administrative agencies performed functions very much like those of the modern political party—they helped to organize support for the republic's political regime" (1975, 6). A restoration of the spoils has therefore received periodic support (see, for example, Peters 1979; Maranto 1991).

But the spoils system could not bear the weight of the discrepancy between such conceptions of its contributions to the regime—increasing citizen attachment and constraining corruption through depersonalized administration—and either the force of the Jacksonian subordination rhetoric or the reality of results. For the spoils system, if not under Jackson then certainly under many of his successors, proved better at bringing the corrupt and immoral into government service—although this assessment has been challenged (M. Nelson 1982, 765; Maranto 1991, 8)—than it was at providing conceptual and structural components for controlling their behavior while in office. The politicization of administration for which it is remembered is thus not in the fundamentals of increasing attachment to the regime or shaping the moral character of its citizens but in the crass, self-interested politicking of the greedy who scrounged for patronage. If public administration as instrument and servant of the people could be bent to this result, how could it ever be trusted, supported, and legitimated as a fundamental shaper of the character of the citizenry?

The Whigs: Administration as the Exercise of Responsible Discretion

Jacksonian ideas about administration, even with their heavy baggage of tensions and contradictions, were clearly triumphant during this turbulent period in the development of American politics and government and in the decades afterward. The ideas did not go completely unchallenged, however. Whig opponents in particular took advantage of the clashes over the Bank of the United States, the presidential protest, and the spoils system to articulate alternative views, with the floor of the Senate proving to be their most effective forum.

Jeffrey Tulis observed that the dispute over the bank, Jackson's protest, and the Senate's reaction "evolved into a deep and serious discussion of the connection of the structure of the bureaucracy to the problem of executive accountability" (1987, 58). In the Senate debate precipitated by Jackson's request to have his protest message entered in the Senate journal, Whig senators spent a good deal of time railing against Jackson's arrogation of the whole executive power to himself. Nevertheless, senators did also deliberate about the structure and status of public administration in the constitutional system, and the Whig view articulated during the debate had very interesting qualities.

Senator George Poindexter, a Whig from Mississippi and the first senator to speak after Jackson's protest was read to the Senate on Thursday, April 17, 1834, observed that the "Secretary of the Treasury, who refused to bend his neck to the yoke of executive power, and to make himself the instrument of violating the solemn obligations of law at the dictation of the Chief Magistrate, was unceremoniously kicked out of office, and another substituted in his place, with a more compliant conscience" (*Register of Debates in Congress* [hereafter cited as *Register*] 1848a, 1336–37). Senator Peleg Sprague, a Whig from Maine, chastised Jackson for designating the Secretary of the Treasury "as the Secretary of the President, and not the Secretary of the law" (*Register* 1848a, 1341).

The following Monday the debate resumed, and Senator Thomas Ewing, a Whig from Ohio, attacked Jackson for speaking "of the Secretaries generally as his Secretaries . . . and thus appropriating those high offices of the law to himself as his sole and exclusive property" (*Register* 1848a, 1405). Senator Ewing also sharply denied that the Constitution vested the president "with any such power" of removal at will, and asserted that "its assumption is against the whole spirit and genius of our institutions.

Its tendency is obvious. It makes the President superior to the law" (1418).

Still later in the debate, on April 30, Henry Clay labeled Jackson's idea that the president possessed the sole executive power and that executive officers were exclusively responsible to him as "altogether a military idea, wholly incompatible with free government." Clay then went on to declare, "There exists no such responsibility to the President. All are responsible to the law, and to the law only, or not responsible at all" (*Register* 1848a, 1575). Finally, in his signature speech in the debate, Daniel Webster proclaimed, "There is, there can be, no substantial responsibility, any further than every individual is answerable, not merely in his reputation, not merely in the opinion of mankind, but to the law, for the faithful discharge of his own appropriate duties" (Wiltse and Berolzheimer 1988, 68).

Responsibility to the law was thus a central theme in the Whig attack on the Jacksonian conception of administration. But Clay, Webster, and their Whig allies articulated a second theme, which emphasized "the importance of the exercise of experienced, informed, responsible discretion as the heart of administration" (Storing 1980, 110). In staking out an early position against the protest message, Senator Theodore Frelinghuysen, a Whig from New Jersey, argued that "when the act of Congress put the public moneys under the discretion of the Secretary of the Treasury, the President did not possess the power of interfering with the full and free exercise of that discretion; much less to substitute his own will for the opinion and conscience of the Secretary" (*Register* 1848a, 1346). Henry Clay contended that "if [executive officers] are bound to conform to the will of the President, and to obey his commands, they cannot be regarded as moral, independent, and responsible beings" (1575). Daniel Webster voiced much the same idea: "And the Protest assumes to the President this whole responsibility for every other officer, for the very purpose of making the President every body, of annihilating everything like independence, responsibility, or character, in all other public agents" (Wiltse and Berolzheimer 1988, 62).

Senator George Bibb of Kentucky delivered perhaps the most interesting, thought-provoking, and surprising speech in the debate, on April 25. Bibb was a Jacksonian Democrat, but in his lengthy speech, he explored the intricate interconnections among responsibility, discretion, and the law facing public administrators. Senator Bibb moved from commentary on the specifics of William Duane's removal, about which he said, "He refused to surrender a duty and trust committed to him by law," to general observations about the duties of appointed officials. He stressed that "where the law itself assigns to an officer the performance of a duty, and the Legislature vests a discretion in that officer, then he is the officer of the law, answerable to the law, responsible for his own conduct" (*Register* 1848a, 1503). After dissecting Jackson's protest, Bibb reached the climax of his speech by elucidating his understanding of "the theory of our Government. Each officer is answerable for his own acts of commission or omission. . . . Each officer swears for himself, judges for himself, is responsible for himself to the public" (1511).

If many of the ideas articulated by these senators ring familiar, it is no accident. Senators Bibb, Clay, Ewing, and Webster in particular examined the records of the Decision of 1789 as intently as had the men who assisted Andrew Jackson in the composition of his protest message. They found intellectual and political kinship with the likes of William Smith, John Page, and James Jackson, who belonged to what Henry Clay labeled "a large and able minority" in the 1789 debate. In fact, Bibb, Clay, and Webster were so emboldened by their examination of the 1789 debate that they were willing to challenge its authoritativeness. Bibb mocked Madison's contention that impeachment provided a "decisive" check on the president. Impeachment, Bibb insisted, "has long since ceased to be any effective protection to the purity of the constitution" (*Register* 1848a, 1510). Clay called the 1789 debate inconclusive; he had argued in early March, in introducing legislation to control executive patronage, that the First Congress had "improvidently" conceded the removal power to the president as "an implied or constructive power" (834). Webster, in turn, had declared in his 1835 speech on the appointment and removal power that "Congress may . . . , hereafter, if necessity shall require it, reverse the decision of 1789" (Wiltse and Berolzheimer 1988, 90).

Their long-running battle with Andrew Jackson drew Whig leaders in the Senate into a searching discussion of the structure and status of public administration in the American regime. In Herbert Storing's interpretation, the conception the Whigs developed was remarkable. "The Whigs saw public administration not as a closed hierarchy leading to the top but as pools of official discretion, loosely connected but largely independent. . . . Sound discretion, not obedience to higher command, is the essence of good administration, though both, of course, are always involved" (1980, 110). Storing compared the Whig conception of the administrator to that of the judge, who is restrained by the limits of the law, and who employs practical reason within those limits to reach a good judgment.

Like their intellectual soul mates from 1789, then, the Whigs sought to define a more independent status for administrators and to anchor that independent status in a particular understanding of the Constitution. But I think that the minority in 1789 made a somewhat greater effort to be specific about the constitutional provisions that could support their understanding of and claims for administrative independence. Although George Bibb vested administrators with independence, responsibility, and discretion, for example, he linked it all directly to the public rather than to provisos in the Constitution, which might have provided a surer and more permanent foundation for the qualities he enumerated. Moreover, the Whigs were closer to accepting an exclusively instrumental function for administration. Thus, although many references to the administrative obligation to fulfill the purposes of the law can be found in the presidential protest debate, it evidences few if any references to the duty of administrators, through their discretion, to shape or refine the law or help to define the purposes the law embodies.

Indeed, many of the Whig paeans to responsibility and fidelity to the law appear to have meant mostly fidelity and subordination to Congress, which makes the law. Webster proclaimed that "the theory of our institutions is plain; it is that government is an agency created for the good of the people, and that every person in office is the agent and servant of the people" (Wiltse and Berolzheimer 1988, 77). The legislature is the supreme agent under "the theory," of course, and Webster continued, "I do not think the Constitution . . . intended to impose any restraint on the legislature, in regard to its authority of regulating the duties, powers, duration or responsibility of office" (89).

Henry Clay similarly placed control over executive power enacted by law with Congress, and argued in his presidential protest speech that "when an officer, no matter what may be the mode of his appointment, or the tenure of his office, is designated by law to perform duties growing out of powers vested in Congress, that officer represents Congress, and is the agent of Congress" (*Register* 1848a, 1577). In his executive patronage speech of 1835, Clay further argued, "The office coming into existence by the will of Congress, the same will may provide how, and in what manner the office and the officer shall both cease to exist. . . . Congress, in pursuit of the public good, brings the office and officer into being, and assigns their purposes" (Colton 1897, 18).

It was John Calhoun, however, who gave clearest expression to the notion that the controlling end of Madison's chain of dependence should rest in Congress's hands. In an 1835 speech on executive patronage, Calhoun offered his own "construction" of the Constitution, that "would put down all discretionary power, and convert the Government into what the framers intended it should be—a Government of laws and not of discretion." Calhoun then proceeded to declare that if his construction "be established, no officer, from the President to the constable, and from the Chief Justice to the lowest judicial officer, could exercise any power but what is expressly granted by the Constitution, or by some act of Congress; and thus that which, in a free state, is most odious and dangerous of all things—the discretionary power of those who are charged with the execution of the laws—will be effectually suppressed, and the dominance of the laws be fully established" (*Register,* 1848b, 555).

Herbert Storing's assessment is, therefore, crucial for characterizing Whig thinking about administration. The practical reason of the judge contains a strong element of instrumental rationality. The "severe limits of the law," after all, force the judge to reach a "good" judgment, that is, a judgment that fulfills the law's purposes. But the leeway, or discretion, permitted the judge within those limits means that the judgment will also contribute, perhaps in only a small way, to refining the law's aims, and thus altering the character of relationships between citizens. The struggle the judge faces in accommodating these two dimensions of judgment can be seen in the Whig effort to articulate a coherent understanding of public administration based on the balancing of fidelity to law (the instrumental) and responsible discretion (the constitutive). It is particularly interesting that Calhoun ultimately rejects the struggle of his Senate compatriots to accommodate the instrumental and the constitutive through a conception of the administrator's job that weds obedience to law with responsible discretion. Instead, Calhoun adopts a constitutional ideology, and within it a conception of public administration, that almost perfectly mirrors the instrumentalism of the Jacksonian view.

As a practical matter of public understanding and political practice, the outcome of the 1834–35 debates was much the same as followed those of forty-five years before. Some of America's premiere statesmen of the time failed again to take advantage of the opportunity to agree to acknowledge explicitly in their political rhetoric, and to embrace fully in the actual operations of government, a more expansive conception of public administration in the regime, one that would encompass its constitutive as well as its instrumental qualities. In this, I think, Jackson's Whig opponents were as much captives of the predominant interpretation of the Decision of 1789 as he was. In an exchange of letters with James Kent, the foremost authority on American constitutional law at the time, Daniel Webster seems convinced by Kent's insistence that "it is too late to call the Presidents [sic] power in question, after a declaratory act of Congress and an acquiescence of half a century" (Wiltse and Allen 1977, 12).

The 1834–35 debates thus failed to alter very much the status of public administration in the constitutional system that had emerged from the Decision of 1789. Consistent with Charles Thach's (1922) later assessment, it remained a question of who—the president or Congress—was the master. The outcome of two highly charged political contests, this way of framing the matter was likely the most important determinant of broad public thinking and political practice for many decades to follow. As it turned out, after Abraham Lincoln, Congress proved to be the undisputed master until the turn of the century.

The Jacksonian Legacy

Some of the political leaders involved in the debates connected with the founding and the Decision of 1789 seemed to recognize public administration as having both instrumental and constitutive attributes. A small handful even advocated grounding the structure and practice of public administration in this recognition. The democratic ideology of subordinate, instrumental administration overwhelmed this perspective, however, creating tensions and contradictions between what was ideal and what was real in politics and governance.

Not surprisingly, the Jackson presidency proved to be a direct response to such a gap between what was publicly pronounced and accepted and what was increasingly practiced with respect to the role of public administration. Yet the Jacksonian response, which centered on strengthening democratic control under the president *and* the party and sharpening the conception of the subordinate administrative instrument, only exacerbated the tensions and contradictions between the developing rhetoric and ideology and the fundamental reality of administration as a vital component in the ongoing construction of the regime. The strains created were particularly acute because the Jacksonian rhetorical response did not fully comport with the Jacksonians' own understanding, intentions, and actions regarding administration.

Although some political leaders did articulate conceptions of administration that seemed to recognize its constitutive role and the tension with its instrumental role, their efforts proved woefully incomplete, especially in translating this recognition to the practice of politics and government. In the presence of such confusion and suspicion about public administration's place in the regime, distrust could not help but increase among political leaders themselves and the public at large. And this, ultimately, could only contribute to weakening the capacity of public administration to support and improve American self-government. Hence, the theoretical and practical challenges public administration posed for American politics and government would have to be confronted again, and would be accentuated by accelerated industrialization and its impact on American society.

4

Perfecting the Neutral Instrument
Merit, Commerce Regulation, and the Effects of Progressive Reforms

What makes the murder of President James A. Garfield such an enduring legend? As part of American folklore, one can find some rendition of it in nearly every college text on American government, particularly in those passages concerning the development of national bureaucracy. Remarkably, it is not the president but Charles Guiteau, the deranged and swindling partisan who gunned down Garfield, who has become the focal point of references to the event. For political reformers of the time, as well as for many who are their ideological descendants, Guiteau seemed to embody the most distinctive characteristics of his political era, even as he proved to be the agent at whose hands the status quo met its undoing. Hence, he stands immortalized not as a madman but as a "disappointed office seeker," and he has secured the place of trigger man in the death of the very spoils system from which he sought to profit.

Of course, the institution of the spoils system survived long past the ten-week death watch over President Garfield; but it did succumb, and Guiteau's crime is more prominent in the story because it energized "public opinion very like a spark on a powder-magazine. It [fell] on a mass of popular indignation all ready to explode" (editorial from the *Nation* quoted in Hoogenboom 1961, 209). The spoils system had to end, because as its opponents proclaimed, the *people* demanded it. Guiteau's attack showed that the spoils system was so evil that it could lead to homicide. The public outcry revealed that the system also defied the democratic ideals then being given a new and vigorous expression.

The Guiteau story helps to illuminate the principal forces behind two laws widely regarded as original pillars in the edifice of the modern American administrative state: the 1883 Pendleton Act and the 1887 Interstate Commerce Act. The debates accompanying the enactment of these statutes also ushered in a new phase of intense struggle with the dilemma that public administration repeatedly presses upon the practice of American government and politics. The collision of democratic ideals and increasingly rapid economic and technological change stimulated this new phase, and important chords that were struck during the resulting dialogues and debates continue to sound today. Before considering how public administration was conceived in connection with the 1883 and 1887 initiatives, and in the much more searching effort of progressives to reconcile democracy and modernity, it is important to explore further the characteristics of this turn-of-the-century display of democracy's expansionary bent, manifested in the civil service reform movement, the effort to alter business-government relations, and the progressivism that enveloped and succeeded both after 1900.

Morality, Efficiency, and Middle-Class Democracy

The reform thrust that traversed the last years of the nineteenth century and the first decades of the twentieth century linked the rather narrowly focused civil service reformers with the more aggressive, far-reaching progressives. It presents an extraordinarily complex picture of diverse and even contradictory ideas and organized ventures. Nevertheless, we can distinguish certain common causes, especially moral restoration and social justice in politics and society, government improvement through more efficient and businesslike operation, and the transformation and intensification of democratic participation in response to the challenges industrialization and technological advances posed for American self-government. The restoration of proper political morals and ethics through reform of the civil service was the particular province of an older generation of reformers. Expanding political power and social justice, through an increase in government efficiency deriving from science and technology, was the motivating force of progressives, who emerged from a new, energetic, and self-conscious middle class. But these areas of concern were not each the exclusive province of one set of reformers. Instead, they were shared with varying emphasis by both the older generation of reformers and the progressives.

Moral Restoration

Over the 220-year course of American political development, each surge in the democratic tide has in essence recreated the original fight for independence. In that fight and its successive recreations, a broad and principled majority goes up against politically distant, entrenched holders of power. An attribute regarded as critical in the popular triumph is the moral superiority of the majority. The elite in power seem exceedingly corrupt and out of touch, while the invigorated majority merely seeks to enshrine such simple virtues as industriousness, honesty, or fair treatment and to realize the principles of democratic rule and individual self-determination. Thus, the patriots of the Revolution had the moral authority of the Declaration of Independence behind them. The Jacksonians sought to restore simple republican virtue and rescue institutions and individuals with crippled moral compasses. Franklin Roosevelt successfully portrayed his opponents as "economic royalists," responsible by their behavior for the political, economic, and social disaster of the Great Depression. Reformers of the 1960s and 1970s successfully affixed a negative connotation to the word "establishment." And from the late 1980s into the 1990s, "career" politicians in consort with "mindless" bureaucrats have become the prime objects of scorn of a diverse collection of reformers, who have sought to exploit broad public frustration with and anxiety about a federal government seemingly out of control and unresponsive to the peoples' needs.

The reformers who led the fight for civil service reform exhibited an acute concern for morality and for the moral degeneracy brought about, they thought, by the spoils system they sought to eradicate. The reformer Julius Bing declared in 1868, "At present, there is no organization save that of corruption; no system save that of chaos; no test of integrity save that of partisanship; no test of qualifications save that of intrigue. . . . We have to deal with evil that is manifest here and there and everywhere" (Hoogenboom 1961, 12). Stating it more succinctly, the pre–Pendleton Act Civil Service Commission, in its 1871 report to the president, charged that through the spoils system, "the moral tone of the country is debased. The national character deteriorates" (quoted in Rosenbloom 1971, 73–74).

After passage of the Pendleton Act, the message from reform leader and interior secretary Carl Schurz was still the same: "In my opinion, the question of whether the Departments at Washington are managed well or badly, is, in proportion to the whole question an insignificant problem overall. Neither does the question whether our civil service is as efficient as it ought to be cover the whole ground. The most important point to my mind is, how can we remove the element of demoralization which the now prevailing mode of distributing office has introduced into the body-politic" (Crenson 1975, 173–74). Putting it all together with passion and hyperbole, the reformers implicated the spoils in everything from the horrific Union losses in the Civil War, to prostitution, to Guiteau's murderous assault.

The reformers were divided somewhat over how civil service reform would work to restore the nation's moral bearings. Those who saw the *individual* as primary moral agent stressed change and moral restoration through persuasion and "exhortation which could direct citizens and politicians toward paths of honesty and virtue" (Karl 1963, 6). Change through civil service reform, by this approach, would be achieved simply by replacing bad employees with good ones. For reformers who emphasized *organizations* or *institutions* as core moral agents, reform would take "the shape of the redevelopment of political institutions and practices or in supposed reversions to institutions which had degenerated from their pure, original form" (6). Civil service reform from this perspective was, congruent with the Jacksonian view, not just a target of opportunity but the engine for altering the nature of the political system and society at large. The only strategy that civil service reformers ever seriously considered was selection of government personnel not by political affiliation but on the basis of merit, as established by competitive examinations and special qualifications associated with educational attainment. Fortunately for the civil service reform movement, this strategy was conducive to either a simple replacement of the bad with the good or a more "fundamental change in the political system by altering the nature of the civil service" (Rosenbloom 1971, 73).

Progressive reformers would appear to stand in contrast to their predecessors because of their concentration on efficiency over moral restoration in their support for continued administrative reform (e.g., Croly 1914, 397–405). Frederick Mosher designates the period 1883–1906 as "government by the good," followed by the period 1906–1937 as "government by the efficient" (1968, 64–79). In Barry Karl's observation, "the early years of the twentieth century saw a transition taking place—from the older emphasis upon sin and corruption to be investigated by vigilantes armed with public virtue to a new emphasis, now upon 'efficiency and economy,' to be investigated by experts armed with technical training and science" (1963, 51). Robert Wiebe (1967, 171) echoes Karl. "Civil service . . . had once been a negative, absolute goal, self-contained and self-fulfilling. Now the panacea of the patrician had given way to the administrative tool of the expert, with efficiency rather than moral purity its objective." Carl Schurz's commentary quoted above further reinforces the contrast.

Yet the seemingly distinct views of civil service and progressive reformers were significantly intertwined. The social control movement, which sought to "employ governmental power to impose homogenous standards of behavior on the entire population," was a significant component of progressivism (Chambers 1980, 114). Indeed, efficiency and science and technology were enlisted in the moral crusade. William Nelson (1982) has argued that reformers built a "new scientific morality," stressing specialized expertise and neutral standards like efficiency, on the ruins of an earlier effort to restore morality to government in the immediate post–Civil War period (also see Chambers 1980, 133–36). Reflecting this, Stephen Skowronek reports that the civil service reformers, "during the Civil War . . . had turned the United States Sanitary Commission into a propaganda instrument for espousing new values of professionalism, self-discipline, and science" (Skowronek 1982, 53). As civil service reform advanced, Senator George Pendleton, an Ohio Democrat, in a speech supporting his own civil service reform legislation, argued that "reform would eliminate . . . the twin evils of political corruption and business inefficiency" (Hoogenboom 1961, 217).

Four years after passage of the Pendleton Act, Woodrow Wilson saw moral recovery as preface to more far-reaching administrative and governmental change. "Civil-service reform is thus but a moral preparation for what is to follow. It is clearing the moral atmosphere of official life by establishing the sanctity of public office as a public trust, and . . . opening the way for making it businesslike" (Wilson 1941, 494). More emphatically, at the very heart of his treatise on progressive democracy, Herbert Croly declared, "During the last quarter of a century general relaxation of American moral fibre has unquestionably been taking place; and in spite of the increasing use of disciplinary measures, the process of relaxation has not as yet been fairly checked" (1914, 207). It was the ideal and the program of progressive democracy, built on a "democratic political organization" that was "fundamentally educational" but also "organized for efficiency" (378), Croly contended, that would not merely check but would cure that moral decline.

As Barry Karl concludes, those "who concerned themselves with honesty and efficiency" were the men who "made the Progressive and Populist platforms. They had fought for civil service reform as well as for expanded governmental regulation and control of public services. They had attempted to reform corrupt governments by the introduction of honest men" (1963, 19). Efficiency was, in a very real sense, itself a moral concept. "The precise meaning of the term was . . . arguable, but its moral significance could hardly be questioned. Efficient administration was 'good'; inefficient administration was 'bad.' . . . The public service, to be good, must be both politically neutral and efficient, and there was more than a little doubt that it could be efficient unless it was also politically neutral" (Mosher 1968, 71).

Democracy for the Modern Age

That the reform efforts stretching across the late nineteenth century and early twentieth century were also supported by a robust democratic impulse seems beyond dispute. But the texture of that impulse was distinctive and important. First, it emanated from the raw, leveling passion of the Populists, combined with, subsumed in, and thus ameliorated by the desire for participation, access, and power of a new professional middle class, the majority core of the progressive movement. More direct democracy—that is, bringing the government and the people closer together—became a special progressive rallying point. Second, however, the drive for participation and access reflected the intention of many reformers, particularly among the diverse professional and economic interests of the middle class, to reinvigorate the pluralist properties of the constitutional system. In William Nelson's (1982) persuasive account, that reinvigoration is a particularly enduring legacy of this era in American political development. Finally, thrown into the mix was the seeming paradox of an antidemocratic yearning of a "patrician elite" to "resume their natural posts of command" (Wiebe 1967, 61). Or, as Barry Karl has described it (1987, 29), progressives sought to develop and control a new, professional elite rule that modern mass democracy could accept.

The civil service reform movement, as described by Stephen Skowronek, was composed of "lawyers, journalists, academics, and clergy. These professionals controlled the executive committees of the reform associations. . . . As a group, they represented a key link between America's old patrician elite and its new professional sector" (1982, 53). The movement as a whole, moreover, "was fed by fears of a partnership of party and industry that would exclude the 'interests of the great middle classes' from government" (52). Although stressing the contrasts between older and newer reformers, Barry Karl nevertheless highlights the fundamental link between the two. "The old reformers had sought to expand democracy; the new sought to preserve it within limits now imposed by science and technology. The groups had a common history, even if they did not always remember it the same way" (1983, 17).

The common historical orientation of all the reformers was readily evident: the American political and governmental system from the very beginning embodied the promise of democracy, but that promise had been systematically thwarted. Progressive historians stressed the popular origins of American democracy, for example, and depicted American political development as reflecting a succession of selfish elites frustrating the search for social justice by the majority (see Herson 1984, 177). Connections between government and upper-class wealth were signs of corruption of popular control, not of inherent structural defects. The Constitution was fundamentally democratic, they concluded, but it had not been put into operation as its designers intended (see Karl 1963, 24).

Certainly, many of the reformers sought "to provide individuals and minorities with protection against what they perceived to be an increased threat of majority tyranny," and thus "to institutionalize pluralism" to address the concern of the founders "that popular power be limited by popular rights" (W. Nelson 1982, 5). Key elements in this push for pluralism may have had their roots in the "more 'pluralistic'" Whig view of American politics (Storing 1980, 110). All of this was consistent, nevertheless, with the growth of a middle class concerned about its political power, a middle class that defined itself on the basis of professional and business interests given concrete form as "associations."

Whether or not public sentiment was increasingly speaking with a pluralist tongue, the central current of reform among reformers old and new during the period was unequivocal: the expansion, and refinement, of *popular* government. Populists sought "to achieve a direct intrusion of the majority into government" (Herson 1984, 170), if possible by dispensing with the "artificial barrier" of "formal political structures" (Wiebe 1967, 61), that is, political parties. Progressives pursued the same end through a number of legal and constitutional changes, such as direct election of senators, direct primaries, and ballot reform, that intensified direct democracy but acknowledged the importance of constitutional forms and thus the "boundaries of popular democracy" (Karl 1987, 28). Hence, perhaps their most important contribution to democratic reform came in the guise of reinterpretations of founding principles of executive leadership (see, e.g., Tulis 1987, chs. 4, 5) leading to the concept of "executive government," with its "efficient organization" for the "rule of the majority" (Croly 1914, 305). All of this would have major consequences for how public administration was conceived of and situated within the constitutional regime.

Neutral Service to the Popular Will

Introductory American government and public administration textbooks rarely miss the opportunity to point out that the word *administration* fails to appear anywhere in the U.S. Constitution. Upon this "fact" many of the texts then stake the claim that public administration was seldom the focus of attention for political leaders and was fairly insignificant in the life of the polity until the establishment of the modern American welfare state by the New Deal. Both the founding generation and the Jacksonians, however, even as they espoused principles of instrumentalism and subordination, in many of their ideas and actions gave administration a prominent place in efforts to shape or reshape the American regime. It is not altogether clear that the reformers of the late nineteenth century and early twentieth century fully grasped this historic constancy to their efforts. By the problems upon which they fixed their attention and the issues that animated their public actions, however, they, like their predecessors, placed public administration and its conception, articulation, and construction at the center of efforts to remake American constitutionalism.

For the civil service reformers, of course, attention to administration was central, because government at all levels was completely colored by patronage, and patronage was *the* insidious evil that had to be exorcised from the body politic. As the reform leader George Curtis put it, "The difficulty is not the abuse of patronage but the patronage itself" (Skowronek 1982, 52). The best way to get at patronage and eliminate it from government and society was to neutralize the civil service, a process Herbert Kaufman has described in starkly effective terms. "The assumption imbedded in the [Pendleton] Act—indeed, in the philosophy of civil service reform—is that the civil service is a 'neutral instrument,' without policy preferences of its own (taken as a body) and without any inclination to attempt to impose any policy on the country. For civil service reformers, the civil service was like a hammer or a saw; it would do nothing at all by itself, but it would serve any purpose, wise or unwise, good or bad, to which any user put it" (1965, 39).

The object of the neutralization of the civil service was the dissolution of partisanship, not only in the selection of administrative personnel, but in the behavior and decision making of administrative officials. Paul Van Riper has argued that this reflected "only a very mild dichotomy between politics and administration." The civil service reformers advocated "the partisan but not total political neutrality of the service. Their doctrine of neutrality was that of the British. Career civil servants were forbidden to play any active party role and were protected from partisan removal and assessments, but they were expected to further the lawful policies of the party in power" (1983, 482). American reformers, in other words, wanted American public administrators to follow the doctrine espoused by the British diplomat Robert Gilbert Lord Vansittart: "The soul of our service is the loyalty with which we execute ordained error" (Denhardt 1993, 252).

Van Riper's argument is bolstered by some of the more complex characterizations of the effects of reform. Carl Schurz, for example, envisioned "presidents and heads of the executive departments" as "respected officers of state having high duties to fulfill" which demanded "strength and ability" (Skowronek 1982, 55). George Curtis argued that "the essential point is . . . to find . . . coal-heavers who, being properly qualified for heaving coal, are their own masters and not the tools of politicians" (Rosenbloom 1971, 79). Curtis's statement is especially provocative. One hankers to ask him if by "their own masters" he meant that these coal heavers were not mere tools of "the people" either but might also seek to shape the purposes for which they were heaving coal.

Van Riper's characterization of the neutrality sought by civil service reformers is, however, more confirmatory of a strong dichotomy than he admits. A public administration that is political yet nonpartisan might seek to shape the polity, perhaps through its discretionary authority, in ways inconsistent with the policies of the party in power but perfectly congruent with the special values and qualities it embodies as an institution, even as it also carries out its ministerial duties as directed by the president, Congress, or the courts. They would be Curtis's coal heavers who were their own masters. In contrast, a civil service that was *totally* neutral, in Kaufman's sense of the complete absence of any policy preferences of its own, would be the one that only did the bidding of the party or majority in power. It would surely be engaged only in the ministerial, or nonpolitical, aspects of administration.

And the latter is precisely what the reformers sought. As David Rosenbloom has stressed, restrictions on the political character of the public service were "intended to insure its impartiality, and to eliminate the possibility that the civil service, either voluntarily or under coercion, could use partisan political activity to subvert the democratic process" (Rosenbloom 1971, 94). For the civil service reformers, protecting the integrity of the democratic process meant not just washing away partisanship from the civil service but thoroughly expunging politics of any sort from administration as well. As Herbert Kaufman explains, "they were anxious to make the best tool possible available to whoever occupied the highest seats in the American governmental system. They conceived of policy and administration as distinct and separate, though related, activities, and they wanted to restrict partisanship to the policy-makers in order to provide a superlative mechanism by which the voters' mandates could be carried out. They perfected the instrument; let the people put it to what use they would" (1965, 39).

This characterization of administration as instrumental by political leaders of this new reform era was as thorough as anything offered by the Jacksonians, with whom they otherwise vehemently parted company. So

too, Herbert Kaufman's assessment suggests, was their idea of administration's subordination to the popular will. Issuing an executive order on
political neutrality three years after enactment of civil service reform,
President Grover Cleveland insisted, "Officeholders are the agents of the
people, not their masters" (Rosenbloom 1971, 97). So thorough was the
acceptance of this conception, in fact, that neither the long rhetorical
campaign of civil service reformers nor the congressional debate on the
Pendleton Act—the principal concrete initiative of the civil service reform movement—generated anything resembling more expansive thinking about the structure of public administration and its standing in the
polity. Indeed, the subordination of the civil service to the people (and,
for some, to the party) as a ministerial instrumentality was the dominant
image conjured up during the debate. The civil service reform effort mir-
rored the tensions and contradictions about public administration's
place in the polity that had been evident in the Jacksonian attempt at republican restoration.

Moral Restoration and Neutral Obedience: The Pendleton Act

Among the lengthiest and most revealing public debates on civil service
reform was the one that took place in December 1882 on the floor of the
U.S. Senate. Reform forces had finally gathered sufficient strength to
push consideration of and final decision on the Pendleton bill. Of the
several notable themes that permeated the debate, one oft-repeated argument was that substantial growth in the size and responsibilities of the
federal government had made it impossible for the heads of departments
and bureaus to know all their subordinates and thus to be able to judge
their capabilities and deficiencies. Hence, even if the spoils system was
not corrupt and destructive (which of course to the reformers it incontrovertibly was), it was no longer practical. Some impersonal, efficient
method for selecting civil servants to meet the government's needs had to
be found. Evidently, the problems of "moral hazard" and "adverse selection" prominent today in rational choice theories of public bureaucracy
(see Garvey 1993, 25–33) were already recognized.

The most deeply entrenched theme was public administration's subordination and service to the people. Proponents argued that this was
best fulfilled by a merit system, which was in keeping with the original
principles and practices of government under the Constitution. Opponents argued that party control and rotation in office was the best way to
maintain "a people's government." Senator Pendleton offered the reformers' case.

The bill has for its foundation the simple and single idea that offices of the Government are trusts for the people; that performance of the duties of these offices is to be in the interest of the people. . . . If it be true that offices are trusts for the people, then it is also true that the offices should be filled by those who can perform and discharge the duties in the best possible way. Fidelity, capacity, honesty were the tests established by Mr. Jefferson when he assumed the reins of government in 1801. He said then . . . that these elements were necessary to an honest civil service, and that an honest civil service was essential to the purity and efficiency of administration, necessary to the preservation of republican institutions. (*Congressional Record* [hereafter cited as *CR*] 1882, 206)

Later in the debate, Senator Daniel Voorhees of Indiana presented a version of the opposition case and seemed to argue that assisting office seekers was one of the duties of elected representatives.

This is a people's government, a representative government. We are sent here by the people who own this Government. I for one am not ready to say the moment I am in place that nobody shall approach me. I am not ready to say that the people who pay the taxes, till the soil, do the work and the voting, shall not have the ear of their representatives and access to their presence anywhere and everywhere. We are their servants, not their masters. A different system is growing up here to that in the days of our fathers. The sooner we return to the old principle that we are the servants of the people and not their masters, the better it will be for us and this country. (*CR* 1882, 355)

Cutting across this major line of division between proponents and antagonists of reform in the debate was the impact of reform on the parties. Indeed, in his history of the campaign against the spoils system Ari Hoogenboom concluded that, "concern over the Pendleton bill's effects on the civil service . . . played second place to its calculated effects on either party" (1961, 243). That concern did stretch the senators' thinking just a bit with respect to the structure of the federal administrative establishment. Many legislators from western states, for example, called for a balanced sectional representation in the federal service through continuation of rotation in office. George Washington certainly pursued a policy of geographic balance in executive appointments (White 1948, 256), and the idea bears resemblance to the concept of representative bureaucracy, which gained prominence in the 1970s (see Rohr 1986, 45, and works cited therein). A public administration regarded as a representative institution would surely break out of the bonds of purely instrumental subordination. Alas, the public record of the debate offers no evidence to suggest that advocates of sectional representation, like Nebraska's Senator Charles Van Wyck, had any such a notion in mind. What they mostly sought was their fair share of the patronage.

Even more provocative was the proposal for "the direct election of officers located outside of Washington" (Hoogenboom 1961, 219), a version of which Senator Pendleton himself introduced as a separate bill. Democratic Senator James George of Mississippi added a twist by proposing "a constitutional amendment providing for the local election of all federal officers" (239). In the House, Representative Amasa Norcross of Massachusetts proposed a constitutional amendment to create a "house of electors to elect or confirm civil officers" (*CR* 1882, 16). Direct election of public administrators is hardly foreign to American political and governmental practice. Today, all but a handful of states directly elect at least some administrative officials, such as secretaries of state, attorneys general, and treasurers. Some states also elect agriculture commissioners, auditors, comptrollers, education commissioners, insurance commissioners, and public utility regulators (see *Book of the States,* 1992).

The election of *federal* administrators would have wide-ranging implications, however. With federal administrators having obvious and identifiable constituencies as the result of elections, could the president or Congress exert any effective control over them? In spite of the Constitution's provision for only three branches, public administration might truly have become the de facto fourth branch of government it has long been touted to be (see Meier 1993). But such exciting implications were never addressed in debate on the Pendleton Act. The idea of electing public administrators was pursued by opponents of the Pendleton bill, less as a serious alternative than as a political maneuver to undercut the reformers' claim that civil service reform was the better way to achieve fidelity to the people's will.

Finally, an issue that also crossed the line between proponent and antagonist and, more importantly, pushed the senators to think more expansively about public administration under the Constitution, was the structure and status of the commission that would oversee any merit system. Pendleton's bill was essentially written by Dorman Eaton and the legislative committee of the New York Civil Service Reform Association (Hoogenboom 1961, 201). It provided for a five-member examining board, serving the president directly during good behavior. Senators raised objections to both the "good behavior" provision and the absence of Senate confirmation of the commissioners in what became another iteration of the struggle over the removal power.

Senators attacking commissioner tenure during good behavior argued that it amounted to insuring "life tenures for civil officers" and created "an aristocracy or bureauocracy [sic] of a class of men beyond the reach of public opinion" (*CR* 1882, 244). Senator John Ingalls of Kansas strenuously urged that the commission "be limited to a distinct and definite term of office, and . . . be held to the American doctrine of direct responsibility to the people, like all other officials. . . . The theory of our system is that when a man is elected or appointed he shall abandon his functions at the end of a certain term to receive the verdict either of the people or of the appointing power as to whether he has discharged his duties well and is fit to fill the place again" (*CR* 1882, 276).

Arguing in favor of tenure during good behavior, Senator Joseph Hawley of Connecticut, having obviously done his homework, sounded remarkably like James Madison in 1789.

> Sir, I would leave the chief with the fullest responsibility. . . . I believe he has and ought to have the power of removal, as he has the power of appointment, and let the full judgment of the country then come down upon him for any failure to do his duty. He has the power to do his duty; he can command abundantly excellent service if you let him, but the moment you put up a barrier between him and his subordinates, and shield him from responsibility, you scatter it, divide it, and destroy it. . . .
>
> To protect us from such results we rely on the principle of responsibility of the chief. . . . Hold him to his duty. (*CR* 1882, 244)

Also opposing fixed terms for the commissioners, and in the process driving home the connection between service to the people, neutralization of civil service, and the dichotomy of politics and administration, Republican senator Warner Miller of New York argued that the Constitution fixed the terms of elective officials because they made policy, and that required direct responsibility to the people. In contrast, "duties which the appointive officer is called on to discharge are usually simply executive or ministerial; they have nothing whatever to do with the policy of the Government or with the methods of government, but with the administration of affairs which are in almost all cases purely clerical" (*CR* 1882, 316).

Senators attacking the design of the commission in the Pendleton bill as a body directly in aid to the president, sought to have the appointment of commissioners subject to the advice and consent of the Senate. This effort, combined with moves to fix tenure, not only of the commissioners, but of most civil officers, thus centered the debate squarely on the removal power. As Senator John Sherman, Pendleton's Ohio colleague, stated it, "the power of removal ought to be checked in some better way than is proposed in this bill" (*CR* 1882, 210). Charles Thach's question thus was again the focus of contention. As Stephen Skowronek rephrased it, "Was the new merit system ultimately an arm of the President or an arm of the Congress?" (Skowronek 1982, 61).

The outcome of the debate on the commission was its reduction in size from five to three commissioners, to be appointed by the president and confirmed by the Senate, and serving for fixed, staggered terms. These conditions have subjected the commission to the push and pull of presidential-congressional struggles over most of its existence (Hall 1965). Remarkably, however, the commission itself gained increasing control over the removal power (Kaufman 1965, 53–56), which all the reformers in 1882 had proclaimed was part of the president's basic executive authority, not to be diminished by the creation of a neutral civil service. This consequence would contribute in its own way to the rift between the rhetoric of an ideally subordinate, instrumental administration and the reality of a public administration with constitutive qualities, as evidenced in actual political and governmental practice.

The debate of 1882–83 was another in the concentric waves on the surface of American political and administrative development, broadcast out from the Decision of 1789. A significant portion of the debate centered on which side could prove that its approach to filling federal offices would create a bureaucracy more obedient to the popular will. Unlike those in 1789 or 1834–35, the discussions in 1882–83 did not stimulate the kind of thinking that grasped the constitutive dimension in administration in a way that might have led to an alternative conceptualization and design for public administration in the American regime. The general intellectual bankruptcy of the spoilsmen must be a major part of the explanation. Debate on the Pendleton Act on the floor of the U.S. Senate took place when the supporters and beneficiaries of the spoils system were at their strongest. An added reason for the narrow focus of the debate may have been the reformers' single-minded attention to only one method of reform. "There was not very much original thought about the best kind of substitute for spoils beyond competitive entrance examinations and security of tenure" (Mosher 1968, 65).

Like the 1834–35 removal power discussions, however, the Pendleton Act debate and the more general civil service reform effort did reinforce the incongruity of the Jacksonian reforms. Reformers and political leaders trumpeted the idea of public administration as purely instrumental and subordinate, in connection with a new and spirited surge of demands for popular control and participation. Yet they also pushed for a neutral, expert administration, because they understood and publicly proclaimed it a vital constituent in the moral and democratic transformation of the regime. For reflective citizens, again, the question was, How could administration be a purely neutral, subordinate instrument of popular will if it was to have a hand in reshaping the moral and behavioral components of that will?

Representation and Management of Societal Interests: The Interstate Commerce Act

The sharpest counterpoint to the dominant instrumental conception of administration came with the struggle over the regulation of interstate commerce and the establishment of a commission to wield that regulatory power. The debate occasioned a spirited exchange of views and ideas among congressmen, other public officials, and prominent private citizens about the proper structure and character, and potential, for public administration in the American system.

The railroads had posed a problem for the American political economy for nearly a decade before Congressman John Reagan of Texas brought focused legislative attention to it in 1878. A version of the story, grounded in economic theory and claiming that the railroads were behind the push for federal regulation (Kolko 1965), remains a key part of the scholarship on the establishment of interstate commerce regulation. Certainly, because the initial law was only weakly restrictive of the railroads, "some [railroad] executives actually welcomed it as protective cover" (Wiebe 1967, 53). But regulatory initiatives in several states had preceded passage of the Interstate Commerce Act (ICA), and these had been fomented largely by the Granger movement, with its blend of moral outrage and naked majoritarianism.

A diverse cross-section of economic interests closed ranks to push for federal regulation (Purcell 1967), and the railroads by and large opposed the final result (Fiorina 1986). Responding to the populist origins of demands for regulation, John Reagan, leaving for his second post–Civil War term in Congress, told his constituents in 1877, "There were no beggars till Vanderbilts and Stewarts and Goulds . . . shaped the action of Congress and moulded the purposes of government. Then the few became fabulously rich, and the many wretchedly poor . . . and the poorer we are the poorer they would make us" (Wiebe 1967, 8).

Reagan had served two terms in the House of Representatives before the war. He resigned from the House to participate actively in Texas's secession from the Union, and he became postmaster general of the Confederacy. After serving a short time in prison at the war's end, he was elected to the House again in 1874. Bringing with him a background as both railway entrepreneur and harsh critic of the railroads and having broad interests in interstate and foreign trade, he assumed the chairmanship of the House Commerce Committee. In the spring of 1878, he successfully steered his committee to favorable action on his own bill "to regulate interstate commerce and to prohibit unjust discrimination by common carriers" (quoted in Fiorina 1986, 33). The bill languished for seven years, through Senate inaction and the Democrats' loss of control of the House in the Forty-seventh Congress (1881–83). Activity and debate was renewed at the end of the Forty-eighth Congress and the beginning of the Forty-ninth, spurred by the Supreme Court decision in *Wabash, St. Louis, & Pacific Railway Co. v. Illinois* (118 U.S. 557) declaring state railroad regulation unconstitutional, and it resulted in the passage of the Interstate Commerce Act in 1887 and the establishment of the Interstate Commerce Commission (ICC) that same year. Originally placed as a bureau of the Interior Department, the ICC gained its status as an independent regulatory commission two years later (Rohr 1986, 95).

A critical aspect of this debate concerned what form the regulation of interstate commerce should take. Having a commission was advanced principally by Illinois senator Shelby Cullom. The alternative was reliance on the "common law" and the courts, and this approach was advocated by Reagan. Reagan defended his approach on the simple populist terms that the courts "were close to the people, and familiar to them" (Rohr 1986, 95) and that as regulatory entities they better fulfilled the fundamentals of constitutional design. As Morris Fiorina has summarized it, "in the best Madisonian tradition Reagan argued that courts were so numerous and dealt with such a wide variety of issues that no single interest would find it practical or possible to control them, though isolated instances of corruption certainly were possible, and indeed were matters of record" (1986, 38 n. 10).

In earlier assessments, the commission idea "had appeared to Reagan an instrument designed to impress the railroad point of view on Congress and the people" (Skowronek 1982, 144). Congressman Reagan and his supporters pressed this and other points of attack as the debate reached its zenith in 1886–87. They expressed concern that a commission could not in practice do what it was being asked to do. This concern reflected in part the enormity of the task, with respect to both geography and the extent of the demand for relief. But it was also an insistence that the commission could not do its job well because it could not avoid falling under the influence of the railroads ("agency capture" in current parlance), no matter how pure, competent, and well-intentioned the commissioners. With respect to appointments to the commission, Reagan observed that the "vast resources" of the railroads enabled them "to control the best legal and business talent of the country, and would enable them to procure influential men in their interest to appeal to the

President in the name of justice and on account of capacity to name such men as would serve their purposes" (*CR* 1886, 7283).

Reagan and his colleagues pressed the attack still further, however, arguing that even if "clothed with a limited discretion," as promised by commission advocates, regulation by commission placed an unwarranted administrative body between the legislature and the judiciary and between the people and the legislature. This would be a body that, if not wholly unconstitutional, was certainly a foreign threat to the American system. "The American people have as a rule great respect for law and for the action of the judiciary, but they are not accustomed to the administration of the civil law through bureau orders. This system belongs in fact to despotic governments; not to free republics" (*CR* 1886, 7283).

Congressman Reagan's commentary on this point is really quite remarkable, because, most likely unbeknownst to him, at nearly the same moment, Woodrow Wilson was struggling with precisely the problem of how to adapt administrative methods used by despotic governments and employ them to help modernize American democracy. Wilson described the situation vividly in a famous 1887 essay: "If I see a murderous fellow sharpening a knife cleverly, I can borrow his way of sharpening the knife without borrowing his probable intention to commit murder with it" (1941, 504). Reagan's contention, however, might have served as a warning to Wilson and others that their efforts would face stiff resistance. Thus, in the view of one commission opponent, Representative Charles O'Ferrall of Virginia, it was better to keep it simple and direct. "The Congress of the United States is the commission created by the people for the enactment of laws, and the courts of the country the tribunals for their enforcement. . . . Let those who have been accredited as the representatives of the people here prove themselves equal to the high duties they have assumed. Let them not stand appalled and paralyzed in the face of corporate power; let them give the relief demanded, assume responsibilities, and not throw them off upon a commission that will be responsible to nobody" (*CR* 1886, 7296).

The reasoning behind the anticommission view in the debate was quite clearly instrumental in its foundations. The people were calling for regulation of the railroads, and the appropriate means had to be found to reach that end; but a commission was too dangerous an instrument to employ, because it could too easily be seized by the railroads for their own purposes. The courts could better serve the public goal of regulation and, like every other political institution, were essential instrumentalities of the popular will. Indeed, as Representative O'Ferrall proclaimed, even the railroads were instruments of the people. "In a word, sir, they are in the intendment of the law the servants and not the masters of the people, and I would act toward them in that fair, just, and equitable manner that should characterize the treatment of a servant, and in return demand of them that consideration due from a servant" (*CR* 1886, 7293).

Commission opponents seemed to be claiming something more, however. Pursuing "administration of the civil law through bureau orders," they contended, would alter the regime. The introduction of bureaucratic structures and the actions of unaccountable bureaucrats would transform the very essence of the American republic. This appears to have been a much more profound concern for commission opponents than which institution would prove the most effective, but their commentary makes it clear that the two concerns could not be severed and considered separately.

Supporters of the commission idea were hardly unified in their conceptions of what the commission should be, but in their diversity they managed to articulate images of the proposed ICC that, among other things, had it fulfilling critical niches in modern American governance beyond what the Congress, presidency, or the courts did, while still expressing and embodying important features of American constitutional structure. Senator Collum regarded the administrative authority embodied in the ICC "as a way to compensate for the deficiencies of a representative body in formulating a regulatory policy" (Skowronek 1982, 146). Hence, Collum and other commission supporters sought broad, vague delegations of authority to the ICC so that the expertise and deliberative reasoning of the commissioners would lead to the most rational regulatory policy.

In written testimony submitted to Senator Collum's special investigative committee, the constitutional scholar and jurist Thomas Cooley, who would become the ICC's first chairman, envisioned the commission as "combining in its management" the interests of the railroads, "constituting . . . a section by itself of the political community," with "the State representing the popular will and general interests" (quoted in Rohr 1986, 104). Rohr points out that Cooley's idea contains a hierarchical aspect, because Cooley used the analogy of municipal government to explain his idea. Municipalities combine state and local power, but the "states are the constitutional masters of local government" (Rohr 1986, 105). Moreover, Cooley, like Representative O'Ferrall, also viewed "corporations as instruments of the state—at least when the state chooses to treat them as instruments" (105). Yet Cooley's conception of the ICC as operating to commingle significant interests in American society seemed to stretch beyond the idea of an administrative entity as simply an instrument of the popular will or of elected representatives. As Rohr concludes, Cooley's subsequent behavior as ICC chairman "carried the clear implication that [the ICC] was ultimately responsible to the Constitution, rather than to the will of elected officials" (110). Indeed, in Stephen Skowronek's estimation, the ICC under Cooley "sought to build administrative authority in order to conserve, protect, reconcile, guide, and educate" (1982, 151), activities much more expansive than those one would associate with a neutral, subordinate instrument.

Other commission proponents advocated the idea that the ICC would mediate between key interests in American society, thus performing a representational function. A professor of economics at Yale, A. T. Hadley, envisioned the commission as an intermediary body between the legislature and the railroads (which was, remember, precisely one of John Reagan's principal fears). In Hadley's view, the commission's function would be "publicity," that is, the commission would represent the interests of the railroads to the public, and the interests of the public to the railroads (Rohr 1986, 97). Similarly, railroad executive Albert Fink pushed for the ICC as "a mediator and counsellor between the railroads and the public" (quoted in Rohr 1986, 97). New York representative Charles B. Baker saw the commission "representing at once public sentiment and the law" (quoted in Rohr 1986, 99). Rohr interprets Baker's views as suggesting that the ICC possessed "its own peculiar constituency, national public sentiment" (99). Indeed, Rohr notes in the records of the debate on the ICC the "remarkable frequency with which the members of the proposed commission were referred to as 'representatives' " (100).

An administrative body that fills a key governing niche, that represents distinctive societal interests, and that, furthermore, commingles core societal interests, not just passively as in an open field of play, but actively as in Cooley's idea of "managing," would appear to be constitutive in its essential nature. This would especially be the case to the extent that it helped to shape the outcome of that interest interaction, by defining or redefining what those interests were.

One other dimension of the debate on the status and character of the commission concerned what powers it would actually wield. John Rohr reports that the emphasis on a common law remedy for the interstate commerce problem brought many participants in the debate to the conclusion that the commission had to be some kind of court. Consequently, by this reasoning, the commissioners deserved the constitutional protection of life tenure. Others saw the commission as a more complex institution (Rohr 1986, 97), wielding a mix of legislative, judicial, and executive powers. Senator John Morgan of Alabama observed, "My judgment is that we have combined very skillfully powers derived from each of these departments of the Government in the hands of these commissioners" (*CR* 1886, 4422). This mixing of powers concerned Morgan. He did not want executive officers wielding legislative and judicial powers, and he offered a cautionary amendment. He warned that failure to clarify the nature of the commissioners' powers would result in the creation of a body of "autocrats."

A concern for the powers that administrative agencies exercise goes to the very heart of the question of public administration's status under the Constitution. The record of the brief debate on Senator Morgan's amendment suggests, however, that senators understood, or at least accepted, the mix of powers they were granting the Interstate Commerce Commission. Senator Samuel Maxey of Texas rang down the curtain on Morgan's amendment by stating, "It is not a matter of the slightest consequence to me whether the powers are called executive, judicial, legislative, or ministerial. We have defined on the face of the bill the powers which are to be exercised by the commissioners" (*CR* 1886, 4422). The senators seemed willing, then, to accept that the commission might exercise substantial authority and influence, under the control of a limited grant of discretion, a formula that Theodore Lowi (1979, 96) holds up as a model of proper administrative arrangement.

In many ways, the debate on the establishment of the Interstate Commerce Commission stimulated extraordinary thinking and deliberation about administration and its proper character and place in the American governmental and political system. That deliberation was especially important because it took place in public, in exchanges among public officials, scholars, and business people. Indeed, the ICC debate elicited most of the major points subsequently advanced in support of independent regulatory commissions as solutions to the administrative dilemma by progressives like Herbert Croly (1914, 363–66; also see Chambers 1980, 242) and by New Dealer James Landis (1938). Commissions should operate with substantial discretion, even autonomy, but only within the narrow sphere defined by their mission and expertise. They should exercise a mix of legislative, executive, and judicial powers, but again only within a narrow sphere, and they should be representative of significant societal interests. The debate also elicited the two central criticisms that have come to dominate both politics and scholarship concerning independent commissions: the threat of interest-group capture (Huntington 1952; Bernstein 1955; Posner 1974) and the problem of vague delegations of power (Lowi 1979).

Despite the impressive content of the ICC debate, its immediate impact on the administrative dilemma was relatively inconsequential. The principal public focus at the time was still on civil service reform—the transformation of the character of the entire executive establishment into a wholly neutral, subordinate, instrument. In the long run, moreover, the debate on the creation of the ICC probably contributed more to public disdain for bureaucracy than to construction of an alternative conceptual foundation for public administration. Although the formula for proper delegation of power that Lowi points to did emerge during the debate, it did not encompass a coherent conception of administration, clearly articulated and anchored in recognition of its instrumental and constitutive qualities and the tensions between them. Several conceptions of the commission that merit categorization as constitutive thinking did surface, but they did not fit together into some overarching idea, nor did the thinkers attempt to make them fit together.

With a chairman of Thomas Cooley's background, the early years of the Interstate Commerce Commission might have generated a conception of the commission as having a constitutive role in American governance, but Cooley's tenure was cut short by poor health (Rohr 1986, 106–10). Of course, the Supreme Court, working through its own version of the dominant instrumental conception, undermined Cooley's efforts anyway (Skowronek 1982, 154–60). Cooley had advanced concept-stretching ideas, to be sure, but he seems never to have tied the ideas together with a unifying argument. The ICC would eventually function in a representative capacity and not only serve but also shape policy aims through its expertise and mix of powers, but this autonomy and policy-making authority went beyond any justification that the founding legislation could have provided (see Lowi 1979, 101–4). When that autonomy and authority in subsequent decades appeared to fulfill John Reagan's prophecy of agency capture, the importance of regarding administrative agencies as subordinate instruments, to be tightly controlled by the people through their elected representatives, was substantially reinforced by the evidence of events.

The establishment of the ICC thus presents a prime opportunity for observing the consequences of the tensions between an ideology of administrative instrumentalism and subordination and the reality of public bureaucracies functioning in ways that noticeably influence the character of the polity. It also provides a prime lesson in the necessity of designing both the parts and the whole of public administration with its essential constitutiveness recognized.

Of course, the ICC was only the beginning of efforts during the Progressive Era to come to grips with the administrative dilemma in American government and politics. The confrontation with modernity took place across a broad front during the apogee of progressive politics. Political leaders wrestled with the tensions and contradictions posed by administration in a liberal democratic regime in issues ranging beyond business regulation, such as the reconstruction of the banking system and improvements to the purity of foods and drugs. Nowhere was the dilemma more dramatic, however, than in the effort to redefine executive power.

Presidents, Popular Will, and Public Administration

President William Howard Taft sent a special message to Congress in June 1912 addressing "the need for a national budget." In his message, Taft argued that "the executive, as the one officer of the government who represents the people as a whole, lacks the means for keeping in touch with public opinion with respect to administrative proposals" (Skowronek 1982, 188). President Taft's point was that a national budget would provide the appropriate vehicle for reinforcing the link between the president and the people, particularly in connection with "a well-considered executive program for governmental activity" (188). In a subsequent letter to the secretary of the treasury with copies to all department heads, Taft claimed authority to require department heads to provide him information in a form that could be the basis of a national budget. "Under the Constitution the President is intrusted with the executive power and is responsible for the acts of heads of departments and their subordinates as his agents, and can use them to assist him in his constitutional duties" (Weber 1919, 90). That Taft had to assert such authority seems remarkable today. At the time, however, the relationship between the president and the executive departments was still fluid, and it would remain so until well into the New Deal.

Historians have judged Taft harshly as president, particularly in comparison with his more celebrated presidential contemporaries. He was demonstrably weak because of his lack of political skills in the face of extraordinary public demands and because of his pursuit of an untenable mix of progressivism and conservatism (e.g., Chambers 1980, 154–60). Taft's crushing repudiation in the 1912 election, in which, as the regular Republican candidate and incumbent president, he won the electoral votes of only two small state, provides ready evidence in support of such a judgment.

Nevertheless, in his efforts to attain more centralized and coordinated budgeting under presidential control, and in the emphasis on the interconnections among the president, public opinion, and public administration that those efforts signify, Taft demonstrated that his progressive thinking was eminently consistent with the answers Theodore Roosevelt and Woodrow Wilson offered to the central political question of the era: how to bring about the governmental centralization and expansion of national administration that rapid industrialization and its accompanying social and economic problems seemed to require. Too late for his presidency, Taft did present a thorough and forceful answer in the "managerial view of the presidency" (Rohr 1989a, 17) that he rendered as Chief Justice in his opinion in *Myers v. U.S.* (272 U.S. 52 [1926]). Roosevelt, and even more so Wilson, constructed their answers through relatively unconstrained constitutional reinterpretation centered on the presidency, leadership, public opinion, and public administration.

Constitutional Reinterpretation

Theodore Roosevelt established the foundation for "progressive" speech and practice concerning the relationship between the president and the public, by making direct yet moderate appeals to the public on issues, especially railroad regulation, that he thought posed a crisis for the American regime. By using the bully pulpit, Roosevelt broke decisively with nineteenth-century practice, altering the rhetorical behavior of presidents and the political practice such behavior reflected for his and subsequent eras (Tulis 1987, ch. 4).

With respect to administration, Roosevelt's redefinition of the president's relationship with the public, and the popular support and electoral stability he enjoyed as president, led him to attempt "to forge an executive-centered reconstitution of civil administration. . . . The neutral civil service was to be transformed into a separate class of citizens, a state caste insulated from party and Congress and dependent in all its interests on executive officers and the President's [civil service] commission" (Skowronek 1982, 179). Skowronek regards Roosevelt's actions as having taken "support for civil service reform . . . beyond a moralistic statement against the spoils system. . . . Giving teeth to the authority granted the President under the Pendleton Act, [Roosevelt] molded the merit civil service into an instrument of executive-centered government" (180). Taking it a step further during his "Bull Moose" Progressive Party campaign in 1912, Roosevelt defined his New Nationalism in terms of "the executive as the steward of the public welfare" (quoted in Milkis and Tichenor 1993, 14). As part of the centralization and administrative expansion this implied, the New Nationalism platform included "a call for national incorporation and regulation of interstate business" (Chambers 1980, 159).

Woodrow Wilson went even further than Roosevelt in transforming presidential practice, specifically regarding the public-presidential relationship. Wilson justified his transformation "with an ambitious reinterpretation of the constitutional order" (Tulis 1987, 118), including a new conception of the nature of executive leadership and presidential power. Presidential power in Wilson's conception derived not from the institutional and legal basis of the office but from public opinion and a popular national mandate (see Wilson 1908, 22–23, 108–10, 127; also Sedgwick 1987, 287–93; Tulis 1987, 128–30). Public administration's authority and legitimacy would come from the same source, primarily indirectly, through elections, but also directly, through "constant public counsel" (Wilson 1941, 501). This only hints at the profoundly complex assessment of public administration and its place in the American polity that Wilson and other progressive thinkers undertook.

Politics, Administration, and Statesmanship: Woodrow Wilson

In major European countries during much of the nineteenth century, scholars and public officials alike undertook a substantial effort to develop public administration. Tocqueville's visit to the United States, ostensibly to study the administration of the American prison system, was certainly a manifestation of this. A distinctive facet of this developmental effort was the conceptualization of what Daniel Martin has described as "multiple differentiations among judicial, legislative, executive, and administrative power. . . . All were different forms of power, and all had separate contributions to make to the polity" (Martin 1988, 632). This suggests that acceptance of a separate institutional sphere must be part of the basis for recognizing administration's constitutiveness. Martin adds that administration in European thinking of the time "was merely one more tool for expressing the will of the state," stressing again the need for multidimensional thinking about the qualities embodied by administration.

On this side of the Atlantic, scholarship began to bristle with activity regarding the development of public administration in the latter three decades of the century, which was happening in conjunction, of course, with civil service reform and interstate commerce regulation, as well as municipal government reform and national budget reform. Scholars and reform activists were fairly well versed on European thinking (see Van Riper 1983; Karl 1987; Martin 1988), although it is not altogether clear to what extent the developing American thinking self-consciously followed that of the Europeans. Certainly Woodrow Wilson had read widely, including the work of Lorenz von Stein, whose *Handbuch der Verwaltungslehre* provided much of the foundation for Wilson's 1887 essay "The Study of Administration." It was the distinction between European thinking on administration and European political values that proved critical.

In the first section of his 1887 essay, Wilson admits that administrative *methods* must be borrowed from the Europeans, because Europe is where the science of administration developed. But borrowed methods had to be grafted onto new roots, "adapted, not to a simple and compact, but to a complex and multiform state, and made to fit highly decentralized forms of government" (Wilson 1941, 486). John Reagan's position on this question, articulated during the debate on interstate commerce regulation, strongly implied that the prospects for such adaptation might not be as favorable as Wilson believed. Yet Wilson had an answer of sorts, insisting that the methods had to be "radically" Americanized, "in thought, principle, and aim" (486).

Such an adaptation of methods seemed plausible to Wilson, for, as he expounded in the second section of the essay, administration was separate from politics. "Most important to be observed is the truth already so much and so fortunately insisted upon by our civil service reformers; namely, that administration lies outside the proper sphere of *politics*. Administrative questions are not political questions" (Wilson 1941, 494, emphasis in original). Wilson had also addressed the separation of politics and administration in *Congressional Government,* wherein he insisted on "the drawing of a sharp line of distinction between those offices which are political and those which are non-political" (Wilson 1981, 180).

It was in his exploration of the politics-administration dichotomy that Wilson gave expression to a distinctively instrumental view of public administration. Thus, in the 1887 essay, he compared administration to the "methods of the counting house" and to "machinery" (Wilson 1941, 494). John Rohr connects Wilson's instrumental conception of administration to his preference for the parliamentary form of government (1986, 75). "An instrumental view of administration fits neatly into a model of government that rests on legislative supremacy. The people elect their representatives, who, acting in their sovereign capacity, pass laws which are duly carried out by the Public Administration" (85). But Wilson's treatment of the instrumental dimension of administration was not a simplistic one. In *Constitutional Government,* he acknowledges that the executive was regarded "as little more than an instrumentality for carrying into effect the laws which our representative assemblies originate." But he went on to insist that "it is by no means a necessary inference that [those who administer the law] shall be in leading strings and shall be reduced to be the mere ministerial agents of a representative assembly" (1908, 15). Moreover, Wilson proceeded to point out that "no part of any government is better than the men to whom that part is entrusted. The gauge of excellence is not the law under which the officers act, but the conscience and intelligence with which they apply it, if they apply it at all" (17).

In his disquisitions on the politics-administration dichotomy, Wilson did not just give expression to an instrumental conception of public administration. They reveal his struggle to work out the problem of importing and safely adapting the methods of "despotic governments" to American circumstances, placing those methods into the hands of a well-trained administrative elite—Roosevelt's "state caste"—and giving those hands sufficient space to operate without violating the principle of popular sovereignty. In doing so, Wilson wrestled with delineating the place of public administration, with its instrumental *and* constitutive dimensions, in an American democracy facing "those enormous burdens of administration which the needs of this industrial and trading age are so fast accumulating" (Wilson 1941, 501–2).

As Kent Kirwin has explained, in his 1887 essay Wilson first made an "evolutionary distinction" between politics and administration "according to which politics has gradually diminished to the point of leaving little but administrative tasks for government" (Kirwin 1987, 393; also see Storing 1980, 97). Political questions, in the sense of fundamental constitutional issues about the nature of the state and the best form of government, had essentially been settled. The United States was then faced primarily with governing, that is administering, a "full-fledged popular democracy" (Kirwin 1987, 393). This was the source of Wilson's statement, "It is getting to be harder . . . to *run* a constitution than it is to frame one" (Wilson 1941, 484).

Hence, the conscious, determined development of public administration, supported by a science of administration, was vital to the "political advancement of the American polity" (Kirwin 1987, 396). Wilson then initiated the necessary intellectual development in the second section of his essay by attempting to craft an "analytical distinction" between politics and administration (Kirwin 1987, 394). It was here in part that Wilson engaged in the struggle to reconcile the instrumental and constitutive aspects of public administration. Kirwin points out that, "after asserting that administration is a separate realm and proclaiming it to be purely instrumental or mechanical in character, [Wilson] admits that 'in any practicable government' [Wilson 1941, 495] it is impossible to establish lines of demarcation between administrative and political functions. The reason is that *in practice* administration is deeply embedded in law" (Kirwin 1987, 394–95, emphasis in original). Public administration's instrumental quality, in the sense of means-ends rationality, apparently still lies at the core, however, because to speak of it in practical terms "is to speak of it with reference to some end," and it is law "that *gives* public administration its definition, that *provides its ends,* and establishes the basis for the choice of means" (395, emphasis added).

So public administration is the practice of government, the matching of "special means" to "general plans" (Wilson 1941, 497). Public administration is nevertheless permeated by politics, or "the evaluative" (Kirwin

1987, 395), "because the administrator should have and does have a will of his own in the choice of means for accomplishing his work. He is not and ought not to be a mere passive instrument" (Wilson 1941, 496). But Wilson did not remain satisfied with this formulation (see Cook 1995 for a more detailed reconstruction of Wilson's administrative theory). By 1891, during the second cycle of his Johns Hopkins University lectures, public administration had become for Wilson "indirectly a constant *source* of public law" (quoted in Rohr 1986, 68, emphasis in original). Rohr adds that, in his attack on separation of powers in the 1891 lectures, Wilson rejected the traditional identification of administration as executive and simply an agent "of the law-making organ." Instead, "the administrative power" included "duties of provident protection and wise cooperation and assistance" (quoted in Rohr 1986, 69).

As both Rohr and Kirwin also point out, Wilson chose to tackle the politics-administration dichotomy in connection with his concern for the classic problem posed by popular rule. The problem was "to establish structural arrangements affording an unhampered expression and an unhampered implementation of the popular will" (Kirwin 1987, 396). Paradoxically, however, public opinion could interfere with the efficient implementation of the popular will. The answer was in part reliance on the government official closest to public opinion—the president—who therefore could direct as much as respond to it (Wilson 1908, 127). But the answer was also "an autonomous civil service, the members of which are obedient to their superiors who, *at the top,* are responsive to the representatives of the people" (Kirwin 1987, 397, emphasis added). Hence the separation of politics, which is the expression of popular will, and administration, is necessary. "The dichotomy . . . would rescue government from the vortex of popular sentiment and grant the nation's leaders sanctuary from meddlesome public opinion" (Rohr 1986, 73). The result would be "an obedient hierarchical bureaucracy *and* a civil service infused with the American spirit of individual liberty" (Kirwin 1987, 397).

As Kirwin also explains, this is Wilson grappling with the problem of responsible administration. The issue of responsibility was at the heart of the Decision of 1789 and the Jacksonian-Whig debate over administration's proper place in the regime. Wilson's extended argument on the matter recalls the Whig position, emphasizing informed, responsible discretion. "Large powers and unhampered discretion seem to me the indispensable conditions of responsibility" (Wilson 1941, 498; see Doig 1983).

Finally, what Wilson sought to insure, in Rohr's view, was that it would be "always in the interest of the administrator to have [the] broad view of the needs of the community rather than those of his superior alone" (Rohr 1986, 74). Rohr concludes that Wilson equated administration with "statesmanship" (cf. Storing 1980, 98). As Wilson argued in 1890, when the people and their legislative representatives were engaged in making choices about appropriate means and deliberating about the effectiveness of institutions, this was best ventured "under the guidance of men trained in the observance of political fact and force." Such men were "the heads of administration" (Link 1969, 7:519).

Administrative Stability and Social Improvement: Herbert Croly

The struggle to reconcile the instrumental and constitutive qualities of public administration was also evident in the works of such "militant" progressives (Karl 1983) as Herbert Croly, which were more widely disseminated than Wilson's. That they should both be pursuing this reconciliation is rather remarkable, because Croly was no devotee of Wilson and his New Freedom platform. Croly supported Theodore Roosevelt's New Nationalism, and he was sharply critical of Wilson, because he regarded Wilson's progressivism as conservative, an attempt to restore a political and social order in which substantial restraints on government had been in force. Croly saw instead a need for a new political order, in which old bonds of constitutionalism and political tradition would be broken, releasing in government an energy that would tackle the formidable social problems of modernity.

In attempting to define the role of public administration in the new social and political order, Croly wrestled with the same question as Wilson did: how to conceptualize administration and properly situate it in the regime when it was clearly both instrumental and constitutive in character. Croly pursued the matter extensively in *Progressive Democracy* (1914), in a chapter revealingly titled "The Administration as an Agent of Democracy." Croly began by explaining how traditional American two-party democracy had not only interfered with genuine popular rule but had also enfeebled administration. He then addressed the deep-rooted American revulsion toward powerful administrative officials. He argued that progressive democracy did not seek "ordinary bureaucratic government" (351), which is based on coercion, the sort of government prevalent in Europe. Instead, because progressive democracy is based on popular political power and "the consent of public opinion, administrative action cannot very well become an agency of oppression" (353). This is precisely the same as Wilson's argument that other governments' administrative methods can be safely adapted without the importation of their despotic ideas.

Croly then drew a sharp distinction between "the administration and the executive" (1914, 354). Under progressive democracy, the executive is "essentially a representative agency," whose "primary business is that of organizing a temporary majority of the electorate, and of carrying its will into effect." The executive is "primarily a law-giver and only secondarily an agency for carrying out existing laws" (355). Croly's definition of the executive parallels quite closely Wilson's description of the role of the president in *Constitutional Government*. Croly proceeded to argue that because the "organization of majority rule" by the executive is temporary and "fluid," it "might degenerate into a succession of meaningless and unprofitable experiments, which would not get enough continuity either to accomplish stable results or to teach significant lessons" (359). Hence, a critical role is defined for public administration. It assists the executive "in converting his program into well-framed and well-administered laws" (356), and it serves "as an agency of political continuity and stability" (358).

The founders, particularly Alexander Hamilton, acknowledged the role of public administration in maintaining regime stability (I explore this matter in chapter 5). Many scholars have since developed it further (see, for example, Long 1952; Marx 1957; Wood 1988; Terry 1990). Croly's characterization of administration as an agency of stability captures both its instrumental and its constitutive qualities. He sees the stability and permanence of administration as providing it the opportunity to gain knowledge and experience from the programmatic experimentation of progressive democracy. The knowledge and experience then guide the popular will and the programs of temporary executives away from stalemate and toward the goal of real, permanent social improvement. In the process, administration has a teaching function to perform. This requires "an element of independent authority." Indeed, Croly argued that the "conscientious and competent administrator of an official social program would need and be entitled to the same kind of independence and authority in respect to public opinion as that which has been traditionally granted to a common law judge" (361). Like the Whigs, then, Croly drew parallels between the administrator and the judge. As John Rohr has expressed the idea, "the skills of the administrator who listens to the public in some sort of open forum, however informal, are not altogether unlike those of the judge" (Rohr 1986, 53).

Thus, Croly conceived of public administration as instrumental because it functions as an agent of the popular will and its representatives, in pursuit of the end of enlightened social improvement, an end "demanded by prevailing political and economic conditions and ideals" (1914, 358). But he also argued that administration, through its stability, knowledge, scientific expertise, and experience, would play a vital part in defining the exact meaning of that enlightened social improvement. In his defense of independent commissions, he favorably compared the administrative court to the regular court, based on the administrative court's duty "to discover and define better methods of social behavior and to secure cooperation in the use of such methods by individuals and classes" (368). More demonstrably, he then described administration "as the instrument of a social program." But in being so, "it must have a hand in creating the social experience which it is also recording" (371). Finally, Croly argued that the "administrator must manage to be representative" (372), by keeping "articulate with the democracy, not by voting expedients, but by its own essential nature" (373).

The Dilemma of Progressive Reform

As the works of Woodrow Wilson and Herbert Croly help to demonstrate, the Progressive Era was incontrovertibly a great intellectual watershed for public administration in American government and politics. At no time before or since have scholars and intellectuals who were also public figures and political leaders engaged in such a broadly and deeply searching enterprise to understand the nature of public administration and situate it properly within the constitutional regime. Because public figures and political leaders were involved, at least some of the enterprise was conducted in public view. It is, therefore, especially perplexing to realize that, in its impact on public thinking and political action, the Progressive Era served largely to reinforce the prevailing conception of administration as purely instrumental and subordinate to the popular will. By doing so, it further reduced the likelihood that political leaders and an attentive public would arrive at an understanding of public administration that embraced its constitutive bearing. This in turn would perpetuate the tensions and contradictions generated in the lengthening history of the American struggle with the administrative dilemma, intensifying their corrosive effects on public support for a recognizably coherent public administration that could contribute effectively to the maintenance and improvement of the regime.

Several explanations stand out in any attempt to interpret the perverse impact of the progressive enterprise. First, the civil service reformers and the progressives achieved their aim, which was to strip away political party as the master over administration. But they failed to replace the party fully and forcefully with another master. Clearly, the president was conceived as the most likely and appropriate alternative. Roosevelt's behavior as president stressed this, and Taft gave the idea a decisive constitutional interpretation in the Myers case.

Wilson's conception of the president as party and national leader, however, along with his extended scholarly examination of the nature of administration, led him to be more ambivalent about the notion that administration was strictly subordinate to and the instrument of the president. Indeed, in *Constitutional Government,* Wilson stated that the president "may be said to administer the presidency in conjunction with the members of his cabinet, like the chairman of a commission" (1908, 66), and he later labeled the cabinet the president's "executive colleagues" (76). The consequence of Wilson's ambivalence on this matter, the result of his insistence on the separation of politics and administration, was presidential administrative action that featured "abandonment of the idea that administrative control required independent and imposing executive machinery . . . [and a] turn toward a cooperative system that would join President and Congress through reliance on party and department heads" (Skowronek 1982, 195).

It is important to reiterate that such action was not inconsistent with Wilson's ideals, since in his attempt to see a way around the debilitating effects of separation of powers, Wilson "preferred that the president and Congress be fully integrated into, and implicated in, each others' activities. . . . Cooperation was especially necessary because the president lacked the energy he needed, energy that could be provided only by policy backed by Congress and its majority" (Tulis 1987, 123). But to include department heads as critical components in such a cooperative system would seem to contradict directly the doctrine of separating politics and administration. Thus, by 1916, "Wilson's cooperative partnership of President and Congress in administrative affairs had turned into an aggressive congressional counteroffensive for control over civil administration" (Skowronek 1982, 198). By the end of the First World War, an "institutional stalemate" prevailed, "with administrators themselves being asked to make policy decisions in a political system defiant of authoritative controls" (209).

This could not have had a positive effect on popular regard for public administration in the face of much political speech and official action that continually proclaimed administration the subordinate instrument of the president or Congress, and ultimately of the people's will. Moreover, the situation was exacerbated by the character of progressivism itself. The movement consisted of a wide array of groups with interests and agendas that often overlapped but were nonetheless distinctive. Many of these were already well organized and professionally managed, and so were well primed for engagement in political action. When civil service and progressive reforms sufficiently disengaged the political parties from control of administration, many of these groups moved in to fill the vacuum. The overall structure and individual agency design of federal administration has always reflected extensive group influence, of course, but the achievements of progressivism extended and regularized group influence still further, making interest groups one of the new masters of administration. The result of this group influence was to involve agencies in policy making, in a way that flew in the face of the dominant ideology and rhetoric of instrumental, subordinate administration.

A second component explanation for the perverse impact of the progressive intellectual enterprise also centers on Woodrow Wilson. As part of his aggressive constitutional reinterpretation and redefinition of political leadership, Wilson set some astonishingly high objectives for such leadership. In his 1887 essay he pointed out that the "bulk of mankind is rigidly unphilosophical, and nowadays the bulk of mankind votes. A truth must become not only plain but also commonplace before it will be seen by the people who go to their work very early in the morning. . . . [To] get a footing for new doctrine, one must influence minds" in an extremely "multifarious" populace (1941, 493). Similarly, Wilson argued in *Constitutional Government* that the "object of our federal system is to bring the understandings of constitutional government home to the people of every part of the nation, to make them part of their consciousness as they go about their daily tasks." If this is not realized, "we have failed as constitutional statesmen" (1908, 197).

Wilson of course had in mind the president as the leader who could attain these aims. Thus, he argued in *Constitutional Government* that the president was "the one person about whom a definite national opinion is formed and, therefore, the one person who can form opinion by his own direct influence and act upon the whole country at once" (1908, 127). It is something of a surprise to discover, then, that Wilson did not seek to fulfill these objectives for political leadership with respect to defining the proper place for administration in the regime. Public administration is rarely mentioned in Wilson's campaign rhetoric or his public speech as president, and he made no attempt as president, at least as evidenced by his published papers, to instruct public opinion about the character of public administration as he had come to understand it (see Cook 1994, 23–31).

Perfectly good reasons for Wilson's behavior come to mind, of course. The press of issues and events and the constant need to win votes, both during a campaign and during service in office, always require the candidate's or president's immediate attention. Furthermore, Wilson's commitment to the separation of politics and administration and his "preoccupation" with political, including party, leadership "dictated his working theory of executive organization and devolution. It was the simple and cogent theory of reliance upon the heads of departments" (Macmahon 1958, 113). Wilson reasoned that if department heads were "not necessarily political officers at all" (1908, 76), then they could concentrate on thinking about administration, even including administrative appointments, which Wilson regarded as a crushing burden on the president (79). The president would attend to politics.

However the role of administration is best understood in theory, then, perhaps in rhetoric and practice it must be treated instrumentally. The perpetuation of the dichotomy means the perpetuation of the contradiction between what the public is told about the role of public administration and what they can readily see of its influence on the shape and substance of the polity.

Finally, the complexity and subtlety of the ideas about public administration that Wilson had developed simply did not lend themselves to effective translation into political speech intended for a general public audience, or to the political practice necessary for governing the diverse, contentious, "multiform" American polity. This, regrettably, is a problem that still bedevils public administration theory today. What did translate more easily, for it is fully evident in Wilson's public speech, was his ambitious reinterpretation of the constitutional order and thus the idea of the president as a direct representative of the people, responsible for interpreting, directing, and expressing the popular will.

To the extent that Wilson did indeed settle much of modern presidential practice, as Jeffrey Tulis (1987) has claimed, his impact on the attention that concerned citizens and political leaders would feel required to pay to public administration was profound. With the exception of Franklin Roosevelt, no president after Wilson has seen it as necessary to address in his public speech the dilemma of public administration in the American system. To the degree that twentieth-century presidents have addressed administration at all, it has been to argue that greater presidential control over administrative structure and process is needed and that performance must be improved to meet the demands and desires of the American people.

5

Serving the Liberal State

Administration in the New Deal
and Post–New Deal Order

Considering all the depictions of President Franklin Roosevelt in American popular culture, perhaps none is more revealing of the impact of the New Deal on American political development than FDR's arrival on stage during the final production number of the Broadway musical *Annie*. Based on the *Little Orphan Annie* comic strip, *Annie* was a phenomenal stage success of the late 1970s, winning numerous awards. In the midst of the number "A New Deal for Christmas," FDR appears as Santa Claus driving a team of orphans dressed as reindeer with names like Perkins, Ickes, Morgenthau, and Cummings. With the help of Daddy Warbucks, he proclaims triumphantly that those happy days that he had promised "are finally here!"

One pop culture success does not validate a political culture phenomenon, of course; but that imagery from *Annie* helps to accent the importance of understanding the contours in the landscape of ideas and actions that constituted the New Deal political order, and their implications for the status and function of public administration in American government and politics. Indeed, it would be difficult to avoid public administration in any description and assessment of the New Deal and its aftermath. As a wealth of New Deal scholarship indicates, Franklin Roosevelt's fundamental intention by the beginning of his second term was to place public administration at the heart of a new American political system.

FDR's New Deal essentially extended the work of the progressives by clarifying and strengthening the subordination of public administration to the presidency. In the effort to go further than the progressives in re-placing party politics with administrative and programmatic politics, the New Deal also strengthened the instrumental linkages of administration to organized groups. By placing administration at the foundation of the modern American state, the New Deal created a dramatic clash between the ideology and rhetoric of a subordinate, instrumental public adminis-tration and the reality of a public administration increasingly influential not just in the selection of means but also in the definition of public pur-poses. Not surprisingly, this exacerbated rather than calmed the tension between the instrumental and constitutive that is at the core of the dilemma that public administration as an institution poses for the Amer-ican constitutional system.

Characterizations of the New Deal

For general interpretive purposes, scholarly characterizations suggest that the New Deal can be understood in one of two ways. Either it was re-active, that is, an extemporary response to the Great Depression and the threats it posed for the American system; or it was purposive, that is, a substantial structural and functional alteration of American govern-ment, politics, and economics with a relatively clear aim and at least a rough plan of action. The interpretation of the New Deal as reaction has its locus in impressive mid-century historical research. The depiction of the New Deal that emerged from this research was that of a pragmatic re-sponse to the evils of the Depression. By some accounts it was an oppor-tunistic, stumbling, groping response, and by others a more coherent pragmatism (see Kessler 1989, 160). Carrying the reactive characteriza-tion a step further, Russell Kirk, a chronicler of American conservatism, argued that it was not FDR who swayed the mass of Americans to follow him in the course he chose to preserve American constitutionalism but instead FDR who "was swayed [by the public] to adopt the course he took." Hence, Americans "were not thrown far out of the course of their established political and moral habits," nor "stampeded out of their sound civil habits by the hardships of the depression" (quoted in Eden 1989a, 24).

It is no secret that FDR brought to his administration a fairly loose and improvisational style. Among other things, he sometimes had aides working at cross-purposes, and he preferred to allow cabinet members and close advisors to debate and disagree openly in his presence. This im-proved the chances that he could witness a full venting of views on any important issue. It also weakened potential rivals to his power (see, for example, Arnold 1986, 89–91).

Often cited also is FDR's reference to "bold, persistent experimentation" in a 1932 speech at Oglethorpe University, and his insistence that it is common sense, if one fails when attacking a problem, to try one method after another. "But above all," he exhorted, " try something" (quoted in Kessler 1989, 160). But a careful reading of the speech reveals that FDR was referring to "experimentation in means, not in ends (if such a thing were possible)" (Kessler 1989, 161). Indeed, although the New Deal contained plenty of improvisation and experimentation, and certainly not all of it successful, it was far from wild, unguided, purposeless experimentation. If the New Deal was purposive, not experimental in ends, then FDR had fundamental principles and aims in mind to serve as guide. Historian Barry Karl has argued, for example, that Roosevelt had a plan for his second term that was intended to transform presidential administration fundamentally (Karl 1989, 187–88).

In truth, of course, the New Deal was both reactive and purposive. Peri Arnold argues that the purposive New Deal was a consequence of the improvisational New Deal. "Roosevelt was like a juggler with a dozen balls in the air. Initially he wowed the electorate with his boldness.... Coordinating his creations was the President's next task" (1986, 89). Similarly, Karl concludes that FDR had come to regard the improvisations as "makeshift necessities, not virtues" (Karl 1983, 156), leading him to seek the help of experts in formulating new and more rational forms of administrative organization. More sharply, the historian Alan Brinkley contends that the lack of "any single principle" about the relationship between the state and capitalism, combined with the shock of the recession of 1937–38, "forced a serious reevaluation among American liberals of the policies and philosophy of the New Deal" in search of "a coherent vision" (1989, 86, 87; also see Karl 1983, 158–61). And John Rohr captures the New Deal's dual character especially well when he writes of "the pragmatic style of the New Dealers, who were busy running real government institutions as they thought and wrote about the new order of American politics they were creating" (1986, 55).

Both the improvisation and the purpose must be kept in view when considering the New Deal and its legacy, but the latter must draw the lion's share of attention in an assessment of the impact of the New Deal on the conception and treatment of public administration in American politics. Like the founders and reformers before him, Roosevelt expressed relatively consistent intents and purposes for his reforms, and public administration was a central element of them. These intents and purposes were given their most complete expression in the initiatives of the so-called "Third New Deal," FDR's plans for his second term, which were intended to go far beyond the more improvisational efforts of his first term (see Karl 1989). Consistent with the efforts of his predecessors, FDR's objectives encompassed the refinement and advancement of democracy, and—a distinct but not entirely separate goal—the definition, institutionalization, and perpetuation of a modern liberal program.

The Democratic Meaning of the New Deal

In a speech delivered at Roanoke Island, North Carolina, on August 18, 1937, Franklin Roosevelt excoriated opponents of the New Deal. He accused them of attempting to undermine the will of the people as expressed in the landslide 1936 election, and he labeled them "American Lord Macaulays." By likening them to the Tory leader who had disparaged American popular government, FDR portrayed these opponents as seeing their "anchor for salvation of the Ship of State" in a select class of educated men who were deeply interested in the security of property and the maintenance of order. Roosevelt then declared, "Mine is a different anchor. They do not believe in democracy—I do. My anchor is democracy—*and more democracy.*" As he began to draw the speech to a close, he claimed that his opponents rejected "the principle of the greater good for the greater number, which is the cornerstone of democratic government." Roosevelt then assured his audience, "I seek no change in the form of American government. Majority rule must be preserved as the safeguard of both liberty and civilization" (1938, 331, 333, emphasis added). Such was the tumult of the 1930s that Roosevelt could safely defend himself against charges that he was engaged in an effort at formal change, when one could only conclude that formal change is exactly what he was attempting. The nature of FDR's defense is crucial to understanding the democratic character of the reform thrust of the New Deal.

Sidney Milkis comments that "Roosevelt was the first statesman to 'appropriate' the term *liberalism* and make it part of the common political vocabulary. In doing so, however, he reworked—some claimed perverted—the elements of the old faith into modern form" (1993, 49). It is easy to see from the Roanoke Island speech why Roosevelt could be regarded as perverting the American liberal creed. For many, that creed entailed liberty and individual rights as first principles. Democracy, that is, broad popular participation in the choice of leaders, meant nothing if individual liberties were seriously restricted. Indeed, implied in one's civil rights was not only the right to vote but also to otherwise influence the government. The liberal creed held, in short, that individual rights were the foundation of democratic government. Yet here was FDR declaring nearly the converse, that democracy was the protector of individual liberty. As inverted—or perverted—as that sounded to many, FDR was in fact tapping into a powerful and venerable sentiment. As Charles Lind-blom stated it, "historically, people have turned to democracy primarily as a guarantor of personal liberty" (Lindblom 1980, 1). Indeed, some scholarly interpretations portray the intentions of many of the founders in almost precisely the manner stated by FDR: they chose a constitu-tional design based on popular sovereignty to serve as guardian of the liberty they held so dear (see, for example, Diamond 1975; Rohr 1986, 78–79).

Philosophically, the New Deal was democratic to its core. Taking the long view, the political energy of the New Deal was readily reconcilable with Tocqueville's vision of an irresistible democratic tide pushing on through the generations. Whereas the progressives represented the first attempt to reconcile this inexorable democratic expansion with the reali-ties of advanced industrialization and a more populous, more interde-pendent world, the Great Depression gave FDR—the most thoughtful and ambitious progressive inheritor—the opportunity to advance much farther, if not to complete, that reconciliation. For FDR as much as for the American people, the Depression was "a blessing in disguise" that al-lowed for the adjustment, and then the application, of founding princi-ples to the altered conditions of the day (Kessler 1989, 163). The adjust-ment involved the modernization of American democracy by attaching it more closely to the president. This was consistent with the efforts of FDR's progressive forerunners. But the New Deal also encompassed something more distinctly Rooseveltian: expanding the definition of po-litical liberty to include a broader range of rights.

A New Majority Consensus

Taking an "unfamiliar angle," Robert Eden contends that the "New Deal mounted a sustained challenge to the ruling ethos of the preceding Re-publican era." Revealingly, Eden insists that FDR forced the Democratic party—the party of Jefferson—"to choose once and for all between ha-tred of *arbitrary executives* and love of free and solitary enterprise" (Eden 1989b, 55, emphasis added). Roosevelt understood that he faced the task of building a new majority consensus and that any such consensus had to be built on the basis of a new standard of "democratic honor," a standard that included placing "arbitrary executives" in positions of leadership.

Franklin Roosevelt's essential task was to transform the deeply rooted conception of democratic honor that prevailed at the beginning of the New Deal, a conception of honor embodied in the Horatio Alger stories: a solitary, courageous individual overcoming incredible obstacles and even multiple failures to obtain wealth and comfort and the admiration of the community. These were (and still are) the sorts of people honored with public acclaim by the Republican ruling ethos. But FDR was convinced that this conception of honor and its accompanying majoritarian consensus on values was at the root of the mess that was the Great Depression. Thus, in Eden's interpretation, Roosevelt sought a change in the accepted conception of democratic honor that would mean a newly inclusive ruling ethos and a broad changing of the guard signifying that new types of people were being granted public laurels and the honor of ruling.

Roosevelt's alternative conception of democratic honor incorporated a "civil or social courage in guiding complex enterprises," not "stoically, minimally, or unobtrusively," but with dashing good cheer (Eden 1989b, 59; also see Wills 1994, 70–79). This was, of course, precisely what FDR personified, and it led logically to making the president the guardian of the new conception of democratic honor, thus binding the "organized electorate" to the national government and, thereby, registering its acceptance of New Deal centralization (Eden 1989b, 60). The traditional conception of honor reflected the task of taming a wild and mostly uninhabited continent and saw this as primarily the work of solitary entrepreneurs. "Roosevelt reinterpreted the task of subduing nature as a cooperative task in which the main actors were not individual entrepreneurs but, rather, organized groups" (59). Part of the reinterpretation involved redefining the task. It was no longer taming the wilderness, but managing "tamed" resources effectively (e.g., Brinkley 1989, 99, 109; Kessler 1989, 163). The fundamental, culturally ingrained American struggle to control nature so as to promote the general welfare and attain relief from want was handed to a more broadly inclusive cast.

The New Deal bestowed the honor of recognition and support as public leaders not only on the likes of corporate executives but on union leaders, farm association representatives, reformers, social activists, and professionals—including liberal lawyers and management experts, *and*, although to only a limited extent when compared with today's standards, to the African Americans and women among them. Indeed, the establishment in the Democratic party of "special divisions" for women, blacks, and labor (Milkis 1993, 62–68), and FDR's reliance on ostensibly nonpartisan groups in his campaigns, represent well this dimension of the New Deal conception of democratic honor. Such efforts had their roots in the similar drive of the progressives to democratize American politics by expanding the sphere of participation to more economic and social interests. The associational or corporatist structures of both "New Era" progressivism and the early New Deal (see Eisner 1993) were one distinctive manifestation of this modern pluralist orientation. All of this came together to form one of the central features of postwar politics, famously interpreted by Theodore Lowi in his near epithet of "interest-group liberalism."

Although seemingly quite disparate, these several elements of a new code of democratic honor were consistent with Tocqueville's general conception of democratic honor (see esp. Tocqueville 1988, 616–27). They reflected Roosevelt's effort to alter and reinvigorate the *spirit* of the American people and to establish a new majoritarian consensus on basic values—a new "moral authority" built on "the morale of a political majority" (Eden 1989b, 61). Hence, the New Deal represented a very powerful democratic current. But what of the nature and focus of that current with respect to American constitutional and political foundations?

Presidents, Majorities, and Economic Rights

An inkling of the answer can be seen in Roosevelt's positioning of the president at the center of the new conception of honor, an indication that FDR drew upon his progressive and Democratic (including Jacksonian) roots. Furthermore, like "most progressive reformers during the first three decades of the twentieth century," FDR believed that Thomas Jefferson and Alexander Hamilton "stood for two contending theories of government that animated later political controversies in American history and still lay unresolved before them" (Milkis 1993, 21). Jefferson, along with James Madison, represented and had carried out in 1800 the construction of barriers against governmental consolidation and strengthening of the executive. Hamilton, in contrast, sought a strong, even dominant executive, to check an overreaching republicanism. Roosevelt's response, born in part of his ambition to lead the country, was to recognize "that Jeffersonian ideals would have to be applied to modern problems in such a way that these ideas were respectful of Hamilton's 'genius' for sound administrative practices" (22). FDR articulated his effort to do just that in his address to the Commonwealth Club in San Francisco on September 23, 1932 (see Milkis 1993, 38–40, on its origins).

As Charles Kessler notes, the "seriousness of the Commonwealth Club address is apparent from the beginning" (Kessler 1989, 161), when FDR declares that he intends to speak "not of politics but of Government," and "not of parties, but of universal principles." What FDR then proceeded to do, consistent with his and his advisors' reformation of progressive thought, was to "give new meaning to the Hamiltonian tradition by infusing it with a democratic purpose" (Milkis 1993, 41). This democratic purpose was the energetic definition and advancement of individual rights—not the traditional rights, particularly property rights, understood by both Hamilton and Jefferson—but *economic* rights, particularly "the economic freedom of individuals to earn a living" (quoted in Milkis

1993, 41). Thus, FDR offered both a modernization of Jeffersonian ideals through an "economic declaration of rights" and a democratization of Hamilton's energetic, executive-led nationalism. This democratization would come about by tying the "enlightened administration" necessary to insure the sustenance and protection of the people's economic rights to the presidency, which, as Andrew Jackson, Theodore Roosevelt, Woodrow Wilson, and even William Howard Taft had argued, enjoyed a direct link to the people and the support of a national electoral majority.

Like his progressive forebears, then, and even Jackson, FDR sought to use the presidency, and public administration, to give shape, substance, and guidance to the inevitable democratic tide. Throughout the construction, refinement, and defense of the New Deal, Roosevelt labored continuously to "establish a government responsive to the needs of the majority," and a presidency "with authority over [its] domain," to ensure that responsiveness (Milkis 1993, 111).

The New Deal's Programmatic Liberalism

For the "economic constitutional order" announced by Roosevelt in the Commonwealth Club speech to come to fruition, however, several other things had to happen. First, FDR had to convince Americans that his brand of progressivism and his plans for governing were consistent with values and principles which they held dear. He accomplished this by drawing forward Jeffersonian ideals and using the language of rights to portray his objectives. By doing so he linked his progressivism to constitutionalism and interpreted it as "an *expansion* rather than a *subversion* of the natural rights tradition" (Milkis 1993, 43, emphasis in original). The outcomes of the 1932 and 1936 elections confirmed, at least to FDR, that the American electorate was indeed convinced.

Second, Roosevelt had to label his program distinctively and banish to the political wilderness any opponents who might claim the same label. FDR achieved this by adopting the title "liberal" and forcing his opponents to accept the designation "conservative." As long as the American people valued the ideas of progress and upward mobility, *conservative* would spell at least some political difficulties for those who bore that label (see Rossiter 1962; Patterson 1967). This was an especially meaningful achievement, for the American political creed was fundamentally liberal. According to John Dewey, the creed consisted of two strains of liberalism—laissez-faire and humanitarian—with the former dominant and the latter associated with personal and voluntary effort (Dewey 1936, as cited in Milkis 1993, 304–5). FDR successfully raised the political status of humanitarian liberalism and redefined it in connection with

government activism, generating a still-increasing sharp competition between the two streams of liberal thought—now in the guise of liberalism
and conservatism (Milkis 1993, 305).

The combination of these two achievements was the construction and
political legitimation of "programmatic liberalism" (Harris and Milkis
1986; Milkis 1993, 38–51), which encompassed an expanded list of
rights—mostly concerned with economic security—that were defined,
delivered, and protected by positive government action, particularly executive initiative. Such an idea of rights stood in contrast to the more traditional conception of rights as "natural," and requiring protection *from*
government interference. Because FDR sought to put his stamp on the
American polity, a stamp of historic proportions that would reduce the
likelihood of recurrence of something like the Great Depression, and because his expanded conception of rights was predicated on programmatic initiatives by government, placing it at the whim of electoral politics and a democracy of localized parties, his brand of humanitarian
liberalism had to be protected in ways that would sustain it beyond the
time in which he could reasonably expect to serve in office. Safeguarding
programmatic liberalism in this way required additional achievements.

Because of the party tradition in American politics, which was strongest at the local level, New Deal liberalism had to be attached to a political
party or, to be more precise, one of the parties had to become the programmatic liberal party. Equally as important, the party of liberalism
had to become and remain the majority party, through a true party realignment. However, the American party system was far too decentralized to be easily controlled from Washington. It was also strongly en-
sconced in Congress, which, by virtue of the Constitution's design, made
it relatively resistant to long-term presidential control. Party government, FDR also came to conclude, was simply too fickle and unpre-
dictable to be the anchor of the New Deal. Hence the preservation and
even extension of programmatic liberalism had to be entrusted to an institution that would be relatively immune to changes in electoral fortunes and party control. That institution was public administration.

This strategic assessment only added to the importance of administration's role in the New Deal scheme, a role already central because the
rights defined by FDR were programs not "formally ratified as amendments to the Constitution, nor . . . fully codified in statutes and policies"
(Milkis 1993, 50). They required "enlightened administration" not only
for their fulfillment but for their long-term upkeep and repair as well.
FDR's expanded definition of rights thus reoriented the role of the national government and placed executive-led administration at the core of
that reoriented role. Roosevelt's pursuit of a protected humanitarian lib-

eralism led to the emergence of an "administrative constitution" (Milkis 1993, 145), an overlay of redistributed powers and newly defined rights that did not depend on formal amendment of the original document.

It is important to stress, in anticipation of my more general argument, that under the emerging administrative constitution, public administration was an *instrument of partisanship,* and it was so in a manner not very different from the Jacksonian conception. The nature of the partisanship under the New Deal transformation was, however, notably different.

Woodrow Wilson's subtle and probing examination of the appropriate role for public administration in the American regime seems never to have manifested itself in his rhetoric and actions as president. This is in part explained by Wilson's commitment to the separation of politics and administration, in which expert professional administrators could safely be left with responsibility for the details of running the government, while the president was to attend to politics and political leadership, that is, the development of basic principles and policy wholes and the mustering of support for them. His commitment to party leadership and to governance by a party majority in Congress is also part of the story.

Franklin Roosevelt served in Wilson's administration as assistant navy secretary, and he was a serious student of Wilson's presidency. Like Wilson, FDR faced the problem of how best to exercise party leadership and to govern through the party system. Intending to bring about a transformation to a progressive social program, he opted for vigorous party leadership in the short run, both to transform the Democratic party into the party of liberalism and to achieve a true partisan realignment that would make the Democratic party the majority party. This realignment, however, was intended to *end* party politics and partisan realignments (Milkis 1993, 110), because, as FDR suspected and as it was fully confirmed during his fight to liberalize the Democratic party, the party system would not facilitate but only stand in the way of achieving and sustaining a liberal social program.

Knowing this, FDR sought to make the president the center of national electoral politics *and* the engine for the programmatic liberal transformation of American government and politics. Public administration, so vital to the creation and sustenance of that liberal program, would be closely attached to the president. Through the New Deal, in other words, FDR sought "a blending of partisanship and administration, one in which administration would become a vehicle for partisan objectives; for liberal partisanship" (Milkis 1993, 51). Bringing about this administrative partisanship and keeping it in check required "tying the administrative state to the presidency" (103). At the heart of Roosevelt's endeavor in this regard was his attempt at executive reorganization, pursued with the help of the President's Committee on Administrative Management (PCAM), the Brownlow Committee.

Executive Reorganization and the New Deal Conception of Administration

Amid minor disagreements about how it all was started, and by whom, scholars of the presidency and public administration agree that executive reorganization that shifted power to the presidency was critical to adjusting the American constitutional scheme to twentieth-century conditions. As Peri Arnold has argued, for progressive reformers the Constitution posed a problem, because it "had not been written to cope with large-scale administration" of the kind the modern world seemed to demand (Arnold 1986, 10). That problem required a shift in "the proper locus of administrative authority in the American regime" from Congress to the president (3), to reconcile expansion of government capacities with basic constitutional structure, particularly separation of powers (see Arnold 1994, 6–13). Similarly, Theodore Lowi points out that the "traditional" regime was Congress-centered, as intended by the Constitution. In Lowi's analysis, the traditional system was not overturned until the New Deal. The "President's Committee on Administrative Management was the first of many efforts to adjust an eighteenth-century constitution to the twentieth century." The central theme of the committee was that the new powers of the national government had to be centralized in the hands of the president to ensure that administrators would exercise those powers responsibly (see Lowi 1985, 2; also see Mosher 1968, 80).

Alexander Hamilton was, of course, the first to seek to define under the Constitution an energetic, independent executive with substantial—although not exclusive—authority over administration. On that basis, John Rohr (1986, ch. 9) argues that the New Deal pursued a constitutional political science like that of *The Federalist*—pragmatic and adaptive. The focus of the pragmatism and adaptation was the constitutional legitimacy of the modern welfare state that emerged under the banner of the New Deal. Rohr concludes that the New Dealers secured a substantial well of legitimacy for the expanded administrative power they sought (also see Milkis 1993, 102–4). However, additional procedural safeguards for individual rights subsequently had to be put in place (see Rohr 1985, ch. 10).

The Brownlow Report's Conception of Administration

As a number of scholarly analyses stress, the report of the President's Committee on Administrative Management was influenced by the ideas of all three members of the committee that wrote it—Louis Brownlow, Luther Gulick, and Charles Merriam, but the report was most strongly shaped by the ideas of Gulick. Richard Stillman argues, for example, that Gulick's infamous acronym PODSCORB (planning, organizing, directing, staffing, coordinating, reporting, budgeting) served as the basis of the committee's report (1991, 116). Indeed, the PODSCORB idea appears in the opening essay of Gulick and Urwick's *Papers on the Science of Administration* (1937), which began as a "group of essays gathered to provide a common language for the [PCAM] staff," and a "tool kit of administrative principles" (Arnold 1986, 97).

If Luther Gulick's ideas formed the core of the Brownlow Committee's report and the executive reorganization legislation that followed, then it was inevitable that the report would focus on a president's needing the help of a more tightly structured, more effectively controlled, and thus more efficient administrative apparatus. For Gulick, PODSCORB defined what the *chief* executive did (Stillman 1991, 115–16). Under Gulick's "new Nationalist" progressive creed, the president was the chief political leader *and* the chief administrator, and as such was the elected official most likely to revitalize the American system of government through more centralized power. More precisely, the modernization of American liberal democracy would occur through effective public administration. The solution to the problem of responsible government in the twentieth century rested with administrative reform, meaning more centralized presidential control (Milkis 1993, 109).

This idea that administrative reform and the tightening of presidential power and control through executive reorganization was in service to American democracy permeates the Brownlow Committee's report (Rohr 1986, 147, 252 n. 54). At the close of the report's introduction, the committee forthrightly states, "There is but one grand purpose, namely, to make democracy work today in our National Government; that is, to make our Government an efficient, up-to-date, and effective instrument for carrying out the will of the Nation" (Arnold 1986, 104). The nature of that national will, moreover, was quite clear to them: "the constant raising of the level of the happiness and dignity of human life, the steady sharing of the gains of our Nation, whether material or spiritual, among those who make the Nation what it is" (Rohr 1986, 149).

This was quite consistent with the New Deal notion, articulated as far back as FDR's Commonwealth Club address, that the principal task of government was the effective management of the nation's resources to prevent destitution and want. Making the point more emphatically later, the committee insisted that the "whole basis of reorganization must not be the superficial appearance but the integrity of the social services underneath, *which are the end of government*" (Rohr 1986, 149, emphasis in original).

Rohr finds "the explicit mention of the purpose of government as something other than the protection of individual rights" in the Brownlow Report "a textbook example of the triumph of administrative means over liberal ends." It is, he contends, inconsistent with American constitutional tradition (Rohr 1986, 148, 149). Rohr argues that this marginalization of individual rights required a corrective, which "thoughtful" New Dealers provided in the 1941 Attorney General's Report on Administrative Procedure (112, 149, and ch. 10). Although not denying Rohr his point, I would reiterate that through the New Deal, FDR and his supporters sought and achieved a transformation in the *conception of rights* and integrated it into a social services or welfare conception of the positive state. In other words, insuring the delivery of basic social services, now often referred to as the social "safety net," was the same as protecting and advancing individual rights. "With the advent of the New Deal political order, an understanding of rights dedicated to limited government gradually gave way to a more expansive understanding of rights, requiring a relentless government identification of problems and the search for methods by which these problems might be solved" (Milkis 1993, 131). This identification of problems began with FDR's articulation of a "Second Bill of Rights," addressing economic security; but by the 1960s and 1970s it had expanded much farther, to encompass broad health, welfare, and "quality-of-life" problems that reformers argued required delineation of additional basic rights as part of their resolution.

The Brownlow Report did not spell out the precise manner in which administration would fulfill its role as servant to the democratic will of the nation and the nation's demand for services. Historian Alan Brinkley (1989) describes a struggle between two contending liberal conceptions of the state that was carried on from the late 1930s to the end of World War II. The regulatory state view promoted relatively extensive government intervention in the economy through actual management of economic institutions, to correct the problems of capitalism and protect the interests of the public. The compensatory government view advocated much less state intervention, relying instead on programs that would stimulate demand and thus economic growth, and on welfare programs that would appropriately distribute the fruits of that growth. The compensatory government view, built on a core of Keynesian economics, prevailed, partly as a result of the bad experiences of state management during World War II (Brinkley 1989, 100–111). These two conceptions of the state, it is nevertheless clear, were consistent with the Brownlow Report's idea of administration as serving the people best by being under the close, coordinated control of the president.

The conception of public administration in the Brownlow Report was, then, decisively instrumental. Administration was to be the principal device with which to meet the demand for the "effective delivery of promised services" in the positive state (Rohr 1986, 137). This instrumental conception was expressed quite explicitly, as in the passage from the report's introduction quoted above, and in its later insistence that the "national will must be expressed not merely in a brief, exultant moment of electoral decision, but in persistent, determined, competent day-to-day administration of what the nation has decided to do" (Milkis 1993, 10). But the instrumentalism was also manifested subtly yet perhaps most fundamentally by the committee's reference to "those who make the Nation what it is." I read this phrase to mean that the committee saw the public, or more specifically the majority, as defining or *constituting* the polity. The committee clearly does not include public administration and public administrators here. Instead, administration and administrators are to serve those who define and redefine the character of the nation. Administration is to do this particularly by insuring the "steady sharing" of mostly material "gains" under the direction of the president, who can most coherently articulate the aspirations of "those who make the Nation what it is." In this characterization and in other passages in the report, the committee sustained, and even intensified, the progressive separation of politics and administration and the instrumental image of public administration it entailed.

Civil Service Reform and the Nature of the Administrative Instrument

Scholars differ somewhat on the extent to which the product of the Brownlow Committee's labors reflected Franklin Roosevelt's ideas and intentions. Sidney Milkis observes that FDR found "in the members of the President's Committee on Administrative Management . . . steadfast loyalty and a shared vision of presidential government" (1993, 108). Barry Karl contends that "Roosevelt's personal influence on the recommendations [of the committee] was great" (1983, 157). Peri Arnold, however, relates Luther Gulick's denial that the committee was co-opted by FDR, and Arnold concludes that any presumption about "the specific details of the committee's recommendations [being] specified by Roosevelt beforehand conflicts with the facts of his past record in administrative coordination" (1986, 107).

Whatever the exact relationship, what FDR shared with Brownlow, Gulick, and Merriam at the most basic level was a conception of the American regime, and of public administration's role in it, that was necessitated by the stresses they saw imposed on democracy by modern society. "FDR was committed to moving the political system from a government order based on *constitutionalism* to one emphasizing *public administration*. Or, more accurately, FDR hoped to transmute constitutionalism, so that it was less legalistic and more open to centralized planning. Planning would not be directed at efficiency for its own sake; rather, the goal was to make American democracy more directly responsive to the developing interest in government-provided social services" (Milkis 1993, 110, emphasis in original). Each of the five principal recommendations in the Brownlow Report, constituting the core of the executive reorganization plan FDR proposed in 1937 and pursued in one way or another even after the bill's defeat, gave concrete expression to the New Deal conception of administration. Public administration moved to a central place in the regime, but it became, more fundamentally than ever before, an instrument in service to an externally defined purpose. The Brownlow Committee's recommendation regarding civil service reform, and subsequent actions taken in this area, are particularly illuminating on this score.

The Brownlow Report is famous for its recommendation that the merit system be extended "upward, outward, and downward" to cover most of the positions in executive agencies not responsible for policy determinations, and then for separating personnel administration from the merit system by the creation of a single administrator responsible to the president. The committee also recommended the creation of a citizen board to serve as a watchdog over the merit system. The interpretation of these proposals by (mostly Republican) critics of the New Deal was that they were intended largely as a patronage effort to reward loyal Democrats with permanent federal jobs. Many feared that FDR was bent on creating a national political machine. The Hatch Act of 1939, which sharply curtailed the involvement of federal administrators in presidential and congressional election campaigns, was the response.

This worry was apparently misplaced, however. FDR "was more interested in orienting the Executive Department for the formation of liberal public policy than he was in developing a national political machine, and the insulation of federal officials from party politics was not incompatible with such a task" (Milkis 1993, 138). Indeed, Louis Brownlow defended these proposed actions as a necessary part of moving from the "negative, protective" phases of civil service reform associated with the patronage abuses of the spoils system to the "positive," progressive phase. The latter could be expected to bring with it a federal administration and administrators dedicated to the programmatic liberalism of the New Deal political order (Milkis 1993, 116).

As I argued in chapter 3, the consequence of a totally neutral, instrumental public administration, as conceived by nineteenth-century reformers, was to relegate administration to ministerial, nonpolitical tasks. This attempt at complete separation of politics from administration simply could not be sustained in practice, however, as the experience of the progressives revealed. The Jacksonians, in contrast, attached public administration as instrument to the president and thus the parties. This served the parties' interests, because administration was a source of party sustenance through patronage. But it also served the Jacksonian objective of restoring republican virtue and, in keeping with Jeffersonian tradition, kept public administration's political and governing role circumscribed. The Jacksonian conception nevertheless posed its own dilemma, for the restoration of republican virtue meant that public administration would have some role in shaping citizen qualities and sensibilities. That the Jacksonian method—the spoils—seemed to produce exceedingly immoral and corrupt results in the public service, and politics more generally, seemed to contradict the notion that the bureaucracy could legitimately contribute to the character of the polity.

Like both their mid- and late-nineteenth-century predecessors, the New Dealers conceived of public administration as an instrument in service of democracy. Unlike the civil service reformers but like the Jacksonians, however, New Dealers sought not a neutral but a dedicated instrument. Rather than simply neutralizing administration so that it served whatever master sought to use it, New Deal reformers specified the master of the administrative instrument. The New Deal reforms thereby brought politics and administration back together, in recognition of Roosevelt's vision that "the line between lawmaking and administration would grow fuzzier," with the president assuming "an expanded role in the more 'streamlined' democracy of post-Depression America" (Milkis 1993, 121). The balance of power and authority shifted, in short, and the president became more influential in both policy and administration, albeit with the safeguards of the civil service reforms and the Hatch Act securely in place. This New Deal conception of public administration as the central instrument of a programmatic liberal state has been sustained, with modifications, in the post–New Deal political order.

Congressional Debate on Executive Reorganization

Like the installation of the Constitution and the Jacksonian and progressive reforms, the New Deal reform effort sparked a major congressional debate centered at least in part on questions about the status and role of public administration in American government and politics. Not surprisingly, the Brownlow recommendations, as they were pronounced in the legislation FDR submitted in January 1937, became the principal fields of battle, particularly during deliberation on the floor of the Senate. The reorganization initiatives, even as modified by supporters of executive reorganization, prominently Senate floor manager James P. Byrnes of South Carolina, generated sometimes heated exchanges and substantial opposition. They proposed to expand presidential support staff, improve the executive's planning and management capabilities, extend the merit system and reorganize the civil service system, extend the president's reorganization powers and bring the various agencies, boards, and commissions under closer presidential control within twelve executive departments, and reconfigure auditing functions to improve the fiscal accountability of executive agencies to Congress. The exchanges in floor debate were sufficiently vehement and the opposition substantial enough that the Brownlow recommendations in their original legislative form went down to defeat, when the House voted 204–196 to recommit the legislation in early April 1938. This happened despite House passage the preceding December of legislation granting the president six new assistants and renewing reorganization authority that had lapsed in 1935, and despite Senate passage of the full, albeit modified, reorganization bill by a 49–42 vote in March.

Scholars have examined the steady crescendo of trouble and eventual collapse of the initial push for executive reorganization of the Third New Deal, both immediately after the fact (Altman 1938; Rogers 1938) and more recently (Karl 1963, 1983; Pohlenberg 1966; Arnold 1986; Milkis 1993). It is worth recounting some of the contextual factors they have pointed to in explaining the defeat of the 1937 reorganization bill, because doing so also sets the stage for characterizing the congressional debate over how public administration as a concept was treated by supporters and opponents of executive reorganization.

Foremost among these contextual factors was that reorganization got tangled up in the political battles over other "big ticket" items FDR pushed the Seventy-fifth Congress to consider. This included, especially, the so-called "court-packing plan," in which FDR sought authority to reorganize the judiciary, including an expansion of the number of justices on the Supreme Court, to allow better response to the increasing demands for judicial review spurred by New Deal programs. Also included was a proposal to create seven regional natural resource planning authorities, an idea consistent with the New Deal emphasis on economic security through proper resource management rather than new exploration and exploitation. FDR launched both of these in February 1937, a month after introducing the executive reorganization legislation, and the latter was pushed back on the congressional calendar, as the House and Senate took up the seemingly more far-reaching proposals first.

That these initiatives somehow interfered politically with the reorganization effort is really quite ironic. Sidney Milkis contends, for example, that the court reform proposal "prepared the constitutional ground" for the proposals made by the Brownlow Committee (1993, 113). Yet it is also clear that the rhetoric and substance of arguments against the court-packing plan, and important elements of the opposition coalition, were readily transferable to the fight over executive reorganization. Similarly, Barry Karl (1983, 166) points out that the proposed regional planning system and FDR's reorganization effort were inextricably linked, but this linkage made the fears of centralized power raised by the former generically applicable to the Brownlow Report's recommendations as well. Indeed, in crucial respects, court reorganization, regional planning, and executive reorganization were all parts of FDR's endeavor to remake the presidency and establish an "administrative constitution" to fulfill the tenets of modern liberalism (Karl 1983, ch. 8; Milkis 1993, ch. 5). The congressional debate over executive reorganization thus was destined to recapitulate the substance and rhetoric of the contests over court packing and regional planning. The latter two went down to defeat in July 1937 and March 1938, respectively. (See Milkis 1993, ch. 6, for an assessment of what the Third New Deal achieved despite these setbacks.)

Two other factors contributed noticeably to the character of the congressional debate on executive reorganization. First, sensing that reorganization was a sensitive issue, the Democratic leadership in both chambers delayed bringing the legislation to the floor for debate. This allowed opposition outside Washington to build and sharpen. Also, the vagaries of congressional scheduling brought legislation to the floor that tied up activity still further. A prominent example was the filibuster by some southern senators against an antilynching bill (Patterson 1967, 193). Second, the economy slipped into recession in August 1937. By the time FDR returned his attention fully to congressional action on his executive reorganization plan, it was in the context of a special congressional session he had called in November to deal with the recession. The effect was to create "a new atmosphere of mistrust, since it raised doubts about Roosevelt's economic policies, and these doubts, in turn, evoked defensive language from the administration" (Karl 1983, 157).

In many respects, then, the parameters for congressional deliberation on executive reorganization had already been established by the time floor debate finally began in earnest at the end of January 1938. The major themes and stratagems had been honed during the debates on other issues that had occurred throughout the previous year. One important feature of the established terrain for the debate was the increasingly coherent and effective conservative counterattack on the New Deal. Although it would have been fallacious to speak of this opposition to the New Deal as "an inflexible conservative coalition voting as a bloc on every issue" (Patterson 1967, 220), at its core were the "irreconcilables," conservative congressmen of both parties in both houses who considered themselves "the bulwark against the New Deal" (212). Throughout the nearly three months of full floor debate, it is clear, opposition to the executive reorganization bill was in part energized by the drive simply to stop Roosevelt and the New Deal, so as "to 'conserve' an America which [the opponents] believed to have existed before 1933" (viii).

During such a lengthy and complex debate, of course, a wide variety of arguments were advanced. Particularly noteworthy for the reorganization debate was the continuation of the traditional distinction between legislative and executive views on the purpose of reorganization. In a March 1 speech, Senator Harry F. Byrd of Virginia expressed the legislative view precisely, by laying down certain "fundamental principles," the first of which was that "Congress [should] go clearly on record that *economy* is one of the main objectives of any reorganization of the Government" (*Congressional Record* [hereafter cited as *CR*] 1938, 2590, emphasis added). In anticipation of this argument, Senator Byrnes tried to dispel the notion that reorganization would result in substantial savings, unless, he declared, "we . . . stop appropriating money for functions." He contended that no senator should believe "that by regrouping Government organizations, by consolidating them, and by abolishing a few of the existing commissions, a large percentage of the total appropriations can be saved. It cannot be done" (*CR* 1938, 2506). Instead, such restructuring would provide "that the President can know what is going on in this organization or that organization" (*CR* 1938, 2502), or, as FDR stated it to Louis Brownlow, "The reason for reorganization is good management" (Milkis 1993, 107).

Also plainly evident in the debate were the numerous but not untypical attempts by congressmen to protect their pet programs and key constituencies by exempting particular agencies from the president's reorganization power. This activity was encouraged in part by the modifications, specifically exempting certain units, which FDR allowed Byrnes to make. It also reflected an opposition tactic to "eventually . . . amend the bill beyond recognition" (Patterson 1967, 221) with a relentless series of proposals to exempt additional agencies.

James Patterson's description of the antireorganization forces in the Senate and the tie that bound them points, however, to the most pervasive substantive themes in the reorganization debate. These forces, led by Senator Burton K. Wheeler of Montana, a "tried and true progressive veteran" who viewed himself as "the true defender of liberalism in the [Democratic] party" (Patterson 1967, 114, 115) and who thus became "a consistent foe of the Third New Deal" (Milkis 1993, 126), consisted of "Republicans, conservative Democrats, and moderate Democrats fearful of excessive centralization of power" (Patterson 1967, 221). The question of whether executive reorganization as proposed by FDR presented too great a threat of centralizing power in the executive emerged time and time again during the debate on reorganization.

In a fascinating exchange between Republican senator William Borah of Idaho and the majority leader, Alben Barkley of Kentucky, on March 15, Borah proclaimed, "A democracy is a peculiar institution. It does move slowly and it necessarily moves with great deliberation. . . . A democracy moves slowly in order to present the views of the masses whom we represent. I would infinitely rather take some time and obtain the judgment of those whom we represent than to move with the celerity which we are witnessing in other parts of the world" (*CR* 1938, 3400). In response, Barkley stated, in part, "One of the things which it seems to me will preserve democracy is for democracy to be efficient, responsive, and ready to serve the people. I do not think there is any question of democracy or autocracy involved in simply authorizing the President to transfer a bureau from one department to another" (3400).

Everyone at the time understood, of course, that Borah's reference to "other parts of the world" meant the dictatorships that had arisen in the crippled democracies of Germany, Italy, and perhaps even Russia. Eleven days earlier, Senator Arthur Vandenberg had similarly argued, "The intended creation of a civil-service dictator," and the "creation of Executive control over public expenditures," were "unfortunate and ill-advised concentrations of Executive authority under any circumstances. They are particularly unfortunate and ill-advised at a difficult moment in our history when the crying need of the hour is an assurance to America that we are not going farther down the road toward authoritarian, centralized, one-man government in the United States" (*CR* 1938, 2813). Other senators voiced similar warnings before, after, and in between Vandenberg's and Borah's statements, but the conflict in views about the essential character of American democracy given voice in the Borah-Barkley exchange proved to be behind most of the expressions of fear of an authoritarian threat.

Barkley's response to Borah was the very incarnation of the progressive struggle against "traditional" democracy. In the progressive conception articulated by Senator Barkley, American democracy should be efficient, responsive, and oriented toward serving the very basic needs and wants of the American public generally. Recall that it was Herbert Croly who had argued that such basic public wants and needs were distinctively different in a modern, industrial age. As Democratic senator Joseph C. O'Mahoney of Wyoming similarly argued with clarity during the reorganization debate, "the people of the United States . . . are not content with a government which merely restrains the inhabitants of the land from injuring one another. They want a government which helps them to do the things they want to do, and helps them to live the sort of lives they want to live; and the pressure never ceases" (*CR* 1938, 2826). The response to this unceasing pressure, argued Croly, the progressives, and their New Deal progeny, was a less fettered, more energetic executive, which would formulate the most rationally organized, efficient, and thus most effective actions—the modern, democratic Hamiltonianism expressed in FDR's Commonwealth Club address.

Borah's contention that American democracy needed to be appreciated as slow, deliberative, and founded on popular opinion expressed through representatives, symbolized most of what the progressive movement had battled to overcome, and it showed how difficult the task of importing the methods of "despotic governments" and adapting them to American needs really was. The antireorganization forces held to a legislative-centered rather than an executive-centered view of American democracy, emphasizing decentralization and a clearly delimited executive power. As Senator Vandenberg stated it, "the gravest errors—in terms of hazard to the administration's own objectives—usually have found root in the departure from democracy and in the substitution of government by Executive decree for our traditional processes of representative and decentralized government" (*CR* 1938, 2813).

The reorganization debate was, therefore, the occasion for a vigorous public probing of that fundamental Jeffersonian-Hamiltonian tension that interlaces the structure and conceptual foundations of the American regime. This should not come as a complete surprise, since FDR's efforts, particularly with respect to the Third New Deal, were aimed precisely at resolving that tension in favor of a progressive vision. But the Borah-Barkley exchange hints at another fundamental point of contention in the reorganization debate: the relative powers of the president versus the Congress in the constitutional system, specifically as manifested in control over administration. FDR's reorganization proposal "touched very centrally" on what had evolved into a "delicate balance of power" (Milkis 1993, 121).

Senator Byrd addressed this issue head on during his principal speech against the reorganization bill. He argued that "to give the President the authority to abolish or modify, in whole or in part, a function of government, involves a great surrender of power by the Congress. A function of government is a policy of government. Congress is the sole agency to determine a policy of government" (*CR* 1938, 2592). Similarly, Senator Josiah Bailey of North Carolina argued that the time had come "for Members of Congress . . . to assert their power in order that it may be known in the United States, and particularly in [the] departments, that the power is ours and not theirs; that the responsibility for the Government and its policies [is] upon the elective and the constitutional representatives of the people and not upon those whose offices we create and to whom we give public funds for distribution for the public benefit" (2710). Finally, Burton Wheeler, in a lengthy speech and exchange with Alben Barkley that served as a bridge between the two main areas of contention, argued, "If we are to have a democratic republic . . . we are going to have inefficiency in government, but the answer to those who are saying we cannot function under a democratic government . . . is not delegating our powers to a President . . . or to the executive branch. The answer to the evils of democracy is more democracy, and have it intelligently and honestly applied" (3023).

What undergirded these invocations of congressional authority, the historian Frank Freidel has observed, was that opponents "saw reorganization as weakening their own power and prerogatives in relation to those of the president. They did not want Roosevelt to gain firmer control over his own administration" (1990, 276). Or, as Sidney Milkis (1993, 121) has concluded, reorganization opponents were not just expressing "irrational fears" but acting on an institutionally based partisanship, grounded in tradition and the Constitution, in response to the very real threat that policy and administration would be reunited under the president's control. If this was to be the case, Burton Wheeler argued, "let us adjourn the Congress and let the departments do the legislating for the people of the United States" (*CR* 1938, 3023).

It is not just coincidence that the battle over executive reorganization is reminiscent of the contest between Andrew Jackson and Senate Whigs. Both confrontations involved very popular presidents leading a wave of democratic sentiment toward systemic reform in congruence with a particular conception of the regime. Both involved efforts to attain greater presidential control over administration and to restructure administration so that it would be an effective instrument in service to the conception of the regime being pursued. Both saw a vigorous congressional counterresponse, embodying contending ideas about the nature of

American democracy and a struggle over the relative power and authority of the president and Congress under the Constitution, especially with respect to the control of administration. The executive reorganization debate even involved the issue of presidential removals from office, several actually exercised by FDR, as well as the threat of such action in connection with the proposed creation of a single civil service administrator to replace the civil service commission.

Nevertheless, one feature of the executive reorganization debate made it different from the 1835 confrontation and the similar debates probing basic regime questions during other times of political change, reform, and development. That feature is the stunning absence of any attempt to articulate alternative ideas about public administration and its place in the regime. To be sure, there was the occasional glimmer, such as Representative Noah Mason's characterization of "government administration" as "vital activities affecting the welfare and the very destiny of this Nation" in his attack on the proposal to abolish the Civil Service Commission in favor of a single administrator (*CR* 1938, 1232). Such glimmers never grew much brighter, however, and the ideas behind them were not developed more systematically or coherently.

The reorganization debate also probed distinctions between strictly executive officers and those who performed quasi-legislative and quasi-judicial functions, in connection with the proposed civil service administrator and the proposed auditor general to replace the existing comptroller general. This probing followed the Supreme Court decision in *Humphrey's Executor v. U.S.* (295 U.S. 602 [1935]), however, and thus was dominated by its reasoning. In the end, then, the representatives and senators of the Seventy-fifth Congress never actually confronted the challenge of trying to define for themselves what constituted an executive officer.

Overall, the only conception of public administration apparently given any credence in the reorganization debate was that of an instrumental, subordinate institution. Indeed, the two most prominent words used to characterize administration and administrative agencies were *mechanism* and *instrumentality*. Although, as I have explained, considerable debate ensued over the extent to which administrative agencies were instruments of the president or the Congress, or perhaps more precisely, what administrative units were the instruments of which branch, at least a plurality of representatives and senators even accepted the notion that administration was solely the tool of the president. The several debates, beginning with those in 1789, on the status of public administration in the American regime, and especially the very powerful progressive and New Deal conception of administration as the president's foremost tool for the management of a modern democracy, seem to have squeezed out of public thinking any glint of an idea that public administration might have any other role in the regime than servant to popular demands.

The Third New Deal thus succeeded in securing the acceptance of an executive–centered administrative hierarchy, for never again would a debate like that over the reorganization bill take place in Congress. That is, never again would Congress be the principal forum for debate about the nature of public administration and its place in the regime. To the extent that debates about the status and design of administration occurred later in the New Deal and during the post–New Deal political order, they were confined mostly *within* the executive branch, often in connection with the work of presidential commissions following the precedent of the Brownlow Committee. To be sure, since the New Deal, Congress has engaged in some fascinating debate about the design of administration, in connection, for example, with the passage of the Atomic Energy Act and the Administrative Procedure Act, both in 1946, and in connection with post–Watergate reforms, such as the Civil Service Reform Act and the Ethics in Government Act, both passed in 1978. But for the most part, the kind of diverse, searching, concentrated debate about the design and placement of administration in the regime evident in the earlier congressional debates, never reappears.

The New Deal in Perspective

In his unprecedented effort to make liberalism the core public philosophy and to realize the benefits of an active social program of progressive democracy, Franklin Roosevelt of necessity confronted the dilemma that public administration as a political institution poses for the constitutional system. His response was to complete the progressive enterprise, principally by more firmly linking administration to presidential control, as a way to insure that the expanding administrative apparatus remained responsive and accountable to the public will. FDR also furthered the intentions of the progressives by accelerating the transcendence of party politics. Again, this was principally connected with the effort to establish, protect, and sustain programmatic liberalism by making administration its institutional platform and placing it under the control of the president. Another of the consequences, however, was a strengthening of the ties that bound administrative agencies to organized interests, especially those of a liberal persuasion that were part of the New Deal coalition.

The New Deal did not resolve the dilemma administration poses for the regime. Indeed, in significant ways it intensified the tensions and contradictions created by the progressive reformation project by broadening the gap between perception and reality, between the conception of administration that had come to dominate American political ideology and rhetoric and how administration in actuality functioned. Two contradictions were prominent in the New Deal's reforms.

First, although an administration conceived of as the instrument of modern liberalism would not be involved in designating the purposes of the liberal state—those would come primarily from the president, as leader and interpreter of the public will—such a distinction could not be sustained in practice. By making public administration the custodian of liberal partisanship, FDR really did meld politics with administration, perhaps to a greater extent than he realized. As Frederick Mosher quite some time ago incisively pointed out, "many of the objectives of governments . . . were social, not readily measurable, and difficult for [an elected] legislature or executive to define with any degree of exactitude" (1968, 76). This left to the discretion of bureaucrats not just the identification and development of means to achieve given public policy objectives, but the designation, or at least refinement, of those objectives themselves. Thus, "during the New Deal period and the war which followed it most new policies and programs were initiated in the executive branch, often, if not usually, well below the levels of political appointees" (82). Policy subgovernments linking interest groups, agencies, and congressional committees formed in response to this reality, and they were soon thereafter attacked as perversions of popular control of government. In particular, they clearly violated the understanding of a subordinate, instrumental public administration.

Second, and perhaps even more profound, FDR seemed to conceive of administration—the instrument of modern liberalism—as also having a hand in shaping the liberal aspirations of American citizens. This is implicit in the notion that administrative agencies would be responsible for the upkeep and repair of the liberal programs which they administered. This concept was taken even further, however: "Roosevelt and the architects of administrative reform hoped to cultivate a federal work force dedicated to advancing the cause of New Deal reform" (Milkis 1993, 116). Part of that cause would be "to cultivate amongst the American citizenry an appreciation of government planning and extensive public service" (110). In other words, to perpetuate programmatic liberalism, administration would have a central role in fashioning and fortifying the public's liberal sensibilities. It would help create a more liberal polity.

Recall that the Jacksonians had a similar conception of the role administration would play in their reform endeavor: the public service would be the instrument of a republican restoration, but in that earlier case the federal work force would also help to cultivate in the populace the simple values and virtues that were the foundation of that restoration. It is in just such a conceptualization as this that the distinct but interconnected qualities of public administration, the instrumental and the constitutive, clearly surface. Andrew Jackson does not appear to have grasped this. Woodrow Wilson did, however, and Franklin Roosevelt may have also. But like Wilson, FDR did not put forth in his public speech any effort to communicate this understanding. Instead, the fundamental message of his public speech, and the work of his expert committee, was that administration was the tool of the public's social service and economic security aspirations. The president, in turn, would be the personal and organizational embodiment of those aspirations and would control the administrative instrument in quest of them. The reality, again, was quite different. Administrative agencies were actively and extensively involved in defining what constituted liberal goals and the interractions with citizens that would give shape and substance to those goals.

By expanding public administration, increasing its capacity and competence, placing it at the center of a reformed political and governmental system, and linking it to a great work, that of restoring an economy to health, establishing the rudiments of broad–based economic security, and defeating worldwide fascism, Franklin Roosevelt generated for American public administration a great well of legitimacy and public support. These were purchased at a very high price, however. As the politics of the recent past and of the present have revealed, the bill has come due.

Politics and Administration after the New Deal

The post–New Deal political order is distinguished by three political movements that share roots in the turbulent politics of the 1960s and overlap across political time in their influences on how Americans think, talk, and act regarding politics, government, and public administration. The first and most substantial of the three, which reached its ascendancy in the late 1960s through the mid–1970s, proved in many respects to be the next wave in the democratic reform impulse. Encompassing important elements of the politics of the New Left and seeking the further expansion and institutionalization of programmatic liberalism (Milkis 1993, chs. 8, 9), this reform effort is a contemporary manifestation of Dewey's humanitarian liberalism. The movement gained control of and altered fundamentally the character of the Democratic party, but its primary organizational vehicle was, and remains, a peculiar manifestation of the special interest group—the "public interest group" or "public lobby" (Berry 1977; Harris and Milkis 1989). Overall, the movement continues to exert a profound influence on the process and substance of American politics and government.

The second movement, associated with the conservative Republican presidencies of Richard Nixon and especially Ronald Reagan and with the rise of a "New Right" emulating the organizational and political strategies and tactics of liberal public interest groups, reached its first plateau of power in the 1980s and a second in the mid–1990s. It stresses governmental decentralization and deregulation in most economic regulatory areas and selected social regulatory areas, representing a contemporary form of laissez–faire liberalism, although it has also sought greater governmental influence and regulation of behavior in highly volatile areas of social relations. From the late 1970s to the present, the liberal public lobby movement and its conservative opposition have engaged in a continuing and often fierce political battle to define the character and aims of the American polity and to control the modern administrative state as the means of realizing those aims (Eden 1989b; Milkis 1993, ch. 11).

Overlying this institutional and ideological combat, a third movement has come to prominence. It emphasizes less what modern American government should be doing and much more how it should go about doing it. Spurred on by static or dwindling financial resources and widespread public perceptions of governmental irrelevance and incompetence, elected and appointed officials, academics, and a new breed of entrepreneurial social reformer—the consultant—have loosely joined forces and borrowed ideas from the tumultuous restructuring of the American economy, with the intent of "reengineering " or "reinventing" the administration of public programs and the delivery of public services (e.g., Barzelay 1992; Osborne and Gaebler 1992).

The concepts, language, and reform measures of all three movements, in a dizzying mix, have become accepted, even deeply ingrained, elements of American politics and government as the nation closes in on a new century. Advocates of all three, moreover, have in one way or another characterized their efforts as countermoves against progressive and New Deal politics and governance. Yet all three rest fundamentally on the conception of politics, government, and public administration bequeathed by progressive and New Deal reforms.

A New Liberalism and Its Instrument

The "New Politics" of the reformers who reached the apogee of their influence in the late 1960s and 1970s stressed participatory democracy, territorial and functional decentralization of government, an expanded panoply of rights, legal formalism, suspicion of administrative discretion, and rejection of interest-group pluralism and the self-interested basis of its political activity (Brand 1989). Although not necessarily members of the New Left themselves, the reformers drew much of their agenda from New Left critiques of American politics. The intersection of this agenda with the organizational and institutional infrastructure established under the New Deal political order generated a dialectical synthesis (Harris and Milkis 1989, 56) that expanded and radicalized the legal and institutional edifice of the New Deal (Milkis 1993, 195).

This synthesis might usefully be labeled an expansion of the New Deal welfare state to include "quality of life." The quality of life, beyond the economic security provided by the New Deal, was a growing concern of the increasingly affluent, suburban middle class of the 1960s and 1970s (Hays 1987), and it was part of Lyndon Johnson's vision of a Great Society (Milkis 1993, 181). Reformers thus concentrated much of their effort on defining an expanded panoply of rights that included the "collective" rights associated with protection against the dangers of industrial capitalism, the "civil" rights and entitlements associated with the special circumstances and needs of "discreet and insular minorities," and the "procedural" rights associated with the care and exercise of collective rights and entitlements (Melnick 1989, 195–201). The procedural rights also reinforced the drive to expand citizens' influence in the governmental process. The result was a reinterpretation of democracy "as a policy-making process [or a] process for popular control of policy making" (Lindblom 1980, 1). Democracy was no longer just a guarantor of personal liberty.

All of the new rights required, at a minimum, the same kinds of positive programmatic actions and protections as the New Deal economic security rights, especially expanded agency missions, new agencies, and even new organizational designs for agencies (e.g., Ackerman and Hassler, 1981). The conception of and regard for public administration in this context is therefore illuminating. Lyndon Johnson's Vietnam betrayal and Richard Nixon's election convinced the new liberal activists that the presidency could no longer be trusted as the institutional expression of public opinion and the faithful overseer of an administration that was the institutional home for programmatic liberalism. Moreover, administration as an institution was itself suspect, because it was associated with FDR's liberalism and it was fully implicated in the subgovernment arrangements driven by the self-interested politics of interest-group pluralism. Wary of both the presidency and public administration, these new liberal activists who came to prominence in the 1970s fashioned "a new institutional coalition" (Milkis 1993, 227; also see Melnick 1989) of congressional subcommittees, courts, and public interest groups. This new arrangement better embodied the vision of democracy the activists sought and more effectively controlled the administrative power deployed in the name of programmatic rights. The latter result was to a considerable extent realized, moreover, because under the "reformation of administrative law" (Stewart 1975) that accompanied the new arrangement, congressional subcommittees, the courts, and citizen groups were (and still are) more extensively involved in the details of administration. Such an "enhancement" of the "representative character of government action" was not meant "to restrain administrative power but, rather, . . . to reshape it as an agent of democracy" (Milkis 1993, 211). Or, as Martin Shapiro has stated it more starkly, courts extended their influence over the details of administration, "to reduce the independence and discretionary scope of a mistrusted bureaucracy and to subordinate it to more control by the regulated, the beneficiaries of regulation, and the public at large" (1986, 461–62).

The conception and treatment of public administration in politics and government by the new liberalism was hardly much different than under the old liberalism of the New Deal. Administration remained a dedicated instrument of programmatic liberalism, although its institutional master was now largely that coalition of congressional subcommittees, public interest groups, and courts. Administrative agencies were sometimes working partners in this coalition (Milkis 1993, 240, 282), but the heightened legal formalism imposed by statute and judicial opinion and restrictions on administrative discretion that the coalition put in place made it clear that public administrators were to regard themselves and their agencies as simply the delivery vehicles for the will of the people as given expression in the liberal programmatic desires of group activists, judges, and members of Congress and their staffs.

Return to Administrative Orthodoxy

With his election in 1968, Richard Nixon brought conservatives and Republicans to power at a time when the new liberalism was still coalescing and gaining strength and momentum. He thus had a chance to stem the tide, and, indeed, he intended to reform the executive branch in such a way as to distance it from the liberalism of the Kennedy-Johnson years. Nixon expected his reform effort—the "administrative presidency" (see Nathan 1975, 1983)—"to reconstitute the executive [branch] into a more centralized and independent instrument of government" (Milkis 1993, 233). His 1968 election victory was very close, however, and, despite his 1972 landslide reelection, Nixon faced a Democratic Congress during his entire presidency, part of twenty-four years of divided party control of the federal government broken only by Jimmy Carter's single term. Nixon was not, moreover, a hard ideologue. He envisioned himself as

"Disraeli to the Great Society," managing rather than departing from or undoing programmatic liberalism (Milkis 1993, 223, 224). It thus fell to Ronald Reagan, a more clearly focused and less personally ambitious conservative, to make substantial progress with a conservative counterattack.

Freedom and liberty were central themes in Ronald Reagan's public speech as both candidate and president, and he sharply questioned, as he had done since his 1964 nomination speech for Barry Goldwater, whether a vast edifice of government programs representing a wide array of rights truly meant greater freedom and personal autonomy. Reagan questioned fundamentally both the philosophy and the organizational and institutional infrastructure of programmatic liberalism, as created by the New Deal and elaborated by the reformers of the 1960s and 1970s.

The conservative movement Reagan led featured a three-pronged attack that included *defunding*, through tax cuts and shifting of budget priorities from domestic welfare to national security and defense, *devolution* of programs to states and localities (with reductions in fiscal support), and *deregulation*, picking up on initiatives of the Carter years in economic regulation and extending the thrust to important areas of social regulation, including environmental quality and workplace health and safety (Benda and Levine 1988). After an initial spate of legislative successes, this path to reform proved increasingly difficult. For this reason, and because the infrastructure of programmatic liberalism was so extensive and deeply rooted, Reagan turned to his own more aggressive and effective version of the administrative presidency.

The essence of the Reagan administrative presidency strategy was to make the federal bureaucracy a more manageable and obedient servant of the conservative agenda. An important tactic centered on shrinking the size of the domestic program and regulatory bureaucracy through defunding, devolution, deregulation, and privatization. But more important was the effort at tightening overall control, through budget and regulatory review and clearance procedures and through personnel policies that placed political appointees deep into the career civil service. These policies insured that all appointees, even at the cabinet level, remained loyal to the Reagan agenda rather than to the agenda of program advocates inside the agencies or among activist groups (Benda and Levine 1988; also Durant 1992, ch. 2). While the battle to "debureaucratize" the federal government and dismantle the infrastructure of programmatic liberalism was being fought largely to a draw, the Reagan effort to impose tighter control and even reshape the policy outlook of the federal administrative establishment was realizing much greater success. The result was the return of the presidency to a mastery over administration similar to what FDR had fashioned (Milkis 1993, 262), and with that return came the reimposition, with a vengeance, of the "administrative orthodoxy" of hierarchically organized controls on administration (Durant 1992).

Despite significant successes, the conservative Reagan "revolution" failed to vanquish programmatic liberalism. Indeed, Sidney Milkis has argued that it "actually extended in important respects the *institutional* inheritance of liberal reforms" (1993, 262, emphasis added). From the perspective of how public administration is conceived and treated, the outcome has been an even more sharply honed instrumental status. Administrative agencies operate in a web of formal controls initiated by both statute and presidential executive order (see Garvey 1993, 191–200) that complement the informal pressures exerted by a constellation of political masters inside and outside government. Hence, public administration is now more than ever regarded as simply a mechanism for the delivery of benefits and services (and often judged a very ineffective one at that). The political engagement of administrative agencies amounts at most to defending the programs they operate. That administrative agencies might effectively engage in deliberation on, and thus help define, the central purposes of the regime and, further, guide the formulation of appropriate public actions, is patently rejected (see Rourke 1991).

A New Paradigm?

The governmental and political arrangements put in place by the new liberalism and by Reagan conservatism have proven to be a highly volatile mix. Describing the combination as "modern factionalism," a system "of the activists, by the activists, and for the activists," Hugh Heclo has argued that "it is possible for activists to win and lose in their struggles over the levers of government without really engaging the general public in a decisive argument about the choices" (Heclo 1989, 311, 314). That American government and politics is not in touch with what troubles American citizens and is not engaged in tackling those troubles (and is too ineffectual to succeed at it anyway) is the animating critique of a varied collection of public officials and intellectuals calling for a new way of thinking about government—a new model or paradigm of governance. Much of the criticism, and much of the interest in taking government in a new direction, arose among the nation's governors, including Bill Clinton, who further pursued his affinity for the ideas of this movement once he reached the White House.

Assessing current circumstances, national leaders in this movement have pointed to what they regard as a useless obsession with disputing the ideological arguments of the past two decades, indeed of the past half-century, over *what* government should be doing (how much or how little), and this preoccupation has led incumbent politicians to ignore the real problems of citizens and to cripple *how* government goes about the work of addressing those problems. Contending that we "do not need another New Deal, nor another Reagan Revolution," and supported by the words of public officials calling for a new vision of government, the chief prophets of this movement, David Osborne and Ted Gaebler (1992, 23–24), state the case forcefully. "Our fundamental problem today is not too much government or too little government. We have debated that issue endlessly . . . , and it has not solved our problems. . . . We do not need more government or less government, we need *better* government. To be more precise, we need better *governance*" (also see Gore 1993, 2, 8, emphasis in original).

Because this movement has sought to distance itself decisively from past conceptions of government and public administration, the content of the new paradigm of governance it claims to offer deserves scrutiny. Perhaps the principal conceptual and metaphorical device employed by Osborne and Gaebler is the distinction between "steering" and "rowing," borrowed from the long-time privatization advocate E. S. Savas. This recalls the politics-administration dichotomy, and indeed, Osborne and Gaebler specifically discuss "separating" steering, which involves policy decisions, from rowing, which involves service delivery (1992, 34–37). But they also argue that governments that steer "actively shape their communities, states, and nations," (32); and they discuss at length "community-owned government" and "empowerment," which involves government's aiding people in defining their goals as well as in finding the means to achieve them.

Osborne and Gaebler do not shrink from stating exactly what they mean by governance. It is "the process by which we collectively solve our problems and meet our society's needs. Government is the instrument we use" (24). Further, governance means " 'leading' society, convincing its various interest groups to embrace common goals and strategies" (34). Theirs is a resolutely instrumental conception of government and politics, in which the nation's problems, needs, goals, and norms of behavior are identified and defined through some mysterious process external to governing, or they have all been determined in the past and will never need any further consideration or refinement. Politics and government, in this view, are simply the art of persuasion: elected officials and other leaders convince groups to accept these predetermined problems, needs, goals, and norms. Public administrators are not involved even to this extent. They are responsible for "policy management," that is, finding the proper techniques and strategies to deliver products and services to citizen-customers (Barzelay 1992) in a manner that does not violate norms such as accessibility, responsiveness, and equity.

To be fair, the most thoughtful strains of the reinventing government movement manifest at least a vague recognition that democratic government and politics involve not just the satisfaction of the needs and wants of citizen-customers for a varied package of products and services but the never-ending project of a people to develop and refine its character. But, in appropriately associating many of the contemporary weaknesses in the responsiveness and effectiveness of American government to the institutional arrangements of the modern factionalism that emerged in the 1970s and 1980s, proponents of reinventing government have completely dispensed with political theory as the basis for a theory of government. In place of political theory or ideology as the foundation for a philosophy of government, they have sought to substitute a cascade of new principles of management, drawn largely from business, that does not even amount to a coherent theory of management. This is hardly much different from the path many progressive reformers pursued in building the now-despised "bureaucratic paradigm" (Barzelay 1992), and predictably this approach has further reinforced an instrumental conception, not only of public administration, but of politics and government as a whole.

From the perspective of public administration and its place in the regime, then, the political movements of the post–New Deal political order have only sharpened and extended a subordinate, instrumental conception of administration. They have, further, sustained the New Deal's success in expunging from public debate any coherent alternative conception of administration's role that might acknowledge its constitutiveness. Despite the greater array of controls on public administration imposed by both liberals and conservatives, however, public agencies are involved in shaping public aims and relations between citizens in ever more subtle and complex ways. The rift between public understanding and political rhetoric on the one hand, and governmental and political realities on the other, has grown, and the public swings back and forth between revolt and anomie.

6

Recovering a Constitutive Understanding of Public Administration

How shall the 'public sector' be made public and not the arena of a ruling bureaucracy of 'public servants'?" The Students for a Democratic Society posed this question in their 1962 manifesto, *The Port Huron Statement*. The authors of the document went on to answer their own question by calling for "steadfast opposition to bureaucratic coagulation." More revealingly, however, they advocated minimizing "the bureaucratic pileups . . . by local, regional, and national economic *planning*—responding to the interconnection of public problems by comprehensive programs," while also promoting "experiments in *decentralization*" that would restore to people the "personal capacity to cope with life" (see Miller 1987, 364, emphasis in original).

The tension between the desire for centralized efforts to dispel chaos and overcome inaction and the desire to keep government closely tied to people in their every day lives is unmistakable in this "New Left" statement of aspirations. Yet it is hardly unique. Across the past three decades, survey research has shown repeatedly that majorities of Americans claim to want less government, and thus lower taxes and fewer government services, while also insisting that government be powerful and effective in fighting long-smoldering problems and attacking new threats as they arise (see, for example, "Opinion Roundup" 1987; "Public Opinion and Demographic Report" 1993). In short, Americans seem to want what public bureaucracy does but not what it is, namely, complex organizations housing officials who at least sometimes make independent decisions that affect people's lives.

It is not just the New Left and its remnants, but all the children of post–New Deal liberalism, who find themselves in a "love-hate relationship with administrative power" (Milkis 1993, 211). The American public's ambivalence about public administration and its place in both their private and public lives is not simply a product of the New Deal and its aftermath, however. It has roots in the struggle of American political leaders, from the founding onward across successive episodes of regime development and transformation, to comprehend and respond to the distinctive institutional character of administration, a character marked by an especially acute tension between the instrumental and constitutive qualities that typify all political institutions.

To be sure, the fixation on the instrumental dimension of administration, which is at the heart of the public's ambivalence and even hostility, has assumed its sharpest, most expansive form during the twentieth century, as the size and reach of the federal government have grown. This is hardly surprising, signaling as it does the convergence of the irresistible democratic impulse, the hegemony of economic progress, and the lengthening reach of economizing thought. First recognizable in the Progressive Era, this convergence has culminated in the programmatic liberal expression of what E. E. Schattschneider (1960) called the "socialization of conflict": problems previously defined and treated privately are identified as public goals (or ends), and public solutions (or means) are sought to address them. The solutions have come in the form of benefits and protections packaged as government programs. But programs must be administered, and to lessen the chances that these programs might be administered arbitrarily, and to expand the scope of the solutions they offer, "formula decision making," "formalistic analysis," and the language of economics rather than law (see Lowi 1993a, 156–57) have become central administrative design features. This is politics and public administration on automatic pilot (see Weaver 1988).

The acutely mechanistic approach to public policy in this arrangement involves a public administration intendedly devoid of any "independent judgment" (Morone 1990, 128, 141). This is clearly contrary to both the historical and the current realities of the function of public administration in the regime. The contradictions and confusions about the role of public administration in American government and politics which began deep in the Republic's past continue to be sustained by current arrangements. As the United States reaches the end of the twentieth century, the driving force of the democratic impulse has intersected with other social and political forces and events to generate a regard for and treatment of public administration that is thoroughly instrumental, and it is so in two distinctive yet nested meanings.

First, public administration is the principal object of contention between activists within the modern factional regime because it is the principal vehicle for delivering what political leaders and the public most prize about the modern state: the benefits and protections (and punishments and costs) it bestows (see Rohr 1986, 184). Second, these warring factions roughly divide along the fault line between the humanitarian and the laissez-faire streams of American liberalism. The combatants seek to wield public administration as a weapon in a war to secure control of the state, the kinds of services it dispenses, and the means for dispensing them (see, for example, Milkis 1993, 242, 296; also Ginsberg and Shefter 1990, chs. 2–6).

For all the money, energy, and toil invested in this war to insure that public bureaucracy as servant is under "political" control and responsive to the public will as pronounced by political activists, American citizens are no more comfortable than they ever were with an extensive presence of public bureaucracy in their lives. Indeed, they are as anxious and antagonistic as ever toward public "ministers" who seem to threaten both individual freedom and collective self-determination (Morone 1990, 141). And perhaps they should be, for a closer look at the intensely instrumental regard for and treatment of public administration suggests that perpetuating the contradiction between the conception and reality of public administration in American politics has been constitutive of a frustrated, dependent, unimaginative citizenry who suffer from weakened political institutions that are unlikely to sustain strong aspirations to self-government.

Instrumental Administration and Its Consequences

The faceless bureaucrat, the rigidly rule-bound and unresponsive public servant, the threatening labyrinth of corridors (and now electronic message options) of the government agency—these are all part of the imagery of public bureaucracy deeply imbedded in American culture. All are, of course, in some way connected to real traits in bureaucratic organization that may become pathological, but they have been magnified beyond all proportion as the instrumental conception of public administration has flourished. This disproportionate reaction to public bureaucracy is most pronounced in the applications of technology to administration, and it illuminates one of the principal repercussions of a myopic understanding of administration.

Problem Displacement and the Vicious Circle of Control

In addition to searching for automatic, formulaic administration of solutions to societal problems, Americans have repeatedly sought technological solutions that are as devoid as possible of human involvement. These technologies have, nevertheless, required "experts" and "managers" of one kind or another to make them work; the combination of expert and technology in administration has reinforced among citizens the sense of loss of control, even of subservience, to machines and to bureaucrats. In a very real manifestation of the formative effect of tools on tool users, Americans have allowed their character as a people and their interactions with one another to be dictated by the formulas and technologies they have devised to address their problems.

This profound sense of loss of control of who we are, how we act, and how we govern ourselves is not due to the tyranny of the machine or the bureaucrat, however. It is grounded in the mechanistic, instrumental, orientation itself. As William Leiss has stated it, "we are not tyrannized by the complex technical knowledge incorporated in our society's administrative structures; we simply expect too much of it" (1990, 22). The instrumental conception of politics, but especially of administration, embraced by American political leaders with increased intensity across the generations, has served as the repository for expectations for resolving the dilemmas of liberal democratic governance. These dilemmas became increasingly challenging and perplexing with the growing complications of postindustrial society. But if the task of governance was simply to craft the proper tools, in the form of public agencies and the public servants in them, and maintain proper control of those tools so that the fundamental goals of the regime could be attained, then the increasingly polycentric problems that were arising simply required more sophisticated tools, and more sophisticated controls on the use of those tools.

Embracing this definition of liberal democratic governance shunted aside the central dilemmas of democracy and replaced them with the problem of imposing democratic controls on administration, and each successive wave of administrative reform generated increased anxiety about control, responsiveness, and accountability. The result has been an upward spiral in collective worry about the control and accountability of the administrative establishment and about the manipulation of that establishment for partisan political purposes. An increasingly vicious circle has emerged in which anxiety about control and accountability of public administration has led to more extensive, more complex controls, which in turn have increased the bureaucratic distance between administrators and the public they are expected to serve. This distance then raises new worries about control and accountability and brings about the introduction of another layer of controls (see the very similar characterization in Schoenbrod 1983, 824). An expanding share of valuable political and governing resources is consumed in creating and tending this complex matrix of controls, with no noticeable improvement, in the aggregate, in the relationship between the public and public administrators, or in individual or systemic capacity for self-government. Indeed, precisely the opposite would appear to be the case.

Early manifestations of such effects of an instrumental conception of the liberal democratic governance problem are clearly evident in the Jacksonian reform effort. The practice of rotation in office and the nascent bureaucratic mechanisms that the Jacksonians put in place seemed to increase the aggregate accessibility and comprehensibility of administration, and they clearly had beneficial effects for the regime. The organizational norms, operating routines, and controls on behavior introduced by Amos Kendall and others, for instance, allowed for the retention of some administrative capacity and efficiency in face of the greater turnover induced by rotation. Rotation and the spoils system in turn helped the growing public bureaucracy maintain public salience, and with it an important measure of legitimacy with a population that was expanding rapidly in its size and diversity.

The spoils system was not, on the other hand, an easy system to navigate, which raised questions about how much more accessible public employment had really become for any given individual, beyond the effects of the sheer increase in number of positions available. Nor did the spoils necessarily produce a more open, dynamic relationship in the face-to-face encounter between administrator and citizen. And it is not at all clear that administrative subordination to party, through the president or Congress, produced policy formulation or implementation that was much more consistent with the popular will than had the system that preceded it. Unfortunately, research that can shed light on these issues has yet to be undertaken.

In addition, the incipient bureaucratization, aimed as much at limiting corruption as increasing efficiency, combined with rotation to produce substantial administrative incapacity and inefficiency; the Union Army during the Civil War is perhaps the premiere example of this effect (but see Van Riper 1958, 43–44). A more serious consequence was that, because of rotation and routinization, fewer and fewer administrators had the sense of responsibility and the experience to understand and effectively deploy the practical judgment that lies at the core of administration as a political enterprise and of the contributions it makes to the regime. Moreover, the eventually corrupt outcome of the spoils seem-

ingly contradicted the Jacksonian pledges of moral restoration and subjugation of administration to the public will and interest. Hence, a new
reform effort appeared, imposing new control arrangements and creating new and more complex challenges for accessibility, comprehensibility, and effectiveness.

The consequences for the vitality and fortitude of American aspirations to self-government are, however, most pronounced under the present system of controls and political relationships. Despite the greater
openness to public influence, healthy skepticism, and "bottom-up reorientation of political forces" it exhibits (Heclo 1989, 298, 302), American
politics and government are—to paraphrase Theodore Lowi's longstanding critique—open, accessible, intelligible, and beneficial for the organized, but an impenetrable, coercive enigma for the unorganized (see,
more recently, Lowi 1993a, 154–55). The complex matrix of political relationships and administrative controls built up around programmatic
rights requires high-velocity, campaign-style political activism pursued
from a platform of sophisticated organization.

Organization provides to political interests, as it always has to pressure
groups (see Ornstein and Elder 1978, 69–79, for example), the financial,
leadership, and motivational resources needed to marshall the forces, including media access, that are necessary in any effort to define and install
new programmatic rights or to maintain and defend programmatic
rights already won. This characteristic of the policy process does not appear to be very much of a reform of the self-interested basis of modern
pluralist politics sought by the activists of the 1960s and 1970s. From the
perspective of the individual citizen, moreover, the benefits of this system
of modern factionalism are concentrated on and enjoyed by relatively
narrowly defined groups, while the burdens are diffuse, growing, and
borne by an increasingly precarious middle class (see Phillips 1993).

Furthermore, the procedures and requirements for administrative
rule making that constitute a central feature of the current system, although important for opening up administrative decision making to a
wider range of public viewpoints and bringing bureaucratic expertise
into direct contact with the public's views, are nevertheless now so com-
plicated and drawn out that influence rarely comes from anything but
well organized, directly affected constituencies who have the resources
and stamina to maneuver through the process successfully. This situation
is a mockery of the "reformation" of administrative law (Stewart 1975)
that was central to the push by the reformers of the 1960s and 1970s to
expand and protect newly defined rights and enhance popular participation. Lowi has called this outcome the "derangement of procedure"
(1993a, 158–59).

Over the course of the past generation, then, the cycle of worrying about accountability and control of administration, imposing new controls on administration in response, and spawning new and more elaborate concerns about accountability and control, has created an arrangement of administrative controls and political relationships that is nearly incomprehensible and inaccessible to average citizens. Moreover, they see it as preventing them from enjoying the full benefits of the administrative state, to which they believe they are entitled. This generates all sorts of expectations of bad faith between public administrators and their fellow citizens (but see Katz et al. 1975; Goodsell 1994, ch. 2), and it presents serious barriers to meaningfully broad-based citizen engagement in politics and public life (Harris and Milkis 1989, 297–309; Milkis 1993, 250–55).

In addition, the administrative controls that by now have reached their most elaborated patterns, and the political interactions that have reached their most convoluted, high-velocity forms, have revealed themselves to be serious obstacles to the effectiveness with which administrative agencies fulfill their "missions" (e.g., Moe 1989). The fundamental structure of American governments, particularly the separation of powers, has from the beginning produced local, state, and national administrations fragmented in their structure and operational capacity. This has led to what Harold Seidman called the search for the "philosopher's stone" of coordination (Seidman and Gilmour 1986, ch. 10). Further complication and aggravation of this fundamental condition, ironically, thwarts fulfillment of the instrumental conception of administration on which the rules and procedures and arrangements are predicated, a point not missed by advocates of reinventing government. Far more serious, however, is that the complex, unwieldy matrix of controls and political relationships has weakened administrative effectiveness in the hidden but critical constitutive contribution that administration can make better than any other political institution: rethinking and redefining the polity's goals and the citizen relations that give them meaning, in light of both current exigencies and collective choices already made and legitimated (see Rourke 1991, 1992).

Constitutional Space, Democratized Administration, and Policy Design

An exclusively instrumental conception of administration, it must now be clear, especially of administration as a pillar in the foundation of the peculiarly American version of the modern welfare state, has served to cut off that institution from the liberal democratic constitutionalism of which it is a part. This has forced political leaders, public administrators, and scholars into a long and arduous search for legitimating arguments to reconcile and thus artificially reattach administration to a regime predicated on popular sovereignty and individual rights. As the bureaucratic form came more and more to embody what Americans understood by the term "administration," the legitimating arguments advanced and the structural reforms proposed became more elaborate.

Irrespective of the rate or extent of bureaucratization, however, the dominant view in American politics has always been that administration is foreign—an alien in a democratic land. This seems to be especially so with respect to good administration, that which is effective both in meeting goals and in helping to shape those goals and the citizen interactions that embody them. At the time of the founding, those who embraced republican government most ardently regarded strong administration as monarchical. By the turn to the twentieth century, political leaders concluded that administration was more dangerous still, because it was by then clearly bureaucratized. They perceived that its potential for despotism was then much greater, and so it had to be domesticated, harnessed, and controlled or it would undermine the democratic way of life.

The best of the scholarly attempts to reconcile bureaucracy with American liberal democracy have been impressively creative, but all of them in one way or another ring hollow and artificial. More important, the entire reconciliation project has been unsuccessful in finding an arrangement that the American people are comfortable with, largely because it is based on an erroneous, or at least an incomplete, conception of liberal democratic politics. Constituting a liberal democratic regime and engaging in liberal democratic politics consist not only in getting to some predetermined goal and in deciding how best to get there. These are critical dimensions, no doubt, and public administration is particularly vital to the latter. But making and keeping a liberal democratic regime also entails considering and reconsidering what goal to strive for, and thus shaping and reshaping the character of a people. Public administration has a role here, too; and that role, in fact, is unavoidable.

American public administration, even in its current and most bureaucratized form, has a lineage that runs as deep as the Republic's. Public administration is consistent with the idea of the constitutiveness of political institutions inherent in democratic constitutionalism. American public bureaucracy in and of itself does not threaten to control what people think or how they interact with one another, to enslave the populace. It is the notion of citizens as clients or customers, a notion that emanates from the instrumental view of administration, that poses such a threat. American public administration does not need to be artificially reconciled with or grafted onto the regime of the Constitution, or suspended in an increasingly complex matrix of controls. Such controls have been devised, for the most part, to enhance the political power of their creators, rather than to enhance the freedom and sovereign power of the citizenry.

Because American political development generally, and the construction of the administrative state in particular, have not been guided by an understanding of politics or administration that includes a robust constitutive perspective, administration has become separated from the regime. Just as serious, the instrumental perspective has led to legitimating arguments that reconcile administration with liberal democracy principally on the basis of the former's neutrality and expertise, that is, on the basis of means-ends effectiveness. This does not mean that neutrality and expertise are unimportant aspects of public administration. On the contrary, they are crucial considerations. But heavy reliance on them, and the broad grants of discretion it has spawned, has led to the seriously mistaken notion that expertise *is* authority (see MacIntyre 1981, chs. 7, 8; Mitchell and Scott 1987; Cook 1992, 426). It has also allowed the space, or distance, between citizen and government to grow; the limits on power that are so essential to a constitutional regime (Elkin 1993a; Milkis and Tichenor 1993, 12, 16) have, because of the concentration on deploying means to supposedly agreed-upon ends, become dominated by institutions that are less accessible and responsive to citizens and less supportive of the everyday practice of self-government. These institutions are the courts and administrative agencies (see Eden 1989b, 70–71; Sandel 1988, 120).

Maintaining a constitutional space is necessary, to give citizens a sense of psychological distance from the state—a sense that the state in its various guises is not hovering directly overhead—and to give citizens room to grow and to develop abiding attachments to the regime without the coercion of the state. This space also provides the fertile ground in which citizens in a liberal democracy can cultivate institutions of their own making which allow them to shape and control the state but which also serve as a nonthreatening platform for contact between them and the state. Providing such a platform is the role that, in theory, political parties should play, and the role they have played in practice during important episodes in American political development. But the greatly expanded role of federal and state courts and administrative agencies in a system of programmatic liberalism, functioning on an instrumental understanding of politics rather than a comprehensive understanding, fills the constitutional space with brute manifestations of the state. These manifestations give citizens little breathing room and little practice in self-government, and they narrow the pathways for the establishment and reinforcement of civic attachments to the regime.

Working backward from this realization, it is possible to see Alexander Hamilton's conflict with Jefferson and Madison as a clash over the question of which institutions would best form civic attachments and embody a stable, vital, *republican* regime in the long run (see Milkis and Tichenor 1993, 14). Jefferson and Madison argued in favor of legislatures, courts, local administration, and, reluctantly, parties. It was Hamilton's great insight that federal administration, weighing in against factionalism and sectional division, could be one important institutional pathway to civic attachment, and that the design of administration must be sensitive to this. It is clear that Hamilton did not regard administration as the only institution that could cultivate attachments to the regime, but good administration's success in promoting a commercial republic that would bring prosperity to the people and cement their allegiance to the regime was what he prophesied, and most passionately preferred. When Franklin Roosevelt proceeded to turn Hamilton on his head, however (Milkis 1993, 24), and sought to make the unmet economic security needs glaringly illuminated by the Great Depression into basic rights best protected and provided by programs overseen by administrative agencies, the result, especially after the reforms instituted in the 1960s and 1970s, was to expand the presence of federal and state agencies and courts in the constitutional space between state and citizen. This expansion pushed to the periphery other institutions that could cultivate citizen attachments to the regime and maintain its underlying strength, including local administration. A recognizable confusion about the nature of citizenship and the practice of self-government has been the result.

The occupation of that constitutional space by administration has, furthermore, forced attempts to democratize public administration as part of the legitimation search. It may indeed be a very good thing to enhance the voice of employees inside public organizations (see Hirschman 1970) and the voice of citizens outside in their interactions with public agencies. It is also critical, as Woodrow Wilson argued, to make sure administration is connected to popular thought, sensitive to it and adept at reading it. But attempting to transform administration into just another form of democratic politics is something else entirely (see Rohr 1986, 181). Whatever definition of the proper scope of government is in force, public administration is expected to get some things accomplished, not just for customers or clientele but for the whole polity. Engagement in this effort is in fact the source of a great deal of the knowledge and valuable experience, even expertise, of public administrators. Organizational structures and operational modes that lean too far in the direction of citizen participation, democratic process, and deliberation hamper the ability of agencies to accomplish what is demanded of them. This type of organizational reform serves neither public administration nor the regime well. Other institutions are better suited to embody fully—to constitute—the *democratic* spirit.

Lastly, the occupation of the constitutional space between state and citizen by administration, and the efforts to democratize it as a result, reveal the effect that instrumental conceptions of administration and liberal democratic politics have on policy makers' attention to administration when they are designing policy. When working from an instrumental conception, the attention of policy makers to administration, indeed even their conception of the policy-making endeavor itself, is narrowed to the choice or development of means—programmatic, organizational, or institutional—that will achieve already settled ends or will satisfy some social welfare function. The choice may be made by the elected chief executive or by the legislature alone, or by the two in combination, or it may be left up to "expert" administrators. But none of these approaches effectively takes into account the multidimensional demands of administration. These demands include the design of organizational structures and the mobilization of resources, functions that are at the core of the instrumental requirements of administrative design; but they also incorporate the constitutive impacts of administrative choices, especially the formation of particular citizen preferences, the development of relationships among distinctive classes of citizens, and the enriching or debilitating effects on citizen attachments to the regime. Because they are rarely considered in policy design, *unintended consequences* is the commonly used term for these constitutive impacts. When unintended consequences accumulate to the extent that the public perceives them as usually accompanying public policy initiatives, it is a sign that insufficient attention to administrative design is plaguing policy making.

Overall, then, the modern administrative system that has been constructed under this predominantly instrumental conception of administration, operating within an instrumental conception of liberal democratic politics, lacks the capacity to apply administration's distinctive institutional qualities to the complex problems of a postindustrial political economy. American public administrators are pulled away from greater innovation, creativity, and responsiveness, in part by the character of the bureaucratic form of organization, but more by the need to be defensive in a political system in which public organizations are under constant suspicion and subject to a complex matrix of controls, their weaknesses are loudly condemned or completely ignored, and they are rarely respected for their strengths and their contributions to the care and maintenance of the polity.

In a very real sense then, at all levels of American government, public bureaucracies that are insensitive, unresponsive, and incompetent are the *products* of instrumental conceptions of administration and liberal democratic politics. For most of the nation's political development, reformers have approached administration with the working assumption that all that was necessary was to get control of and subordinate it, perhaps by disassembling it in part, and the nation would be restored to greatness. To consider administration constitutively, on the other hand, requires acknowledging that public bureaucracies are fully and legitimately part of the governing complex, that they help shape the regime as well as achieve its goals, but also that their roles are limited. Placing reasonable constitutional limits on what public institutions can and should do places an added burden on citizens, who must come closer to fulfilling the responsibility that the role of sovereign requires of them. A constitutive view also acknowledges the complexity of governing in a postindustrial society, a complexity which might appear to make it impossible for average citizens to engage in self-rule. The easier path is to rely heavily on public administration (which, like the courts, seemingly does not demand too much citizen time and effort in governing), to push administration beyond both practical and constitutional limits, and then to attack, control, denigrate, and fear it when it fails to function well.

Administrative agencies in the United States face a constant struggle to maintain some balance between the conception, generated by the dominant ideology of instrumentalism, that they are simply tools of the popular will, and the reality that they help shape public purposes and the relations between citizens. This is in many respects the way the system has responded to the tension between the instrumental and the constitutive that lies at the heart of the design of a liberal democratic regime, and it may be necessary not to make this tension too explicit. Forcing administrative agencies to deal with the tension may also be the price all American citizens, but especially American public administrators, have to pay to enjoy the benefits of a modern, postindustrial society built on an eighteenth-century framework. Yet the consequences of a pervasively instrumental conception of administration and politics reveal a fundamental reason for attempting to recover and nurture a more complete understanding of administration that captures its constitutive side. Any conception of administration, the history of American political development shows, will invariably have a formative effect on politics, government, and the character of the citizenry. We may become what we do not like. Hence, it behooves political leaders and the attentive public to think long and hard and carefully about the conception they will embrace. To do otherwise will incur unintended and unwanted consequences. Being cognizant of the constitutive qualities of political institutions, most especially public administration, means, in other words, being more attentive to consequences.

The Meaning of Constitutive Administration

An instrumental understanding of administration, initially articulated and formalized under the Constitution by the Decision of 1789, and subsequently reinforced and magnified by several waves of democratic expansion and political reform, has left American political leaders and scholars mostly wringing their hands about the problems of democratic controls on administrative discretion and increasingly ignorant of the possibility that good administration, its design well considered by policy makers, is integral to the regime and the capacity of the people for self-government. It is possible, nevertheless, to reconsider the path American political development has taken in its conception of the role of administration in politics and government and to seek to infuse that conception with a strong constitutive perspective that will illuminate the distinctive contributions public administration can make to the health of the regime. The first step in this reconsideration is to examine the political nature of administration in its most basic sense, to identify, that is, the fundamental elements of a constitutive role for public administration in the American regime.

Regime Attachments and Tempering the Democratic Impulse

Of the many questions examined and debated during the American founding, one was what features of a political and governmental system would best cultivate among a free people a long-term attachment to the regime and allegiance to the government. Another was how such a system could be built upon popular sovereignty and still avoid the fatal excesses associated with democracy. The responses to these questions were many and varied, of course, and the Constitution emerged as the remarkable if imperfect plan to answer them. From the point of view of several of the framers, administration had a pivotal role to play in insuring the Constitution's success with respect to both problems.

For the proponents of the Constitution, two qualities of the plan stood out as likely to win the hearts and minds of the American people. The first was its "aptitude and tendency to produce a good administration" (*The Federalist* No. 68), and the second was its capacity to maintain stability while keeping a proper "dependence upon the people" (No. 37). In the first instance, as Alexander Hamilton argued, administration, or more precisely *good* administration, would, in and of itself, be a key influence on the formation of citizen attachments to the regime. Because of their closer proximity to the people, the state governments would gain most of the advantage over the federal government from this formative effect of administration, "unless the force of that principle be destroyed by a much better administration of the latter" (No. 17). Hamilton expected, and later strove for, that very outcome. He enumerated along the way "various reasons" that "induced" a "probability that the general government will be better administered than the particular governments" (No. 27).

In the second instance, proponents claimed that the Constitution would gain general adherence because it offered, in place of the "irregular and mutable legislation" that characterized the Articles of Confederation, stability in government. Madison saw this as "essential to national character and to the advantages annexed to it, as well as to that repose and confidence in the minds of the people, which are the chief blessings of civil society" (*The Federalist* No. 37). Regularity and stability in public affairs would result from the decreased likelihood that public councils would succumb to the passions, demagoguery, and temporary delusions to which popular government was susceptible. As John Rohr (1986, ch. 3; also see Swift 1993) has demonstrated effectively, the Senate was to play a pivotal role in this regard, providing duration, expertise, stability, and a "due sense of national character." With surgical precision, Rohr has shown that the modern Senate cannot fulfill this role but that in many respects the career civil service can (1986, 32–39). It is also evident that several of the framers from the very beginning saw administration as helping to fulfill this role in the regime (see, esp., *The Federalist* Nos. 72, 76).

Administration, then, is constitutive of the regime in the educative or formative sense—it influences what ideas about the regime citizens hold and it shapes the relations that develop among citizens—because it interacts extensively with citizens on a daily basis and is the institutional setting for much interaction among citizens of various kinds. It thus cultivates, and in some instances undermines, citizen attachment to or identification with the regime. Good administration, administration that is well organized, supported with ample resources, and populated by knowledgeable, practical, and judicious men and women who operate with a steady but not inflexible hand, will encourage good citizen relations and a commitment to supporting the regime (see Kravchuk 1992). Administration without these qualities will erode that commitment. Furthermore, administration is constitutive of the regime in the formative sense because, by virtue of its premiere qualities—stability, durability, the application of knowledge to urgent problems while acknowledging settled law and tradition—it helps to encourage the democratic temperament to value stability, continuity, and practical reason, thus helping to steady the sometimes passionate whim and impulse of democratic decision making (but see Page and Shapiro 1989, on the relatively steady character of modern American public opinion).

Public administration is not simply the means to such ends. In a very real sense it is a collection of those ends, and by its practices it keeps them alive. Administration is the institutional expression of and gives an organized existence to the goals of stability, continuity, and temperance of democratic excess. To the extent one can say that the American polity has achieved these goals, we can point to administration as a concrete manifestation of that achievement. This is what stood at the heart of Tocqueville's appreciation for the political effects of decentralized administration. "Municipal bodies and county administrations are like so many hidden reefs retarding or dividing the flood of the popular will. If the law were oppressive, liberty would still find some shelter in the way the law is carried into execution" (1988, 263).

It is now almost wholly out of favor, as it has been for quite some time, to suggest that democracy needs to be reined in, that the people's immediate wants may not always be in their long-run interest or that popular participation in governing should not be maximized without limit. The current American polity, with its much larger cohort of well-educated citizens enjoying astoundingly better access to information and displaying much greater sophistication, and cynicism, about public affairs, is light years distant from the polity of two centuries ago. Moreover, the stumbling of modern public bureaucracies, and the downright destructive behavior of some, calls into question the capacity of administration to serve safely as the institutional home for stability, continuity, and temperance of democratic whim. We cannot ignore the attacks emanating from an angry mix of "disaffected populism," "contented republicanism," and "private liberalism" (Dryzek and Berejikian 1993), as well as the forward-looking critiques of some of public administration's most thoughtful friends, who have strong democratic leanings (e.g., Adams et al. 1990; Cox, Buck, and Morgan 1994, ch. 16).

The pursuit of ever more expansive democracy, of greater popular participation and control, must not lose sight of some essential traits of democracy, however. Democracy is prone to demagoguery, to the instability of majority cycling, and to a present-orientedness that favors quick, easy, short-term solutions to complex problems (but see Barber 1984). The effort to democratize administration must acknowledge the strengths and weaknesses of popular rule and fully understand how public administration is constitutive of a regime that is predicated on more than simply the force of popular will.

Representation of Objective Interests

One of the most basic, if not *the* most basic, of components in any liberal democratic regime established under a constitution is its scheme for representation. Representation is constitutive because, through elections, it periodically reconstitutes the polity. Through representation, citizens make a choice about how they will be recognized politically, and in the process they become "self-conscious about who they are collectively" (Schwartz 1988, 129). Free, competitive elections are the foundation of the representation schemes in most liberal democracies. Elections thus appear to be the core of what makes representation constitutive. "Consent of the governed, which is the basis of democratic political authority, is periodically reconstituted or reaffirmed through elections of representatives, where citizens actively renew their membership" (Schwartz 1988, 128). By extension, then, elected officials enjoy a special status in liberal democracies, because they personify the reconstitutive or reaffirmative act of representation.

This poses a significant challenge to the legitimacy of administrative power in the United States, where, with the exception of several state government offices, public administrators are not selected in competitive elections. John Rohr has argued that the centrality of elections in establishing public authority is misunderstood. Following Edward Corwin, he stresses that only the Constitution derives its authority from the people. All public officials, elected and nonelected, derive their authority from the Constitution, and Rohr notes that popular election is one of only twenty-two ways of holding office under the Constitution (1986, 185, 260–61 n. 31). To deal with the special legitimacy that elections impart, at least three general ways of establishing the legitimacy of public administrators, and thus recognizing the authority of their decisions and actions, have developed.

The hierarchical, or "overhead democracy" argument, is grounded in a Hobbesian conception of representation as authorization and delegation (see Cook 1992, 405–10, for elaboration). Administrators do not achieve the status of representatives in this scheme, but their decisions and actions can be regarded as authoritative because they are delegated from true representatives, namely elected officials, who are in turn following the supreme dictates of the people. This is, of course, the understanding of the status of public administrators at the heart of the instrumental conception of administration that has been dominant in American political development (also see Lowi 1993b, 262). Administrative authority is predicated on the usefulness of their technical expertise in achieving designated goals. The challenge posed by the idea of over-head democracy concerns (1) how closely administrative decisions and actions adhere to the dictates of elected officials, (2) the efficacy of either internal controls (Friedrich 1940; Meier 1993, ch. 7) or external controls (Finer 1941; Gruber 1987; Meier 1993, ch. 6), and (3) how adept public officials, particularly members of Congress, are in applying external controls (cf. Morone 1985, 293–94; Schwartz 1989; Aberbach 1990).

The pluralist view, in contrast to the hierarchical, rejects the possibility that there is some objective public will or public interest that elected officials represent (see Lowi 1979, 31–41; Morone 1985, 294–96; Cook 1992, 410–14). Instead, only group interests, organized or unorganized, exist; and it is only through the pulling and hauling of these interests in the political arena that an agreement on public policy emerges, an agreement that usually favors some group or coalition over others. One version of the pluralist view of administrative authority overlaps with the hierarchical view in asserting that administrative agencies are simply the vehicles for putting group agreements into effect. Another version, however, depicts administrative agencies as true representatives, in the sense of delegates and advocates, of particular organized interests, hence the idea of the clientele agency. In the most extreme pluralist view, agencies themselves behave like organized interests (see Rourke 1984; Yates 1982).

Finally, the "representative bureaucracy" view presents public administrators as in some sense better representatives than elected officials, in part precisely because they are not elected and thus are not distanced from the people by elections that require compromises or dependence on campaign contributors, who are not in any sense average citizens (Morone 1985, 297). But the representative bureaucracy view mostly turns on the contention that administrators more accurately represent the public demographically—that many of the diverse traits of the populace are more clearly evident in the ranks of public bureaucracy than in the ranks of elected officials (Long 1952, 812–14; Krislov and Rosenbloom 1981; Rohr 1986, 45–50; Rosenbloom 1992, 136–39). A body of representatives that looks like the population it represents in terms of gender, race, ethnicity, and socioeconomic traits, so the descriptive representation argument goes (Pitkin 1967, ch. 4), will think and act on questions of public policy as the whole population would if it were engaged in decision making.

Each of the three arguments attempting to link public administration to representation as a way to give warrant to administrative authority is open to significant attack on its own terms (see Cook 1992; Meier 1993, chs. 6, 7). All three are commonly flawed, however, in that they conceive of representation in instrumental terms. This is inconsistent with basic constitutional thinking and reinforces the kinds of consequences I assessed above. The hierarchical and pluralist arguments are obviously problematic because they are based upon the authorization and delegation models of representation, in which representatives merely follow the orders of either the whole body of the public or of organized interests within it. The representative bureaucracy argument is based on the descriptive model of representation, in which the body of representatives recreates the population at large in microcosm and thus can be expected to do its bidding. None of the three captures a constitutive understanding of representation, which, as explained by Schwartz, involves the ongoing effort of a polity to decide what it is and what it seeks to achieve. Moreover, the concept of representation that prevailed at the founding was at least in part constitutive in just this way, because representation was conceived of by the founders as performing a transformative function. It would "refine and enlarge the public views" (*The Federalist* No. 10), although that could be bad as well as good. It would also bring the major parts of society together so that through deliberation and debate representatives, and ultimately the people themselves, would determine their "true" or "enlarged and permanent" interests in a way that was not just a second-best alternative to direct democracy but an improvement on it that would result in more effective self-government (Pitkin 1967, 191, 194–95; also Elkin 1993b, 132–35).

Public administration functions as a representative institution in just this way. Public administrators engage in deliberation and debate with each other, with other public officials (legislators, chief executives, judges), and with substantial segments of the public at large, not only about what are the best means for achieving designated policy goals, but about what those goals and the larger ends of the polity ought to be. As Norton Long stated it nearly a half-century ago, public bureaucracy "is a medium for registering the diverse wills that make up the people's will and for transmuting them into responsible proposals for public policy" (1952, 810). Calls for public administrators to engage the general public more substantially and effectively in deliberation and debate about not just means but ends as well seek to enhance further this aspect of the representative function of public administration (e.g., Reich 1988).

An important consideration, therefore, in conceptualizing the representative function of administration concerns the nature of the interests that administrators and administrative agencies represent. It is certainly true that many public agencies represent and promote the interests of (mostly) well-organized groups. These are interests understood to be, as James Madison depicted them, formulated out of individual self-interest, opinion, and passion, grouped by common impulse into factions. They are to be controlled and regulated, *by* representation, in the Madisonian scheme, or encouraged and celebrated *as* representation in the modern pluralist scheme.

But Madison's acknowledgement of the existence of "enlarged and permanent" interests, seems akin to what Edmund Burke conceived of as "unattached interests" (Pitkin 1967, 192). In Burke's representation theory, these are broad, relatively fixed interests that are objective and rationally discoverable (Pitkin 1967, 176). Nancy Schwartz similarly describes "broad appropriative interests, such as labor, service, agriculture, and commerce, and deep associative interests, such as cities, states, churches, and schools." Schwartz argues that a representative "speaks and acts for these yet is independent of any of them. . . . Dynamically, representatives can articulate new values and enable political formations to develop and change" (1988, 142).

It is possible to think of public agencies representing not organized agricultural or commercial interests, for example, but the nation's interest in agriculture, commerce and other broad, relatively fixed concerns that are objective and rationally discoverable. Pitkin cautions that this idea can be taken too far. If these broad interests can be determined simply by knowledge accumulation and do not require active decision making, then experts can attend to them and no substantive representation is sensibly in force. If they are matters of questioning and debate as well as of knowledge, then political representation comes into play. If public administrators engage in deliberation and debate among themselves and with other public officials and segments of the general citizenry, they bring their specialized technical knowledge, normative training, and governing experience to bear to help determine the objective interests of the community, study them, and judge how they fit together to constitute the interest of the whole—the public interest (Goodsell 1990; Cox, Buck, and Morgan 1994, 259). Administrative agencies, in other words, represent ideas or rational constructs. They give organized existence to "the environment" or "the economy," for example, and help define how citizens are to relate to one another in environmentally or economically rational ways. In their capacities as implementors, moreover, administrators and their agencies enable political formations to develop and change (see Stone 1985). This dimension of the representative function of administration, with its focus on broad, long-term interests, reinforces the contributions public administration makes to stability in the regime. Its emphasis on rationality reinforces public administration's contributions to the regime through practical reason, which I take up next.

Tradition, Law, and Experience: Social Learning and Practical Reason

One of the most remarkable characteristics of the instrumental conception of politics and administration is how unsophisticated it really is about the nature of liberal democratic politics. The notion that administration is simply the search for and then employment of the appropriate means toward previously determined goals implies a level of harmony incongruent with the conflict and competition engendered by democratic rule. It suggests that the "popular will" is fixed and predetermined and need only be elicited from the minds of the people or their representatives. Modern pluralism essentially emerged as a critique of this simplistic view of democratic governance, but for all intents and purposes it simply replaced "popular will" with "group agreement," leaving administrative agencies still to carry out that agreement, and by extension to be actively involved as contending groups in its creation.

To be sure, pluralism does acknowledge the conflict and competition that are indicative of liberal democracy. In the end, however, it is mostly a variation on the basic instrumental theme. The goals or ends of the polity are still established "out there," separate from governing, by the conflict, competition, bargaining, and accommodation that take place among organized groups. In the pluralist view, governing *is* the competition, bargaining, and accommodation among organized interests (Lowi 1979, 36). It may take place in the legislative, executive, judicial, or administrative arena, and thus legislators and legislative committees, elected executives and their staffs, attorneys at the bar, and administrative agencies can all be understood best as representing organized interests or even behaving politically, just like interest groups. In pluralism's ultimate form, the competition, conflict, bargaining, and accommodation that produce the "parceling out of relative advantage" (Wilson 1975, 93) constitute the be-all and end-all of government; they are what government exists to provide.

The "popular will" is not fixed, however, nor does it simply emerge from the conflict and competition among organized groups. Democratic politics and government does involve conflict, competition, bargaining, and accommodation among varied interests. But it also involves confusion, uncertainty, and therefore the search, by at least some public officials, group leaders, and concerned citizens, for common interests that are not just the lowest common denominator of group agreements. They consist, instead, of "justice and the general good" (*The Federalist* No. 51). In contemporary but discredited parlance, this is the public interest, and it consists at minimum of the democratic consensus, a basic conception of the good society, and the adjustments to these made necessary by experience (Goodsell 1990, 100–101, drawing on Downs 1962 and Pennock 1962, among others; also see Long 1990). Founding agreements, established traditions, and the experience with their consequences, along with the more immediate elements of interaction, conflict, and competition among interests and ideas, are the stuff that create the ends of the polity. When the life of the regime is understood in this way, administration has a substantial role to play.

To characterize public administration, and to defend agency autonomy against charges of runaway bureaucracy, Charles Goodsell has used the metaphor of "the vessel at sea, which is subject to numerous influences of wind, current, and radioed commands from shore, but still sets its own immediate course. Only in this way will the vessel get safely to shore to unload its cargo of effective public policy" (1994, 159). Certainly, public agencies face tremendous expectations derived from the instrumental imagery communicated by Goodsell's metaphor: delivering effective public policy "goods" and doing it well. As Goodsell intends his metaphor to communicate, moreover, within established limits, autonomy and discretion are necessary for public administration to fulfill these expectations. But the administrative enterprise consists of much more than this, which a stretching of the metaphor can illuminate.

For example, ships at sea do not just receive messages radioed from shore; they send them as well. The information on conditions and the captain's judgments contained in such messages may result in alterations to the commands about the course to take, or even at what port to call. Furthermore, on long voyages, ships may make many ports, and the interactions between crews and residents may be the grist for more information and judgment communicated to ship owners and users, which again may alter both strategies and objectives. On the long voyages of colonization of the eighteenth and nineteenth centuries, in which a ship's cargo might have included live plants and animals, the cargo itself would have grown or declined, but certainly it would have been transformed, partly on the basis of the good or poor efforts of the crew. Similarly, public administrators do not make decisions simply about the mode and timing (and they sometimes do not have discretion over such variables) for delivery of public policies completed and prepackaged by legislatures and elected executives. Instead, administrators often work to develop further the definition and substance of both discrete programs and broad strategies for public action, and they may do this in either the presence or the absence of the kind of clear legislative guidance Theodore Lowi has long advocated (further discussed in the next chapter). It might even be best to abandon the vessel-at-sea metaphor altogether, because it depicts an isolation from politics and the public lives of the citizenry that is not the experience of most public administrators (but see Gruber 1987, chs. 4, 6).

It is clear, in any case, that public administration is involved in more than delivering goods and services. It is involved deeply in conservative, restorative, and transformative activity. "Much governmental activity . . . represents an attempt to employ government as an intermediary to alter some set of conditions that has complex origins" (Stone 1985, 486). Much of this kind of activity takes place in the realm of policy implementation, and thus involves public administration directly and substantially. Instead of a "business-firm" model emphasizing the efficient production and delivery of goods and services and based on instrumental rationality, it requires a model of "social learning" (Stone 1985; also see Long 1952, 815–16; Brown and Wildavsky 1984; Stivers 1990, 263–64). The rational foundation of such a model is Aristotle's "practical wisdom" or *phronesis,* "to conjoin knowledge of the principles of right with considerations of what is suitable" (Morgan 1990, 74; also see Stivers 1990, 250, 260–61; Mainzer 1994, 360, 385–86 n. 2). Such practical wisdom is relevant to any "enterprise" (Anderson 1990), but it has special import in the public realm.

Recall that Herbert Storing linked what he labeled "practical reason" to Whig views on public administration. In Storing's version, it involves the application of instrumental rationality—the matching of means and ends—and is combined with a concern for the nature of the ends themselves in light of both experience and an abiding responsibility and morality (1980, 110–12). Practical reason in the public sphere is, therefore, centrally concerned with efficiency, in the sense that Charles Anderson gives it—"fittedness to purpose" (1993, 105). Most fundamentally, it is concerned with "institution fitting," that is, how properly to arrange institutional parts with respect to both their instrumental and constitutive contributions to the regime whole (Elkin 1987, 193–95). Administrative discretion must be well grounded in accountability, that is, in the requirement that decisions be based on the giving of reasons that are linked to clear, substantive rules (the rule of law) and the underlying values and democratic consensus that outline the public interest (Downs 1962; Elkin 1987, 111–12). This accountability is a necessary condition for fostering practical reason in the public sphere and the social learning that stems from it (Stivers 1990, 263–64; also Anderson 1990, esp. chs. 9, 10). A regime function centered on practical reason might then be the legitimate foundation for public administration claims to special education, training, and expertise.

Much of the contribution of administration to the regime which I am trying to describe here can be captured by drawing together material from Woodrow Wilson's lecture notes on public administration and public law. Wilson saw the foundations of administration as "those deep and permanent principles of Politics quarried from history and built into constitutions" (Link 1969, 7:115). With this as its foundation, Wilson identified the field of administrative activity as the field of the "discretionary effectiveness of institutions—the field not of Law, but of the exercise [or realization] of legalized function" (Link 1969, 6:519). Wilson observed that administration rests on essential, or customary, law as well as on legislation. But he also contended that it is indirectly a constant source of public law. "It is through Administration that the State makes test of its own powers and of the public needs, makes test also of law, its efficiency, suitability" (Link 1969, 7:138). In contrast to law, which Wilson characterized as the summing up of the past, administration must be seen as always in contact with the present. It is thus the State's "experiencing organ," and the suggestions or initiatives of administration, Wilson insisted, are one of the most useful means of further developing public law. Because administration sees government in contact with the people, finally, it encounters questions about adjustment, not just of means to ends, but of government functions to historical conditions and, ultimately, to liberty (see Link 1969, 7:116). Administration, then, is integral to the "working constitution" (Long 1952, 816), because it is concerned with what will work in public policy with respect to fitting means to ends, determining the limits of public acceptability, and ensuring fidelity to Constitution, statute, and tradition (Morgan 1990, 73–74).

Public administration is thus constitutive of the regime because, more than any other institution, it encompasses and must grapple with the tensions between the instrumental and the constitutive that are so acute in a liberal democratic polity. Public administration stands at the crossroads of the ideal and the real and must, on a continuing basis, demonstrate affinity to both. It is expected to help insure that planes arrive on time and that hazardous waste sites are cleaned up promptly and thoroughly while also helping to determine why such actions are necessary. It is constitutive in the formative sense, because it helps to develop among citizens an appreciation that popular demands for action must be balanced against prior agreements etched in statutes, tradition, and constitutional principle. But it also offers numerous lessons about making practical adjustments to what stands, in light of pressing needs and the careful assessment of current and future conditions.

Because public administration "sees" government in contact with the people, in Woodrow Wilson's words, indeed *is* government in contact with the people, it is in a position to help citizens cultivate an appreciation for practical reason and to help them practice it. This occurs to some extent now, despite the dominance of the instrumental view of public administration's place in the regime and its consequent overreliance on bureaucracies and courts to get results the qualities of which have not been very thoroughly explored. That such exploration must be expanded, with respect both to the time and resources allotted to it and to the number of citizens involved, seems clear if the capacity for self-government is to be not only preserved but enhanced (Barber 1984; Stone 1985). Public administration released from an overbearing instrumentalism could play an even more effective role (Stivers 1990).

In the institutional sense, public administration is constitutive of the regime because it is the organized expression of the desire and necessity to reconcile, or at least cope with, the tensions between instrumental and constitutive reasoning laid bare by a liberal democratic design. Along with the courts, public administration is also the institutional home for rationality in the public sphere, although unlike the courts, agencies embody a form of practical reason that is both retrospective and prospective and takes account of both historical and social facts (Morgan 1990, 75–79).

Finally, however imperfectly individual agencies and administrators may exercise it currently, public administration as a whole is the active institutional expression of *responsible discretion* in the public sphere, a quality that is itself grounded in practical reason. It really makes little sense to think of legislatures, courts, or elected executives as exercising delegated or discretionary authority. Political leaders and interested members of the public at large can really develop an adequate understanding of discretion, how much or how little is preferable and how it might best be exercised in the public realm, only by observing and even participating in the practice of public administration. In short, public administration *is* the exercise of responsible political discretion.

The aspects of public administration's constitutiveness that I have described here are of course extensively intertwined, and many more connections exist, no doubt, than those few I have identified. What remains to be considered, however, are the necessary conditions for, and the potential consequences of, imbuing our politics with a constitutive understanding of public administration.

7

Bureaucracy and the Future of American Self-Government

In the penultimate chapter of *Progressive Democracy,* Herbert Croly characterized the "democratic political organization" he advocated as "fundamentally educational." He admitted that although it was "designed to attain a certain administrative efficiency, its organization for efficiency is subordinated to the gathering of an educational popular political experience. Indeed, it is organized for efficiency chiefly because in the absence of efficiency no genuinely *formative* popular political experience can be expected to accrue" (Croly 1914, 378, emphasis added).

Even from a late-twentieth-century perspective, Croly's initial juxtaposition of two values—efficiency and education—does not seem all that odd. After all, shouldn't the criterion by which any political organization is judged be its fundamental ability to make effective tradeoffs, such as the loss of some efficiency in favor of an educational political experience? Indeed, it is difficult to avoid seeing politics as a matter of choosing between relatively equally attractive but competing values or ends, such as equality, fairness, and efficiency. To choose one, and to fashion public programs and societal institutions in order to achieve it, inevitably involves losses on the ledgers of other values we hold dear (Okun 1975; Nelson 1977; Calabresi and Bobbitt 1982). Recall that one of the principal arguments of congressional opponents of FDR's original executive reorganization plan was that it weakened the traditional foundations of American democracy in exchange for an increase in governmental efficiency. They thus were able to portray the plan as an unacceptable tradeoff of democracy for efficiency.

Politics as tradeoffs is, however, a manifestation of the instrumental conception of politics and administration; and it should now be clear that, from the perspective of an instrumental understanding, societal ends do not actually come out of nowhere. They are the products of political institutions, particularly elections and legislatures, which aggregate individual or group wants and preferences, often resolving conflicts in favor of the most passionate or powerful (Schattschneider 1960; also see Elkin 1987, 198–99). Other institutions, particularly public administration, are then put to the task of achieving the ends designated. But note how Croly seems ultimately to have expressed a different view of political organization and progressive democratic politics, one which emphasizes arranging public life so that one value—or one kind of conduct or mode of interaction—is supportive of another rather than competing with or replacing it.

It is perhaps wise to take with a grain of salt Croly's typically progressive, and thus almost romantic, embrace of the salutary effects of efficiency, and the social application of the scientific method that underlies those effects (see Croly 1914, 397–405). It does not seem too far-fetched, however, to conceive of the work of political institutions in a liberal democracy, including the work of public administration, as "fundamentally educational." Along with its responsibilities to be organized efficiently in order to grapple with the practical problems that arise every day in the governing order, and to identify and put into effect efficient means to popularly desired ends, public administration contributes to the "formative popular political experience" that sustains and advances the regime. It does so in the ways explored in the preceding chapter, and it is readily conceivable that improvements in administrative efficiency enhance its formative contributions, as Alexander Hamilton recognized when he argued that good administration would foster stronger citizen attachments to the regime. At its foundation, this is the manner of thinking about public administration in a liberal democracy that I have sought to illuminate and develop.

Widespread acknowledgement, but more importantly keen understanding, of this way of thinking about administration, among political leaders and the public at large, can alter profoundly the conduct of politics and government under the Constitution. Recognizing administration's constitutiveness will bring about a reorientation in the education and training of public administrators. It will, more significantly, stimulate changes in the concepts, incentives, and practices of public policy design. And it will, most significantly, be a critical step in the reinvigoration of American self-government.

Educating Public Administrators

Because of the peculiarly ambiguous, open, and fluid character of American government and politics, which derive from the founding and the developmental pathways that followed, American public administration as a distinctive occupation or profession has always suffered from an identity crisis. As the demands and dangers of the modern world have pressed in upon the regime, seeming to require massive, regularized state structures, the identity problem for both the practice and the study of public administration has grown more acute (see Stillman 1991). Certainly, American political culture evinces a strong aversion to the notion of a professional cadre of public servants. This would seem to stem from a mix that includes, at least, the fundamental commitment to limited government, the Jacksonian notion of democratic administration, and concerns about the distorting effects of professionalism (see Meier 1993, 198–201; Mosher 1968, 1978). Despite this aversion, however, the idea of public administration as an intellectual endeavor and scholarly discipline, as well as a professional field with a distinctive ethos, has continued to advance, albeit idiosyncratically, over the past sixty years (see Henry 1990).

It is, therefore, particularly instructive to consider Gerald Garvey's observation that it is critical to take into account the peculiar features of the public policy process—fluidity, shifting issue networks, and the accompanying "shadow bureaucracies" of interest groups, think tanks, and government contractors—all of which feature extensive, ongoing, face-to-face interactions between public administrators and private actors. Under these conditions, what are commonly presumed to be the ethos and ideals of the profession of public administration might better be viewed as "*general obligations of citizenship* rather than as peculiar requirements of the call to public service. Such an identification implies an extension of the public service ethic to all who actually participate in the public policy process, whether from the public or private side of the boundary" (Garvey 1993, 221, emphasis in original). Of course, as John Rohr eloquently explains, public officials are special, because they pledge to uphold the Constitution, something private actors are not required to do (Rohr 1986, 187–94). Yet such an oath does not itself make a distinctive profession. Public administration as a unique "enterprise" and "community of inquiry" (Anderson 1990) or "calling" (see Green, Keller, and Wamsley 1993) cannot be adequately distinguished by its values and ideals. But then, what special skills and perspectives, drawn from their advanced education as well as their work experience, can those who embrace a commitment to work on the "public side of the boundary" bring to the collective endeavor of politics and government? The answer lies in how public administration is constitutive of the regime, particularly in its embodiment and promotion of practical reason in the public sphere. The education of public administrators, and any claims they may make to expertise beyond narrow technical specialties, must center on a commitment to the development and exercise of practical reason in public affairs.

Providing a competent treatise on the nature of practical reason and an educational program that would lay the foundations for exercising it is a task for which I am not adequately equipped. I can only point the reader to Aristotle's *Nichomachean Ethics* (Book VI), Alasdair MacIntyre's *After Virtue,* and Charles Anderson's *Pragmatic Liberalism* and his *Prescribing the Life of the Mind,* among many others. Practical reason cannot really be taught in the context of a program of formal education. As its name implies, it can only be learned through practice. Nevertheless, I will say something about what core elements of formal education for public administrators might lay the foundation for developing a cadre of public men and women skilled in the exercise of practical reason in the public realm (also see Green, Keller, and Wamsley 1993). I do so without any pretensions to being systematic.

First, public administration education must be grounded in political science, but a political science understood in what might be called its classical sense: theory joined to practice, specifically to the practice of liberal democratic politics (Elkin 1987, ch. 10; Anderson 1990, pt. 3; Ceaser 1993; Elkin 1993a, 20–21; 1993b). This approach depends upon a strong grounding in and appreciation for history and circumstance, which in turn requires that substantial attention be paid to moral, ethical, and constitutional foundations (e.g., Burke, 1986; Rohr 1989c; Cooper 1991) and to the historical foundations, development, and immediate political circumstances of different types of administrative organizations and of specific agencies (see, for example, Kass 1990; Morgan 1990; Terry 1990; Wamsley et al. 1990; Garvey 1993). Again, however, the central concern is to support the "maintenance and improvement of the liberal democratic experiment" (Anderson 1990, 195). This means that the empirical research to be taught in public administration education, and supporting administrative practice, is best based on theory that is anchored in these foundations. Thus, such research should be concerned ultimately with questions about what is good and what is bad for a liberal democratic regime like the United States, and why.

Nicholas Henry has argued that into the 1930s political science possessed most of the attributes I have just sketched out and that it was no coincidence that the discipline was dominated by public administration scholars. By the 1950s, however, because of problems in theory, such as the politics-administration dichotomy, and following the emergence of an aggressive positivist approach to political studies, political science and public administration had for all intents and purposes parted company. It is public administration scholarship that most closely resembles the older, and more viable, tradition of political science, Henry argues, particularly in the area of public policy studies (see Henry 1990, 7–11).

Henry calls for the strict organizational and institutional separation of public administration education from any other related discipline, to ensure what he considers the effective education of not just public administrators but public administration educators as well. However, institutional strategizing aside, public administration education and training is not an either-or proposition. It is a conjunction rather than a disjunction, a practical political science in which the "descriptive and explanatory bent of political science [is] harnessed to the marriage of theory and practice" (Elkin 1987, 200). Knowledge about circumstance across a variety of levels of analysis, after all, can be gained most effectively via the "descriptive and explanatory bent" of the empirical political science that is now dominant. Again, however, such empirical inquiry must be guided by the proper context of normative theory and practical concerns.

I conclude exactly the opposite of what Henry has concluded. Every public administration program should be tied closely to, if not housed within, a political science department. Program curricula should be grounded in normative political theory with empirical research of several different designs tied closely to it (Mainzer 1994). Likewise, any graduate program in political science that does not have public administration scholars on its faculty and does not interweave public administration throughout its curriculum is deficient. The study of the moral, ethical, and constitutional dilemmas faced by administrative officials, in the context of particular agencies and their histories and operations, is particularly important.

A wide recognition of the constitutiveness of administration in the regime also points to a second principle for public administration education. Policy analysis must be the central skill promoted and developed by the education and training of public administrators. I do not mean policy analysis as commonly understood, taught, and practiced today. The currently dominant analysis paradigm is based in microeconomics, and it is concerned with designing programs or institutional arrangements to achieve some publicly designated end on the basis of allocative efficiency. It is one of the most distressing aspects of American higher education that this conception of policy analysis dominates the advanced education of many public officials through schools of public policy and public administration.

In contrast to the dominant approach, a proper policy analysis weds the economizing version to what might be called "regime analysis." It is thus concerned with properly fitting programmatic and institutional means to public ends. But it also seeks inquiry into the content of the purposes themselves. It is, therefore, analysis in the context of fundamental regime questions and "regime values" (Rohr 1989b). This is analysis ultimately concerned with preserving and improving the regime; it considers the mix of institutions, and the citizen interactions they foster, that will give proper expression to popular aspirations and will promote interactive problem solving rather than command and coercion (see Elkin 1987, 191–95; Elkin and Cook 1985, 807–10; also Stone 1988). A concrete example from the realm of education policy would be analysis that synthesizes the work of Chubb and Moe (1990), who analyze alternative institutional means for providing education, and Henig (1994), who considers the formative political consequences. Ultimately, combining instrumental analysis—the search for the proper mix of programs and institutional forms to achieve some end—with analysis of the formative effects of that mix of policies, is the foundation of practical reason in the public sphere, and public administrators are in a unique position to understand and exercise it. Just as significant, public administrators are in a position to foster publicly oriented practical reason among the larger citizenry. This is one critical way in which administrators can contribute to the maintenance and enhancement of self-government.

Building the education of public administrators upon these pillars of political study and properly conceived policy analysis is crucial to developing throughout the polity an appreciation for the dynamic tension of the instrumental and the constitutive in administration. The wider recognition of that tension will, in turn, further reinforce support for a public administration education that is based on these core components.

Designing Public Policy

In the parlance of the "new institutionalism," the peculiarly Madisonian foundations of American constitutional design manifest themselves most clearly as a configuration of institutional "incentives." In instrumental terms, these incentives aim at harnessing the self-interested motives that lead to factionalism and tyranny, so that the pursuit of self-interest will steer political actors into a dependence on reason and deliberation, allowing them to envision and commit to the "cause of an enlarged and permanent interest" (*The Federalist* No. 42) and fostering policy based on "moderation, good sense, and compromise" (Cain and Jones 1989, 17; also see Elkin 1993b, 137). In constitutive terms, American institutional arrangements help to form a polity that does not seek to deny or disable fundamental self-interested motives, but which nevertheless prefers to temper self-interested striving in such a way as to ensure the predominance of reason, commitment to a recognizable public interest, and moderation, good sense, and compromise in public action.

I have already tried to show that, specifically in the case of Alexander Hamilton, administration was fundamental to the framers' attempt to explain, foresee, and justify how their constitutional scheme would work. This would seem to be inconsistent with the scholarly consensus, which is that administration was given relatively short shrift in both the crafting of the Constitution and its defense during ratification (see, for example, Derthick 1990, 8–11). The argument is that the framers purposely left decisions about administrative structure and conduct for Congress to decide, albeit within broad parameters, such as specifying that agencies be headed by single administrators subject to presidential superintendence and derive their authority from law (Wilson 1975, 77–78; Lowi 1993b, 262). Yet the framers certainly appear to have attended to administration in considering the design of institutions and the incentives such designs would generate.

The discussions of the structure of the presidency and of the Senate in the *Federalist* papers, for example, read like an attempt to create incentives for elected officials to attend to good administration, to be accomplished by creating a bias in favor of stability through longer terms of office and no limit on reeligibility. Also, the provision for senatorial participation in the selection of top administrative officials indicates an attempt to create an incentive for senators to be concerned about the quality and capacity of these officials, by virtue of both the senators' accountability to the American public, especially the states, and their interest as legislators in selecting officials with sufficient capabilities and independence to check the behavior of the president. In the case of the Decision of 1789, in which Madison played the leading role, vesting removal power in the president created in him a real incentive to take special care that the laws would be stably, effectively, and efficiently executed, the accountability for administration being clearly fixed in the president.

As Bruce Cain and W. T. Jones (1989, 12–15) argue, however, Madison's approach to institutional design was inductive, experimental, tentative, and pragmatic rather than deductive and axiomatic. As is often noted, Madison acknowledged that protecting liberty through an expectation of exclusively self-interested behavior and thus an absolute reliance on harnessing it was impossible. Some public spiritedness, manifested particularly in the selection of representatives, was required of the citizenry (see Diamond 1980, 30). Madison also recognized the limits of knowledge about human behavior and about what designs of political structures would be most appropriately sensitive to the mix of motivations leading individuals to participate in public affairs. Hence, he fully conceded the potential for error and misjudgment in institutional choice and the consequent necessity that the workings of political institutions be closely observed, with an eye toward improving them incrementally. Unfortunately, Madison's recognition of the pitfalls of institutional design has proven all too prescient with respect to public administration, for a combination of initial institutional arrangements, subsequent institutional tinkering, and changes in American society have resulted in an American political and governmental system with policy maker incentives that are "not conducive to good administration" (Derthick 1990, 4).

Assessing Administrative Consequences

A combination of design features and political development has undermined incentives favoring stability in the formation and administration of law. Specifically, a constitutional design based on individual rights *and* popular sovereignty manifested largely through electoral accountability, combined with societal changes reflecting the advance of democratic and egalitarian sentiment, have weakened many of the institutional checks on the influence of general public opinion. In addition, what is regarded as public opinion is now largely amorphous public sentiment seized by, manipulated by, and reexpressed in the passionate opinions of activist elites (whom Madison might have called factionalist leaders—see Heclo 1989). Additional structural changes, such as the Seventeenth Amendment (providing for the direct election of senators), the embrace of the popular presidential primary, the New Deal "economic bill of rights," and postwar "democratizing" congressional reforms cumulatively have served to create incentives for excessive responsiveness to "popular" activist demands. This responsiveness has led to an "extreme pragmatism" in which policy makers constantly pursue policy fixes (Derthick 1990, 216) in response to what Mathew McCubbins and Thomas Schwartz (1984) have labeled "police patrol" and "fire alarm" congressional oversight and information gathering (also see Aberbach 1990). Such an approach to policy making serves to exacerbate the mutability of public policy and devalue stability, one of the core contributions that administration can make to the regime (Derthick 1990, 225).

In addition, a design in which separate institutions share power produces institutional incentives that encourage members of one branch to counteract the ambitions of another branch and thus to engage in competition and struggle over public policy. These basic incentives simply overwhelm whatever incentives may have been built into the system to encourage policy designers to care about good administration. This effect became increasingly evident as the stakes for organized interests rose so dramatically with the expansion in the size, responsibilities, and control of the federal government. Indeed, administration proved to be a major instrument in that increasingly high-velocity struggle, with public officials and their interest-group allies seeking to use bureaucracy to overturn losses they had suffered elsewhere in the policy process or preserve victories they had gained. In some instances, the result was to expand administrative discretion substantially, while in others it was to limit it severely; but in either case interinstitutional competition translated into only intermittent regard for administrative capacity or effectiveness in further shaping or carrying out the law (Moe 1989).

Furthermore, the growth of federal government powers and responsibilities, and the concomitant reliance on administrative power, created enormous incentives for legislators especially to create new programs and new entitlements with little regard for the consequences, administrative or otherwise. The bureaucracy could simply be blamed for what went wrong, and legislators could take the credit for fixing it (see Fiorina 1989).

While situating responsibility for attending to administration more clearly in the presidency and thereby creating the incentive to fulfill that responsibility, as Madison and Hamilton apparently intended, the Decision of 1789 also defined better the terms on which the legislative and executive branches would contend for control of administration. By defining administration in strictly hierarchical terms and thus discounting its constitutiveness, the Decision of 1789 made it justifiable for the president and Congress to use administrative agencies as instruments in their policy struggles with one another. The result, widely recognized and often deplored, is a fragmented, sometimes contradictory administrative establishment, designed better to serve the interests of its political masters than to ensure administrative effectiveness or minimize deleterious effects on the constitution of the citizenry.

Given these realities, Martha Derthick is decidedly pessimistic about the possibilities of overcoming fundamental structural obstacles to good administration. Nevertheless, she advances some "modest proposals" for change. Her proposals center on providing information on agency capacities that may make clearer the potentially damaging administrative impacts of policy proposals and their consequences for constituents. Access to this information might alter the calculus of policy makers enough that they might attend more to administration when designing policy. The burden for making the impacts and consequences recognizable lies, Derthick stresses, with analysts, who must "demonstrate that present policy-making practices have administrative costs of a kind that politicians would care about were those costs to be specified. These are costs not just of inconvenience, disruption, and damaged morale in administrative agencies, but also in wasted money in the federal government's budget and in hardships to citizens" (Derthick 1990, 223–24).

For the analysis of agency capacities to be produced, Derthick argues, elected officials must tolerate the relatively low costs of maintaining small staffs to perform the analyses. Unfortunately, the evidence suggests that the deck is stacked against even this modest regard for administration in the behavior of elected officials. The number of staffmembers in the Office of Management and Budget who are assigned to management rather than budget analysis declined from 224 to 47 between 1970 and 1989 (Moe 1994, 116). The agenda of the leadership that came to power when the Republicans captured both houses of Congress in 1994 included cutting appropriations and staff for the General Accounting Office, which evaluates agency management for Congress (Salant 1995). When the political center appears to support reductions in the size, and the scope of responsibilities, of government, the elimination of agencies is the administrative focus of elected officials. Their attention is not trained on preventing the incapacity of administrative agencies or improving their functions (indeed incapacity is proof of the need for elimination), however strategically counterproductive that may turn out to be (see Durant 1992).

Finally, the thrust to reinvent government is predicated on the notion that the incapacity and ineffectiveness of administration rests with bureaucracy, as a particular form of organization, and its old, tired, rigid, and elephantine ways. Organizational capacity and effectiveness can be restored by adoption of "entrepreneurial" administration and management. Restoration is thus the sole responsibility of agencies and agency heads. This provides presidents and members of Congress with effective cover. They can continue to blame the bureaucracy for deleterious consequences, even when they as policy makers fail to take administrative structure and capacity into account, either in the design of new or consolidated programs, or in their plans for program reductions or elimination.

The point of analyzing the institutional incentives for attending to administration in policy design is not to find ways to eliminate entirely incentives for the fragmentation, diffusion of power, and political manipulation of administration. Such an objective, as Derthick effectively argues (1990, 213–15; also Moe 1989), is not possible, nor would it be wise. Administration will therefore continue to be the object of political contention, especially in a system in which it is subordinated to institutions that are purposely set against one another. The point instead is to determine if something like a Madisonian "balance" (Cain and Jones 1989) can be achieved. Is it possible, in other words, to reduce the incentives to neglect administration in policy design and increase incentives for policy makers to concern themselves with implementation and attend to good administration in the framing of public policy?

The institutional design obstacles are still enormous. As Derthick points out, implementation must be incremental, experimental, and adaptive. This is particularly true for public policy that concerns the regulation and use of complex, high-risk technologies (e.g., Cook, Emel, and Kasperson 1990), where planning for institutional and organizational capacities and impacts is critical (Rosenbaum 1995, 350–54). But the volatility of a "modern factionalist" regime makes for short-sighted, short-tempered, and impatient policy makers. What, beyond Martha Derthick's modest proposal emphasizing information and analysis, might alter policy makers' understanding of the consequences of neglecting administration in policy design?

A healthy recognition of the constitutiveness of administration would transform how policy makers react to the incentives they face. With a firm knowledge of the formative bearing of political institutions generally, and the constitutiveness of administration specifically, policy makers, especially legislators, would be more cognizant of the consequences—wasted money and burdens on citizens—of neglecting administration in policy design. In other words, seeing the constitutive dimension would alter policy makers' calculations of the benefits and costs of alternative policy actions. They would take the administrative consequences of their policy designs into account as a result, and administrative design would be numbered routinely among the central considerations of public policy making. This in turn would provide the foundation of support necessary for the ongoing analytical activities proposed by Derthick.

But how would policy makers come to acquire an adequate understanding of the constitutive dimension of political institutions, and especially public administration? It is certainly not outside the realm of possibility that the scholarly treatment of a subject, and the ideas advanced therein, might have an impact on the thinking of policy makers directly, and indirectly through the education of future political leaders. The influence of Lowi's *The End of Liberalism* in the 1970s and Osborne and Gaebler's *Reinventing Government* in the 1990s are premiere examples. The hope of scholarly impact is an exceedingly slender reed on which to build an effort at institutional change and reform, however, because, although considerable attention and intellectual energy have been trained on understanding the dissemination and adoption of ideas in politics and policy making (see Kingdon 1995, for example), no adequate theory has emerged that could serve as a guide. A more concrete, specific, and action-oriented effort at institutional and even systemic change is necessary to affect policy makers in a manner that would, among other things, bring the constitutiveness of public administration within range of their radar screens.

The Rule of Law and Administrative Consequences

The best-known and thus perhaps most widely debated of such efforts is Theodore Lowi's "juridical democracy." Lowi's "modest proposal for radical reform" is predicated on a reduction in the discretion of administrative agencies (Lowi 1979, 298–313; 1993a). The corrosive effects of interest-group liberalism on the regime which Lowi catalogued in *The End of Liberalism*, including the neglect of administration in policy design because of unguided delegations of power, could only be neutralized, he argued, by a return to a fundamental regard for forms and formalisms. The rule of law—the requirement that the state express clearly the rule on which it seeks to take action—requires the state to make plain the purposes and means for any action. As Lowi states it succinctly, "the institutions of government ought to say what they are going to do to us before they do it; and if they cannot say they cannot act" (1979, 299).

Lowi's operational precept would seem to require policy makers, especially legislators, to take administration into account in policy design. To meet the test of the rule of law, policy makers would have to say something about how the rule behind a proposed action would be put into effect, and how the purposes would be achieved. The effect of this, however, would seem to be to reduce administration to an exclusively instrumental role. Indeed, Lowi defines administration as "a process of self-conscious, formal adaptation of means to ends. Administered social relations are all those self-conscious and formal efforts to achieve a social end" (1979, 22). His conception of the American regime under the rule of law is clearly legislatively centered (Ginsberg and Sanders 1990), and some have charged that it is legislatively absolutist, and highly centralized and hierarchical (see Schaefer 1988, 381–84; but see also Lowi 1988, 402–7, for clarification).

Lowi sounds like a progressive *par excellence* and an unwavering friend of the politics-administration dichotomy when he argues that "broad delegations are a menace to formal organization and to the ideal of the neutral civil servant," and that they make "a politician out of a bureaucrat." This contradicts the "*raison d'etre* of administrative independence—neutrality and expertise." Improving the administrative process through adherence to the rule of law would, moreover, make "administrative power more responsible as well as more efficient" (1979, 304).

More fundamentally, Lowi's juridical democracy and its vision of a regime based on legal integrity—laws that have real, substantive meaning for citizens and articulate, with at least some precision and clarity, rules of behavior—appears to thoughtful critics to be an inappropriate response to the problems posed by the institutional arrangements of the Constitution and the regime developments that have followed. In particular, James Q. Wilson (1990) has argued that juridical democracy is deficient on three counts: (1) Clearly defining and restricting the powers of administrators is inconsistent with a continued commitment to an activist welfare state; such a commitment requires more administrative discretion, not less. (2) Many of the policies modern liberal democracies pursue cannot be reduced to clear rules of purpose and means, because some goals cannot be coherently and compellingly articulated in advance, some goals are in conflict with other goals, and some problems are so complex and interdependent ("polycentric") that the outcome of specific actions cannot be adequately predicted in advance. Hence, public bureaucracy must be "deregulated," that is, granted greater autonomy and discretion (also see Wilson 1994). (3) The incentives faced by all public officials ("risk-averse bureaucrats, demagogic legislators, activist judges") do not favor the articulation of clear rules, because clear rules force the identification of winners and losers, and "our political system thrives on maintaining the illusion that no one need ever be a loser" (Wilson 1990, 571).

But Lowi hardly reads like a champion, or even a passive supporter, of either the scope or the objective of the American welfare state as it is currently configured. As Ginsberg and Sanders (1990, 565) interpret him, Lowi argues that "what the state cannot do well, it should forego, rather than hand an impossibly vague mandate to bureaus, subcommittees, and their clientele groups" (also see Lowi 1971, 210: "chaos is better than a bad program"). Nor does Lowi's steadfast commitment to formalism appear to be founded on what Donald Brand claims is Lowi's commitment to a "sharp dichotomy of a government of laws or a government of men" (Brand 1988, 299). Lowi acknowledges that American legislatures will find it difficult to articulate a clear rule for every policy action, especially in the organic statute for an agency (see Lowi 1988, 402–3). The rule of law, he admits, "could never eliminate all the vagueness in legislative enactments and could never eliminate the need for delegation of power to administrative agencies" (1979, 302). Wilson essentially acknowledges Lowi's argument in this regard but faults Lowi for failing to specify the policy circumstances under which clear rules might be effectively developed and applied, an endeavor Lowi undertook on an independent track with his development of policy typologies (e.g., Lowi 1964, 1972), an effort in which Wilson has also engaged (e.g., 1980; 1989, ch. 9; 1992, ch. 23).

Lowi contends that the likelihood of vague legislative enactments requires the application, as a criterion independent of process, of the rule of law within administrative agencies. This would take place through early formal rule making. The effect, he argues, would be to shift the emphasis from agency-clientele bargaining on individual cases—he applies the term *log-rolling*—to bargaining on the rule. Lowi argues that, although bargaining on the rule would inevitably lead to bargaining on the case (allowing hard differences between winners and losers to be softened somewhat), the latter would then be helpful in refining the general rule (1979, 107–13, 303–4). The end result would be to reduce the "patronizing" effects of the informality of discretion (1993a, 171). Substantial political judgment—the central meaning of politics for Lowi is "the making of choices between good and bad, choices of priorities among competing good things" (1979, 267)—must, however, remain in the hands of administrators.

I conclude from Lowi's argument that a greater reliance on formalism would appear to bring laws and people into closer consort while leaving administration plenty of discretion to adapt to changing circumstances and to undertake the arduous task of understanding and responding to complex, multifaceted problems. Of course, if politics means making hard choices, then Wilson is surely right in arguing that greater adherence to the rule of law would mean making more explicit the winners and losers created by any particular choice. But that seems to be precisely Lowi's point. If institutional arrangements and the prevailing public philosophy create incentives for policy makers that make distancing themselves from the hard choices the norm, then radical reform of the system is required. It will force basic decision making back into the hands of political representatives and the people themselves, rather than leaving it with administrators whose authority and legitimacy is for the most part dependent.

Wilson argues that what would be required to accomplish this would be to change "all other features of the system at the same time" (1990, 571) in a manner that would create a regime foreign to our history and traditions. Lowi sounds like he aims for precisely that with his call for serious political discourse from which a new public philosophy could emerge (1979, 298), guided by political theory (313). The specific steps he advocates, however, hardly seem foreign to the regime: restoration of the Schechter Rule in the Supreme Court's scrutiny of the constitutionality of statutes; restoration of the tradition of codification, in which Congress reviews, updates, and sometimes simplifies statutes on the basis of administrative experience; limited tenure for statutes, which has become widely known and used as "sunset" provisions. Lowi also expected that the move toward embracing the rule of law would have to come through changes in curriculum and philosophy in law schools, the pressure of social chaos resulting from public nonadherence to the rule of law, and the clarity with which interest group demands are already made. Substantial debate followed publication of *The End of Liberalism,* and it continues today, which is exactly what Lowi had hoped to engender.

On the question of the proper function and status of administration in the regime, however, Lowi seems to accept it as fundamentally political, and appropriately so within the constraints imposed by the rule of law and the Constitution's basic commitment to limited government. When Lowi acknowledges the importance of administration in this way, he sounds like the Woodrow Wilson of the Johns Hopkins and Princeton lectures on administration and public law. Lowi describes his idea of juridical democracy as "working toward a fusion of fact and value," which "merely amounts to a fusion of political behavior, public administration, and public law" (1979, 312). He envisions Congress's revising and codifying laws "in light of administrative experience." To acknowledge the collective institutional responsibility of state action under the rule of law and to take seriously the experience of agencies, including policy failure under a clear rule (299), would allow policy makers to "fuse administrative experience" in the refinement of the law (307). It would also, presumably, reduce their temptation to deflect blame and claim short-term credit for quick fixes. Administrative experience, Lowi even suggests, might be among the most effective restraints on the excesses of legislative majorities (see Lowi 1971, 183–84; Schaefer 1988, 381; Lowi 1988, 403).

Reanchoring the regime securely to the rule of law would not only encourage policy makers, especially legislators, to acknowledge and even understand the constitutiveness of public administration, it would imperatively require it. Having to say something substantive about ends and means would force them to consider the consequences of what they seek to do. They could no longer hide behind broad delegations of power, which make for a government and politics empty of all but process and thus constitute the epitome of an instrumentally rational, or "mechanistic," conception of governance (Lowi 1979, 63). Instead, legislators would have to consider the implications of their ends for the character and conduct of the citizenry and its relationship to government. This in turn would require them to think about implementation, about what administrators would actually do, and about how much and what kind of independent judgment would be left up to administration. The ansers to these queries would indicate to them what might be the independent formative impact of administering the policies they devised, that is, the potential consequences of their pursuits.

It is unlikely that this alternative conceptual schema will appear full-blown in the heads of many legislators, but neither would it require that moral and intellectual giants be elected to Congress or to state legislatures. It would emerge from the deliberation that is the hallmark of representative bodies made up of average politicians who collectively possess a diversity of talents and limitations, including more than a modicum of demagoguery (see Bessette 1994; also Elkin 1993b, 134–35). The deliberation, and the result, would therefore frequently be rushed, short-changed, manipulated, and flawed. Elected executives, courts, and administrative agencies operating under the rule of law could, however, provide some of the necessary correctives through their experience and expertise, which, for perhaps the first time, would be cumulative, and through their own well-developed conceptions of what the law, and the Constitution, require. Moreover, Martha Derthick's proposed analyses of administrative capabilities would, under the rule of law, help legislators avoid major mistakes; and the policy makers would have the incentive to support such modest analytical efforts, because, in operating with fidelity to the rule of law, they would demand information and analysis on administrative capacity so that they could choose more carefully and articulate more clearly the ends they sought and the means to be employed. They could also better assess administrative experience with policy operations and policy outcomes.

Legal Formalism and Administration in Clean Air Politics

My own interpretation of the functioning of juridical democracy may seem to many to be decidedly Pollyannaish. Analyses of one particularly prominent public policy case—national air pollution control—reinforce Lowi's assessment of the pitfalls of inadequate adherence to a rule-of-law criterion. The case also lends some empirical support to Lowi's conception of how Congress and administrative agencies would operate and interact if greater commitment to clarity and substance in lawmaking held sway.

In a sweeping critique of the Clean Air Act of 1970 and its impacts, David Schoenbrod (1983) concludes that the very structure of the act created the principal obstacles to its success. He classifies the 1970 Clean Air Act as a "goals statute." Goals statutes "announce goals and authorize delegates to promulgate controls on conduct in furtherance of those goals" (751). Schoenbrod finds this approach to policy design prominent, albeit not unique, in environmental policy and related social regulatory arenas (755).

The impact of a goals approach is distinctive, because it is "written on the relatively abstract level of social priorities rather than conduct" (Schoenbrod 1983, 753). Thus, even though it had "supposedly specific action-forcing procedures," as a goals statute the Clean Air Act's abstractions generated "contention among experts" and masked "the disparate expectations of lay persons." More serious, the act promised benefits without allocating costs, created rights without assigning duties, and, as a result of both, facilitated "wishful thinking in public opinion and legislation" (754).

The underlying reason for these effects was Congress's "refusal to make choices about the present" (Schoenbrod 1983, 754). Instead, "Congress left the choice of permissible conduct to others" (751), specifically the Environmental Protection Agency (EPA), which in turn regulated the states. Hence, the Clean Air Act is really "a law that regulates government rather than sources of pollution" (742), and it places the burden for making fundamental value choices on an administrative agency, which has less visibility and clear accountability and thus less legitimacy than a legislative forum. As Schoenbrod shows, the burden on the agency, in the form of value conflicts and administrative overload and breakdown, produced unpleasant effects.

Principally, the agency was faced with having to "shrink its mandate" under the act so that it could preserve "a portion of its power" and make "the most of its limited resources" (Schoenbrod 1983, 769). It did so by using its discretion in enforcement to avoid imposing the most onerous controls and punishments the act seemed to require. In consequence, timetables were slighted, deadlines were missed, and the legal ramifications were ignored. Congress was only too happy to ratify rollbacks in subsequent legislation, making a mockery of the act's absolute promise of air quality improvement (see Melnick 1992). Worse, from an administrative standpoint, what little credibility the agency had was undermined, because the act left the impression that core value conflicts and technical questions had been resolved (Schoenbrod 1983, 790), thus making it appear that the EPA simply could not do its job of implementation. This failure, in turn, threatened the absolute right to clean air promised by the statute (also see Lowi 1995, 73–74). Moreover, without some guidance from Congress about what polluting behavior was permissible and what was impermissible, neither the EPA nor Congress could learn from the experience in a way that would help develop and refine public policy further with respect to an inevitability: the emission of substances into the atmosphere that are the byproducts of human life.

In place of goals statutes in air pollution control and elsewhere, Schoenbrod advocates the use of "rules statutes," which "state rules of conduct" (1983, 751) and thus confer obligations. The one provision in the 1970 Clean Air Act that approximates a rule of conduct, the requirement for specific emissions reductions from new car fleets, Schoenbrod credits with achieving the largest share of emissions reductions under the act (778). But Congress hedged its bets in this provision by inviting the auto industry to ask for relief if it decided it could not meet the required reductions. The 1977 amendments to the act refined this provision, because "Congress considered what the auto industry could feasibly do and set minimum standards that the industry was seriously expected to meet" (786).

Rules statutes make sure that decision-making authority for fundamental value questions rests where it can legitimately "make value judgments stick" (Schoenbrod 1983, 819), and they provide "a means for the legislature to pursue a mix of goals without conferring too broad a power on administrative agencies" (754–55). But that does not mean that administrative agencies are reduced to the role of police officers on foot patrol. Under a rules approach to air pollution control, the "EPA could have an ongoing role of proposing new rules for legislative consideration, interpreting and enforcing the rules enacted, and exercising power to impose emergency orders on an interim basis when acute risks are discovered" (804). In addition, the experience to be gained from the agency's operating under a reasonably clear, substantive set of rules would be concrete, even practical, in contrast to the "procedural and abstract" experience generated by operation under a vague yet absolute goals mandate.

In an analysis that preceded Schoenbrod's, Bruce Ackerman and William Hassler (1981) attempted to show what had gone wrong with the "technology-forcing" features of the 1970 Clean Air Act and congressional attempts to adjust them in 1977 amendments. For comparison, they used the New Deal model of policy development and implementation, using broad delegations of authority to an insulated, expert agency. They concluded that Congress's attempts to "go beyond the New Deal" in institutional design by creating agencies subject to greater political control and policy direction had led, in the case of the EPA and air pollution control, to actions that were both environmentally and economically flawed. By attempting to give detailed directions to the EPA about the development and implementation of so-called "new source performance standards," Congress exceeded its technical competence and opened itself up to political manipulation by special interests which produced law and policy so bad the courts could not provide a sufficient corrective; and the EPA, because of its origins and organizational design, was not predisposed to try to make the corrections.

In their concluding assessment of the case, Ackerman and Hassler point with approval to the "ends-oriented" agency forcing evident in Sections 108 and 109 of the 1970 Clean Air Act, which did not "require Congress to indulge in instrumental judgments beyond its capacity." Instead, agency forcing generated "a process by which the ultimate aims of environmental policy" could be "clarified over time" (122–23). Ackerman and Hassler then describe how the EPA's operational experience contributed substantially to this goal development and clarification and how Congress engaged in substantial deliberation on basic value questions in 1977 as a result. They argue that the "most important contribution" of an ends-forcing strategy is to improve the quality of congressional deliberations. They see it as having the effect of focusing "congressional debate on the issues Congress is most competent to handle." Instead of indulging in "pseudotechnocratic judgment . . . , Congress [was] encouraged to concentrate on basic questions" (127). In addition, the strategy seemed to allow the EPA to engage not only in the search for means but also in the further refinement of policy ends within some general boundaries. It also encouraged Congress to assess and debate the results with one eye on the next policy step and one on the larger questions of political economy.

Schoenbrod rightly criticizes Ackerman and Hassler for advocating an approach that still fails to specify which parties will be obligated to take what action to achieve the goals the law was intended to achieve. The burden rests exclusively on the administrative agency, leaving it with the job of spelling out the rules "without the concrete guidance that both *confines and justifies* its mandate" (1983, 802, emphasis added). However, the Ackerman and Hassler analysis shows that even under the difficult circumstances created by a goals statute, the EPA contributed, through its operational experience and technical expertise, to the effort to place the fundamental value choices in the right hands, and it helped Congress to face up to making those difficult value choices. So, the EPA also helped to clarify what national purposes should be.

A goals statute approach to public policy, it must be clear, is the epitome of the instrumental conception of administration and the vicious circle of controls heaped upon controls that has resulted from that conception. In contrast, Lowi's rule-of-law criterion and Schoenbrod's rules statute approach acknowledge the constitutiveness of administration and thus its inevitable influence on policy, but they seek to place it within proper bounds to advantage policy making. In air pollution control, a more pronounced and resolute move toward adherence to the rule of law would force Congress to specify conduct as part of its decision making among competing values. This would allow the EPA to contribute even more effectively, over time and through its operational experience, to the refinement of the rules of conduct and broad national purposes.

Constitutive Administration and the Reinvigoration of Self-Government

With this assessment of the possibilities offered by the rule of law, my argument has come full circle, for the question American political leaders have faced since the beginning of the republic remains how to balance the constitutiveness of administration against its substantial instrumental character in a manner consistent with the liberal democratic structure and principles of the Constitution. Lowi's critique and his declaration of reform raised that question anew, and answered it by contending that the source of authority and legitimacy for administration at the national level is clear and unequivocal: it is delegated by Congress in statutes (see, more recently, Lowi 1993b, 262). But this authority and legitimacy can only be secured, Lowi maintains, if statutes have real substance and sufficient clarity about the rules of behavior policy makers intend them to apply, so that administration, understood as government by officials rather than by laws, is properly constrained. The failure of policy makers to ensure these basic features of law puts administration in an untenable position and destroys its authority and legitimacy. Such failure also undermines the very authority and legitimacy of the government generally. This is the situation that has obtained in what Lowi called the Second Republic of the United States. Within the boundaries of law with real substance and clarity of rule, however, administration can, indeed must, act in ways that not only serve the purposes of the law but help to shape those purposes and the character of the citizenry.

Now contrast Lowi's answer with that of John Rohr as advanced in his "normative theory of Public Administration . . . grounded in the Constitution" (Rohr 1986, 181). Rohr argues that public administrators often face situations in which the legal commands and instructions from their political superiors—the president, Congress, and the courts—are in tension or outright conflict, are insufficiently clear, or are constitutionally dubious. Indeed, even in a system where most commands are "clear and legally correct," the most important situations facing administrators are those "wherein the law empowers rather than commands," that is, where discretion is required (259–60 n. 25). These circumstances are proof,

Rohr insists, that administrators need an independent source of authority and legitimacy, and guidance for their discretion, that is grounded in the Constitution and not in statutory delegation.

For Rohr there is plenty of textual and historical evidence that the framers and developers of the American regime intended public administration to be a core institutional component of the constitutional system, even though it is referenced only indirectly in the Constitution, and then only in a subordinate capacity. This constitutional status is in fact the foundation of Rohr's conception of the independent authority, legitimacy, and guidance public administrators should recognize—the normative theory that should direct and teach them. Rohr argues for a conception of public administration as an instrumentality that is subordinate, yet professionally nonpartisan and autonomous and constitutionally independent enough to serve as a "balance wheel" among the competing branches in the separation-of-powers system. Public administration can do this by way of individual administrators or entire agencies, choosing "which of its constitutional masters it will favor at a given time on a given issue" (1986, 182). Public administrators can do this within the discretion they possess, and they may do it in a way that "favor[s] those policies that they think are most likely to promote the public interest," but this must be pursued "against the broad background of constitutional principle" (183).

The great strength of Rohr's conception is also its great weakness. Rohr wants to anchor administrative behavior in the Constitution and encourage the public, as well as public administrators, to understand and judge administrative discretion in light of basic constitutional principles. It is difficult to see how anyone could disagree that this is in close keeping with the heritage of the founding and development of the constitutional system. It is also what a people who had embraced liberal democratic constitutionalism would want. In his conception of a subordinate yet autonomous public administration choosing among constitutional superiors, however, Rohr risks promoting exactly what he professes to abhor, namely, public officials claiming stewardship of the nation and the citizenry. This, he insists, is a "threat . . . to the rule of law" (1986, 185; on the stewardship model, see Kass 1990). Lowi would not, indeed does not, approve (see 1993b, 264).

It is abundantly clear, then, that the central political "problem" public administration poses for a liberal democratic constitutional regime is that administration is the manifestation of the ability of the public—the state, if one prefers—to reach where the law cannot quite grasp and to shape the aims of the polity and the character of the citizenry beyond the expressed intent of the law. Lowi seeks to pull the reach of the state back and into line with what the law can grasp. But even he admits that this calibration can never be exact and, moreover, that public administration is central to the refinement and further clarification of substantive and rule-oriented law. Rohr seeks to legitimate the reach of the state as it stands, but also to ensure that it is guided by the higher law and purpose of the Constitution. Anything more than this, such as what Lowi seeks, means reconstructing the regime, which Rohr finds beyond the work of administrative reform (see Rohr 1986, 186; also see Bryner 1987, 216–17).

Lowi presented his proposal for juridical democracy as the initiation of a discourse intended to craft a new public philosophy. Likewise, Rohr and his companion authors of the Blacksburg Manifesto, in many ways the successors to the New Public Administration movement, promoted it as the initiation of a dialogue about the political and constitutional status of public administration (see Wamsley et al. 1990). The work of both has stimulated a substantial body of additional scholarship, and at least in the case of Lowi, political action as well. Along one important dimension, however, the political discourse and practical dialogue have not gotten very far. Political theorists and social commentators concerned with the future of liberal democratic constitutionalism have paid public administration very little heed, except, perhaps, for the concern about bureaucratic tyranny. That is a serious oversight, for any theory of democratic constitutionalism that does not incorporate, to use John Rohr's label, a "constitutional theory of public administration," is fatally deficient. Drawing on the wisdom of history and the insights of political leaders and scholars, I sketch out very briefly the foundation for such a theory, stressing the centrality of a constitutive understanding of administration.

Democratic Constitutionalism and Responsible Discretion

In a democracy, it is inevitable that the reach of the people, in the guise of the state, will exceed the grasp of the law. This places public administration at the front lines of the contact and interaction between the state and citizens, confronting administrators with numerous opportunities to exercise discretion. The values of constitutionalism—limited government and the rule of law—invariably focus the attention and concern of the people and their political representatives on controlling discretion and ensuring that administration serves designated ends. But a wholesale concern for potentially irresponsible administrative behavior leads to extraordinary efforts to exact control. These efforts are inconsistent with the reality of political life in a liberal democratic regime, and they impair effective governance. It is the value of a constitutive perspective on public administration that it shows administration, and the discretion it inevitably exercises, as not simply a necessary evil but a critical positive force in keeping the regime in good repair and guiding its further development. Recognizing the constitutiveness of administration draws political leaders and the public away from a single-minded concern for control and directs their attention toward the fostering of responsible discretion. Within a general theory of constitutionalism, then, a constitutional theory of public administration is a theory of responsible discretion.

The substantial literature on administrative ethics, from the writings of Paul Appleby onward, has essentially aimed at spelling out the principles that define a responsible administrator. But prior to any enumeration of behavioral standards, a constitutional theory of responsible discretion must be grounded in two founding tenets. First, administrative discretion, to be responsible, cannot be unlimited. If it is, it will ultimately undermine not only public administration, but the regime itself. This is Lowi's core insight. Greater adherence to the rule of law is fundamental. Despite the complexities and uncertainties of a postindustrial political economy and the worldwide commitments and influences faced by a modern nation-state, the rule of law is not too rigid or unadaptable. Moreover, it not only constrains unreasonable demands and expectations that delegation of excessive discretion might place on administration, it also returns liberal democratic politics and the accompanying obligations of citizenship to the center of the American polity. Administrative politics has its own important function in the constitution of the regime, but it is democratic politics, particularly the debate and deliberation associated with legislative forums, that must stand at center stage.

Second, within the boundaries of the rule of law, an adequate sphere of constitutionally legitimate independence for administration must be carved out. This is Rohr's central insight. He connects it to the administrator's oath of office. As important as administration's ministerial functions are to the integrity of the law, in following the commands of political superiors and fulfilling the clear purposes of the law, the discretionary function is the source of the most vital contributions administration makes to the regime. Especially when the bureaucratic form of organization dominates, it is also the source of some risk to constitutionalism and the rule of law. But as long as recognition of the constitutiveness of administration prevails among political leaders and the interested public, that risk will be part of the ongoing debate about the structure and purposes of the regime that keeps the polity vibrant.

Where the state can reach but the law cannot quite grasp, administrators need sufficient security, emanating from a constitutionally grounded legitimation of their independence and authority, to take action. Such independence, set in the context of statutes with clear, substantive rules as required by the rule of law, is in and of itself valuable. It signals broad political respect for administrators and recognition of their worth, and it provides an incentive for them to behave responsibly. This seems to be the real import of Woodrow Wilson's observation that "large powers and unhampered discretion seem to me the indispensable conditions of responsibility" (Wilson 1941, 497). The point, Wilson stressed, was to fix the task and the responsibility clearly and then permit the administrator the independence to act. To grant broad discretion without clarity, and thus to divide and diffuse it, leads to obscurity and "remissness" (498; also see Bryner 1987, 217).

Now, the action administrators choose to pursue may be action to prevent a harm or right a wrong, to fulfill the purposes of the law even if the law does not expressly command it. The action may generate practical experience about the impact of the law which will be helpful in refining both means and ends. The action may include administrators' cautioning political representatives, or even the public at large, that what is being sought by a statute is ambiguous, contradictory, or constitutionally dubious and very likely will lead to serious unintended consequences until the basic questions the issue raises are asked and answered. Finally, it may be action which allows administrators to explore the prospects for juxtaposing seemingly incompatible values, and the institutions that embody them, in ways that are mutually supportive, and thus to meet the test of efficiency and the progressive development of the regime championed by Herbert Croly.

It should be clear now that what I just described is the exercise of practical reason. Recall that administrative discretion must be grounded in accountability, which means that discretionary decisions are based on the giving of reasons linked to clear, substantive rules and to the underlying values and the democratic consensus that constitutes the public interest. A constitutional theory of public administration built on fidelity to the rule of law and a constitutionally legitimate independence defines the prerequisites for these conditions. Public administration operating within such a context can fulfill its most critical regime function: exercising practical reason and fostering its appreciation and practice among the citizenry at large. A move toward a constitutive conception of public administration in American politics and government is thus imperative, because without that understanding administration is severely hindered in the function for which it is well suited: champion of practical reason within the regime. To allow the absence of such a champion to continue is surely to put the regime in peril.

It is important to underscore, finally, that action is the key, because it lies at the heart of public administration. Administration is not a contemplative or academic enterprise. The knowledge it generates and the manner in which it is constitutive of the regime are the results of administrative action, the fulfillment of its need and obligation to act. This goes to the very heart of why it is that *practical* reason is at issue here.

The development and refinement of a constitutional theory of public administration that has as its object the promotion of practical reason through constitutionally anchored responsible discretion, rather than the prevention of an unanchored, irresponsible discretion, is critical to dispelling the sense of loss of control and endangerment to self-government that so vexes the public and political leaders in the United States. Both the public and its political representatives will be able to accept as fundamentally legitimate a status and function for public administration that includes a constitutionally grounded independence, because adherence to the rule of law will confirm the inevitable and vital constitutiveness of administration. In turn, the debilitating contradiction between the reality of administration's formative role in the regime and a doctrine of absolute instrumental subordination to political command will disappear, because the absolutist doctrine will have lost its power. The security provided by adherence to the rule of law and responsible discretion will stand in its stead.

A Vital First Step

The end of the twentieth century has revealed itself to be a time of considerable agitation and flux in American politics, with students of constitutional democracy engaged in a top-to-bottom reassessment and search for new directions, and with American political leaders calling for wide-ranging reforms. The American people are, in essence, locked in a struggle with themselves over who they are and what they will become as a political community. The extended record of their political behavior shows that Americans are a truly pragmatic people (see, for example, Flanagan and Zingale 1994, 135), whose commitment to liberal principles therefore cannot be reduced to one best way of arranging political institutions and policy choices (Anderson 1993, 110). What a tragedy it would be, then, if they so denigrated public administration as to utterly impair its capacity to assist them in their struggle to move closer to realizing their aspirations to self-government. It is the job of theory, scholarship, and political leadership to prevent the tragedy from taking place. The first step must be a broad-based, concerted effort to fashion a constitutional theory of public administration for the American regime.

References

Aberbach, Joel D. 1990. *Keeping a Watchful Eye: The Politics of Congressional Oversight.* Washington, D.C.: Brookings Institution.

Aberbach, Joel D., and Bert A. Rockman. 1988. "Mandates or Mandarins? Control and Discretion in the Modern Administrative State." *Public Administration Review* 48:606–12.

Ackerman, Bruce A., and William T. Hassler. 1981. *Clean Coal/Dirty Air.* New Haven: Yale University Press.

Adams, Guy B., Priscilla V. Bowerman, Kenneth M. Dolbeare, and Camilla Stivers. 1990. "Joining Purpose to Practice: A Democratic Identity for the Public Service." In Henry D. Kass and Bayard L. Catron, eds. *Images and Identities in Public Administration.* Newbury Park, Calif.: Sage Publications.

Altman, O. R. 1938. "American Government and Politics: Second and Third Sessions of the Seventy-fifth Congress, 1937–38." *American Political Science Review* 32 (December): 1099–1123.

Anderson, Charles W. 1990. *Pragmatic Liberalism.* Chicago: University of Chicago Press.

———. 1993. "Pragmatic Liberalism, the Rule of Law, and the Pluralist Regime." In Stephen L. Elkin and Karol Edward Soltan, eds. *A New Constitutionalism: Designing Political Institutions for a Good Society.* Chicago: University of Chicago Press.

Annals of the Congress of the United States, The. 1834. 1st Cong., part 1. Washington, D.C.: Gales and Seaton.

Appleby, Paul. 1952. *Morality and Administration in Democratic Government.* Baton Rouge: Louisiana State University Press.

Arnold, Peri E. 1986. *Making the Managerial Presidency: Comprehensive Planning, 1905–1980.* Princeton: Princeton University Press.

———. 1994. "Reform's Changing Role: The National Performance Review in Historical Context." Paper prepared for the Division of United States Studies, Woodrow Wilson International Center for Scholars, Smithsonian Institution.

Associated Press. 1995. "Republicans Attacking EPA: Agency Targeted as Regulatory Villain, Spending Cuts Sought." *Worcester Telegram and Gazette,* August 7.

Banning, Lance. 1984. "The Hamiltonian Madison: A Reconsideration." *Virginia Magazine of History and Biography* 92 (January): 3–28.

Barber, Benjamin R. 1984. *Strong Democracy: Participatory Politics for a New Age.* Berkeley: University of California Press.

Barzelay, Michael. 1992. *Breaking through Bureaucracy: A New Vision for Managing in Government.* Berkeley: University of California Press.

Benda, Peter M., and Charles H. Levine. 1988. "Reagan and the Bureaucracy: The Bequest, the Promise, and the Legacy." In Charles O. Jones, ed. *The Reagan Legacy: Promise and Performance.* Chatham, N.J.: Chatham House.

Bernstein, Marver H. 1955. *Regulating Business by Independent Commission.* Princeton: Princeton University Press.

Berry, Jeffrey. 1977. *Lobbying for the People.* Princeton: Princeton University Press.

Bessette, Joseph M. 1994. *The Mild Voice of Reason: Deliberative Democracy and American National Government.* Chicago: University of Chicago Press.

Book of the States. 1992. Lexington, Ky.: Council of State Governments.

Bragdon, Henry W. 1967. *Woodrow Wilson: The Academic Years.* Cambridge: Harvard University Press, Belknap Press.

Brand, Donald R. 1988. *Corporatism and the Rule of Law: A Study of the National Recovery Administration.* Ithaca: Cornell University Press.

———. 1989. "Reformers of the 1960s and 1970s: Modern Anti-Federalists?" In Richard A. Harris and Sidney M. Milkis, eds. *Remaking American Politics.* Boulder, Colo.: Westview Press.

Brinkley, Alan. 1989. "The New Deal and the Idea of the State." In Steve Fraser and Gary Gerstle, eds. *The Rise and Fall of the New Deal Order, 1930–1980.* Princeton: Princeton University Press.

Brown, Angela, and Aaron Wildavsky. 1984. "Implementation as Exploration." In Jeffrey L. Pressman and Aaron Wildavsky, *Implementation,* 3rd ed., expanded. Berkeley: University of California Press.

Bryner, Gary C. 1987. *Bureaucratic Discretion: Law and Policy in Federal Regulatory Agencies.* New York: Pergamon Press.

Bullock, C. J. 1895. "The Finances of the United States from 1775 to 1789, with Special Reference to the Budget." *Bulletin of the University of Wisconsin Economics, Political Science, and History Series* 1:117–273.

Burke, John P. 1986. *Bureaucratic Responsibility.* Baltimore: Johns Hopkins University Press.

Burnham, Walter Dean. 1970. *Critical Elections and the Mainsprings of American Politics.* New York: W. W. Norton.

Cain, Bruce E., and W. T. Jones. 1989. "Madison's Theory of Representation." In Bernard Grofman and Donald Wittman, eds. *The Federalist Papers and the New Institutionalism.* New York: Agathon Press.

Calabresi, Guido, and Philip Bobbitt. 1982. *Tragic Choices.* New York: W. W. Norton.

Ceaser, James W. 1993. "Reconstructing Political Science." In Stephen L. Elkin and Karol Edward Soltan, eds. *A New Constitutionalism: Designing Political Institutions for a Good Society.* Chicago: University of Chicago Press.

Chambers, John Whiteclay, II. 1980. *The Tyranny of Change: America in the Progressive Era, 1900–1917.* New York: St. Martin's Press.

Chubb, John E., and Terry M. Moe. 1990. *Politics, Markets, and America's Schools.* Washington, D.C.: Brookings Institution.

Colton, Calvin, ed. 1897. *Works of Henry Clay,* vol. 6. New York: Henry Clay Publishing.

Congressional Record. 1882. 47th Cong., 2nd sess., parts 1–3. Washington, D.C.: U.S. Government Printing Office.

Congressional Record. 1886. 49th Cong., 1st sess. Washington, D.C.: U.S. Government Printing Office.

Congressional Record. 1938. 75th Cong., 3rd sess., parts 1–6. Washington, D.C.: U.S. Government Printing Office.

Cook, Brian J. 1992. "The Representative Function of Bureaucracy: Public Administration in Constitutive Perspective." *Administration and Society* 23 (February): 403–29.

———. 1994. "Administrative Theory and Presidential Rhetoric: Woodrow Wilson and the Instruction of Public Opinion." Prepared for delivery at the 1994 annual meeting of the American Political Science Association, New York, September 1–4, 1994.

———. 1995. "At the Crossroads of the Real and the Ideal: Woodrow Wilson's Theory of Administration." *Administrative Theory and Praxis* 17 (2): 15–28.

Cook, Brian J., Jacque L. Emel, and Roger E. Kasperson. 1990. "Organizing and Managing Radioactive Waste Disposal as an Experiment." *Journal of Policy Analysis and Management* 9 (summer): 339–66.

Cooper, Terry L. 1991. *An Ethic of Citizenship for Public Administration.* Englewood Cliffs, N.J.: Prentice-Hall.

Corwin, Edward S. 1984. *The President: Office and Powers, 1787–1984,* 5th ed. New York: New York University Press.

Cox, Raymond W., III, Susan J. Buck, and Betty N. Morgan. 1994. *Public Administration in Theory and Practice.* Englewood Cliffs, N.J.: Prentice-Hall.

Crenson, Matthew A. 1975. *The Federal Machine: Beginnings of Bureaucracy in Jacksonian America.* Baltimore: Johns Hopkins University Press.

Croly, Herbert. 1914. *Progressive Democracy.* New York: Macmillan.

Dahl, Robert A. 1982. *Dilemmas of Pluralist Democracy.* New Haven: Yale University Press.

Denhardt, Robert B. 1993. *The Pursuit of Significance: Strategies for Managerial Success in Public Organizations.* Belmont, Calif.: Wadsworth.

Derthick, Martha. 1990. *Agency under Stress: The Social Security Administration in American Government.* Washington, D.C.: Brookings Institution.

Dewey, John. 1936. "A Liberal Speaks Out." *New York Times Magazine* (February 23): 3, 24.

Diamond, Ann Stuart. 1980. "Decent, Even Though Democratic." In Robert A. Goldwin and William A. Schambra, eds. *How Democratic Is the Constitution?* Washington, D.C.: American Enterprise Institute.

Diamond, Martin. 1975. "The Declaration and the Constitution: Liberty, Democracy, and the Founders." *Public Interest* 41 (fall): 39–55.

Diesing, Paul. 1962. *Reason in Society: Five Types of Decisions and Their Social Conditions.* Westport, Conn.: Greenwood Press.

Dimock, Marshall E. 1936. "Criteria and Objectives of Public Administration." In John M. Gaus, Leonard D. White, and Marshall E. Dimock, eds. *Frontiers of Public Administration.* Chicago: University of Chicago Press.

Doig, Jameson W. 1983. " 'If I See a Murderous Fellow Sharpening a Knife Cleverly . . .': The Wilsonian Dichotomy and the Public Authority Tradition." *Public Administration Review* 43 (July–August): 292–304.

Downs, Anthony. 1962. "The Public Interest: Its Meaning in a Democracy." *Social Research* 29 (spring): 1–36.

Dryzek, John S., and Jeffrey Berejikian. 1993. "Reconstructive Democratic Theory." *American Political Science Review* 87 (March): 48–60.

Durrant, Robert F. 1992. *The Administrative Presidency Revisited: Public Lands, the BLM, and the Reagan Revolution.* Albany: State University of New York Press.

Easton, David. 1971. *The Political System: An Inquiry into the State of Political Science,* 2nd ed. Chicago: University of Chicago Press.

Eden, Robert. 1989a. "Introduction: A Legacy of Questions." In Robert Eden, ed., *The New Deal and Its Legacy: Critique and Reappraisal.* Westport, Conn.: Greenwood Press.

———. 1989b. "Dealing Democratic Honor Out: Reform and the Decline of Consensus Politics." In Richard A. Harris and Sidney M. Milkis, eds. *Remaking American Politics.* Boulder, Colo.: Westview Press.

Eisner, Marc Allen. 1993. "Demobilization and Development: Models of the State and the Reformation of the U.S. Political Economy in the Interwar Period." Paper prepared for delivery at the New England Political Science Association annual meeting, Northhampton, Mass., April 3–4, 1993.

Elkin, Stephen L. 1985. "Economic and Political Rationality." *Polity* 18:253–71.

———. 1987. *City and Regime in the American Republic.* Chicago: University of Chicago Press.

———. 1993a. "Constitutionalism: Old and New." In Stephen L. Elkin and Karol Edward Soltan, eds. *A New Constitutionalism: Designing Political Institutions for a Good Society.* Chicago: University of Chicago Press.

———. 1993b. "Constitutionalism's Successor." In Stephen L. Elkin and Karol Edward Soltan, eds. *A New Constitutionalism: Designing Political Institutions for a Good Society.* Chicago: University of Chicago Press.

Elkin, Stephen L., and Brian J. Cook. 1985. "The Public Life of Economic Incentives." *Policy Studies Journal* 13 (June): 797–813.

Elkins, Stanley, and Eric McKitrick. 1993. *The Age of Federalism.* New York: Oxford University Press.

Finer, Herman. 1941. "Administrative Responsibility in Democratic Government." *Public Administration Review* 1 (summer): 3–35.

Fiorina, Morris P. 1986. "Legislator Uncertainty, Legislative Control, and the Delegation of Legislative Power." *Journal of Law, Economics, and Organization* 2:33–51.

———. 1989. *Congress: Keystone of the Washington Establishment,* 2nd ed. New Haven: Yale University Press.

Fisher, Louis. 1985. *Constitutional Conflicts between Congress and the President.* Princeton: Princeton University Press.

Flanigan, William H., and Nancy H. Zingale. 1994. *Political Behavior of the American Electorate,* 8th ed. Washington, D.C.: Congressional Quarterly Books, CQ Press.

Flaumenhaft, Harvey. 1981. "Hamilton's Administrative Republic and the American Presidency." In Joseph M. Bessette and Jeffrey Tulis, eds. *The Presidency in the Constitutional Order.* Baton Rouge: Louisiana State University Press.

Flexner, James T. 1969. *George Washington and the New Nation (1783–93).* Boston: Little, Brown.

Foresta, Ronald A. 1984. *America's National Parks and Their Keepers.* Washington, D.C.: Resources for the Future.

Fowler, Dorothy Garfield. 1943. *The Cabinet Politician: The Postmaster General, 1829–1909.* New York: Columbia University Press.

Frederickson, H. George, and David G. Frederickson. 1995. "Public Perceptions of Ethics in Government." *The Annals of the American Academy of Political and Social Science* 536 (January): 163–72.

Freidel, Frank. 1990. *Franklin D. Roosevelt: A Rendezvous with Destiny.* Boston: Little, Brown.

Friedrich, Carl J. 1940. "Public Policy and the Nature of Administrative Responsibility." In Carl J. Friedrich and Edward S. Mason, eds. *Public Policy,* vol. 1. Cambridge: Harvard University Press.

Garvey, Gerald. 1993. *Facing the Bureaucracy: Living and Dying in a Public Agency.* San Francisco: Jossey-Bass.

Ginsberg, Benjamin, and Elizabeth Sanders. 1990. "Theodore J. Lowi and Juridical Democracy." *PS: Political Science and Politics* 23 (December): 563–66.

Ginsberg, Benjamin, and Martin Shefter. 1990. *Politics by Other Means: The Declining Importance of Elections in America.* New York: Basic Books.

Goldsmith, William M. 1974. *The Growth of Presidential Power,* vol. 1. New York: Chelsea House.

Goodsell, Charles T. 1990. "Public Administration and the Public Interest." In Gary L. Wamsley et al., *Refounding Public Administration.* Newbury Park, Calif.: Sage Publications.

———. 1994. *The Case for Bureaucracy: A Public Administration Polemic,* 3rd ed. Chatham, N.J.: Chatham House.

Gore, Al. 1993. *From Red Tape to Results: Creating a Government that Works Better and Costs Less.* Report of the National Performance Review. Washington, D.C.: U.S. Government Printing Office.

Green, Richard T. 1990. "Alexander Hamilton and the Study of Public Administration." *Public Administration Quarterly* 13 (4): 494–510.

Green, Richard T., Lawrence F. Keller, and Gary L. Wamsley. 1993. "Reconstituting a Profession for American Public Administration." *Public Administration Review* 53 (November–December): 516–24.

Gruber, Judith E. 1987. *Controlling Bureaucracies: Dilemmas in Democratic Governance.* Berkeley: University of California Press.

Gulick, Luther, and Lyndall Urwick. 1937. *Papers on the Science of Administration.* New York: Institute of Public Administration.

Hall, Chester Gordon, Jr. 1965. "The United States Civil Service Commission: Arm of the President or Congress?" Unpublished Ph.D. dissertation, American University.

Hardin, Russell. 1989. "Why a Constitution?" In Bernard Grofman and Donald Whitman, eds. *The Federalist Papers and the New Institutionalism.* New York: Agathon Press.

Harris, Richard A., and Sidney M. Milkis. 1986. "Programmatic Liberalism, the Administrative State, and the Constitution." Paper prepared for delivery at the annual meeting of the American Political Science Association, Washington, D.C., August 31–September 3.

———. 1989. *The Politics of Regulatory Change: A Tale of Two Agencies.* New York: Oxford University Press.

Hays, Samuel P. 1987. *Beauty, Truth, and Permanence: Environmental Politics in the United States, 1955–1985.* Cambridge: Cambridge University Press.

Heclo, Hugh. 1989. "The Emerging Regime." In Richard A. Harris and Sidney M. Milkis, eds. *Remaking American Politics.* Boulder, Colo.: Westview Press.

Henig, Jeffrey R. 1994. *Rethinking School Choice: Limits of the Market Metaphor.* Princeton: Princeton University Press.

Henry, Nicholas L. 1990. "Root and Branch: Public Administration's Travail toward the Future." In Naomi B. Lynn and Aaron Wildavsky, eds. *Public Administration: The State of the Discipline*. Chatham, N.J.: Chatham House.

Herson, Lawrence J. R. 1984. *The Politics of Ideas: Political Theory and American Public Policy*. Homewood, Ill.: Dorsey Press.

Hill, Larry B. 1992. "Taking Bureaucracy Seriously." In Larry B. Hill, ed. *The State of Public Bureaucracy*. Armonk, N.Y.: M. E. Sharpe.

Hirschman, Albert O. 1970. *Exit, Voice, and Loyalty: Responses to Decline in Firms, Organizations, and States*. Cambridge: Harvard University Press.

Hoogenboom, Ari. 1961. *Outlawing the Spoils: A History of the Civil Service Reform Movement, 1865–1883*. Urbana: University of Illinois Press.

Huntington, Samuel P. 1952. "The Marasmus of the ICC." *Yale Law Journal* 61 (April): 467–509.

Hyneman, Charles S., and George W. Carey, eds. 1967. *A Second Federalist: Congress Creates a Government*. New York: Appleton-Century-Crofts.

Karl, Barry D. 1963. *Executive Reorganization and Reform in the New Deal: The Genesis of Administrative Management*. Cambridge: Harvard University Press.

———. 1983. *The Uneasy State: The United States from 1915 to 1945*. Chicago: University of Chicago Press.

———. 1987. "The American Bureaucrat: A History of a Sheep in Wolves' Clothing." *Public Administration Review* 47 (January–February): 26–34.

———. 1989. "The Constitution and Central Planning: The Third New Deal Revisited." In Philip B. Kurland, Gerhard Casper, and Dennis J. Hutchinson, eds. *The Supreme Court Review, 1988*. Chicago: University of Chicago Press.

Kass, Henry D. 1990. "Stewardship as a Fundamental Element in Images of Public Administration." In Henry D. Kass and Bayard L. Catron, eds. *Images and Identities in Public Administration*. Newbury Park, Calif.: Sage Publications.

Katz, Daniel, Barbara A. Gutek, Robert L. Kahn, and Eugenia Barton. 1975. *Bureaucratic Encounters*. Ann Arbor: Institute for Social Research, University of Michigan.

Kaufman, Herbert. 1965. "The Growth of the Federal Personnel System." In Wallace S. Sayre, ed. *The Federal Government Service*. Englewood Cliffs, N.J.: Prentice-Hall.

Kessler, Charles R. 1989. "The Public Philosophy of the New Freedom and the New Deal." In Robert Eden, ed. *The New Deal and Its Legacy: Critique and Reappraisal*. Westport, Conn.: Greenwood Press.

Kettl, Donald F. 1988. *Government by Proxy: (Mis?)Managing Federal Programs*. Washington, D.C.: Congressional Quarterly Books, CQ Press.

———. 1993. *Sharing Power: Public Governance and Private Markets*. Washington, D.C.: Brookings Institution.

Kingdon, John W. 1995. *Agendas, Alternatives, and Public Policies*, 2nd ed. New York: HarperCollins College.

Kirwin, Kent A. 1987. "Woodrow Wilson and the Study of Public Administration: Response to Van Riper." *Administration and Society* 18 (February): 389–401.

Kohl, Lawrence Frederick. 1989. *The Politics of Individualism: Parties and the American Character in the Jacksonian Era.* New York: Oxford University Press.

Kolko, Gabriel. 1965. *Railroads and Regulation, 1877–1916.* New York: W. W. Norton.

Kravchuk, Robert S. 1992. "Liberalism and the American Administrative State." *Public Administration Review* 52 (July–August): 374–79.

Krislov, Samuel, and David H. Rosenbloom. 1981. *Representative Bureaucracy and the American Political System.* New York: Praeger.

Landis, James M. 1938. *The Administrative Process.* New Haven: Yale University Press.

Landy, Marc K., Marc J. Roberts, and Stephen L. Thomas. 1990. *The Environmental Protection Agency: Asking the Wrong Questions.* New York: Oxford University Press.

Lane, Robert E. 1981. "Markets and Politics: The Human Product." *British Journal of Political Science* 1 (January): 1–16.

Lasswell, Harold D. 1936. *Politics: Who Gets What, When, and How.* New York: McGraw-Hill.

Leiss, William. 1990. *Under Technology's Thumb.* Toronto: McGill-Queen's University Press.

Leopold, A. Starker, Stanley A. Cain, Clarence M. Cottam, Ira N. Gabrielson, and Thomas L. Kimball. 1963. "Wildlife Management in the National Parks." Washington, D.C.: Wildlife Management Institute.

Lindblom, Charles E. 1980. *The Policy-Making Process,* 2nd ed. Englewood Cliffs, N.J.: Prentice-Hall.

Link, Arthur S., ed. 1969. *The Papers of Woodrow Wilson.* Princeton: Princeton University Press.

Long, Norton E. 1952. "Bureaucracy and Constitutionalism." *American Political Science Review* 46 (September): 808–18.

———. 1990. "Conceptual Notes on the Public Interest for Public Administration and Policy Analysis." *Administration and Society* 22 (August): 170–81.

Lowi, Theodore J. 1964. "American Business, Public Policy, Case Studies, and Political Theory." *World Politics* 16 (July): 677–715.

———. 1971. "A Reply to Mansfield." *Public Policy* 19 (winter): 207–11.

———. 1972. "Four Systems of Policy, Politics, and Choice." *Public Administration Review* 32 (July–August): 298–310.

———. 1979. *The End of Liberalism,* 2nd ed. New York: W. W. Norton.

———. 1985. *The Personal President: Power Invested, Promise Unfulfilled.* Ithaca: Cornell University Press.

———. 1988. "Response to Schaefer." *Administration and Society* 19 (February): 399–412.

————. 1993a. "Two Roads to Serfdom: Liberalism, Conservatism, and Administrative Power." In Stephen L. Elkin and Karol Edward Soltan, eds. *A New Constitutionalism: Designing Political Institutions for a Good Society.* Chicago: University of Chicago Press.

————. 1993b. "Legitimizing Public Administration: A Disturbed Dissent." *Public Administration Review* 53 (May–June): 261–64.

————. 1995. *The End of the Republican Era.* Norman: University of Oklahoma Press.

Lowi, Theodore J., and Benjamin Ginsberg. 1990. *American Government: Freedom and Power.* New York: W. W. Norton.

Maass, Arthur A., and Lawrence I. Radway. 1959. "Gauging Administrative Responsibility." In Dwight Waldo, ed. *Ideas and Issues in Public Administration.* New York: McGraw-Hill.

MacIntyre, Alasdair. 1981. *After Virtue: A Study in Moral Theory.* South Bend, Ind.: University of Notre Dame Press.

Macmahon, Arthur W. 1958. "Woodrow Wilson: Political Leader and Administrator." In Earl Latham, ed. *The Philosophy and Policies of Woodrow Wilson.* Chicago: University of Chicago Press.

Mainzer, Lewis C. 1994. "Public Administration in Search of a Theory: The Interdisciplinary Delusion." *Adminstration and Society* 26 (November): 359–94.

Maranto, Robert. 1991. "Thinking the Unthinkable in Public Administration: A Case for the Spoils System." Presented at the annual meeting of the American Political Science Association, Washington, D.C., September 1–4.

Marini, Frank. 1971. *Toward a New Public Administration.* Scranton, Pa.: Chandler Publications.

Marshall, Lynn. 1967. "The Strange Stillbirth of the Whig Party." *American Historical Review* 72 (January): 445–68.

Martin, Daniel W. 1988. "The Fading Legacy of Woodrow Wilson." *Public Administration Review* 48 (March–April): 631–36.

Marx, Fritz Morstein. 1957. *The Administrative State.* Chicago: University of Chicago Press.

McCubbins, Mathew, and Thomas Schwartz. 1984. "Congressional Oversight Overlooked: Police Patrols versus Fire Alarms." *American Journal of Political Science* 28 (February): 165–79.

McWilliams, Wilson Carey. 1995. *The Politics of Disappointment: American Elections, 1976–94.* Chatham, N.J.: Chatham House.

Meier, Kenneth J. 1993. *Politics and the Bureaucracy: Policymaking in the Fourth Branch of Government,* 3rd ed. Pacific Grove, Calif.: Brooks/Cole Publishing.

Melnick, R. Shep. 1989. "The Courts, Congress, and Programmatic Rights." In Richard A. Harris, and Sidney M. Milkis, eds. *Remaking American Politics.* Boulder, Colo.: Westview Press.

————. 1992. "Pollution Deadlines and the Coalition for Failure." In Michael S.

Greve and Fred L. Smith, Jr., eds. *Environmental Politics: Public Costs, Private Rewards.* New York: Praeger.

Milkis, Sidney M. 1993. *The President and the Parties: The Transformation of the American Party System since the New Deal.* New York: Oxford University Press.

Milkis, Sidney M., and Michael Nelson. 1994. *The American Presidency: Origins and Development, 1776–1993.* Washington, D.C.: Congressional Quarterly Books, CQ Press.

Milkis, Sidney M., and Daniel J. Tichenor. 1993. "The Progressive Party and Social Reformers: The 'Critical' Election of 1912." Paper prepared for delivery at the 1993 annual meeting of the American Political Science Association, Washington D.C., September 2–5.

Miller, James. 1987. *Democracy Is in the Streets: From Port Huron to the Siege of Chicago.* New York: Simon and Schuster.

Mitchell, T. R., and W. G. Scott. 1987. "Leadership Failures, the Distrusting Public, and Prospects of the Administrative State." *Public Administration Review* 47 (November/December): 445–52.

Moe, Ronald C. 1994. "The 'Reinventing Government' Exercise: Misinterpreting the Problem, Misjudging the Consequences." *Public Administration Review* 54 (March–April): 111–22.

Moe, Terry M. 1989. "The Politics of Bureaucratic Structure." In John E. Chubb and Paul E. Peterson, eds. *Can the Government Govern?* Washington, D.C.: Brookings Institution.

Morgan, Douglas F. 1990. "Administrative Phronesis: Discretion and the Problem of Administrative Legitimacy in Our Constitutional System." In Henry D. Kass and Bayard L. Catron, eds. *Images and Identities in Public Administration.* Newbury Park, Calif.: Sage Publications.

Morone, James A. 1985. "Representation without Elections: The American Bureaucracy and Its Publics." In Bruce Jennings and Daniel Callahan, eds. *Representation and Responsibility: Exploring Legislative Ethics.* New York: Plenum Press.

———. 1990. *The Democratic Wish: Popular Participation and the Limits of American Government.* New York: Basic Books.

Mosher, Frederick C. 1968. *Democracy and the Public Service.* New York: Oxford University Press.

———. 1978. "Professions in Public Service." *Public Administration Review* 38 (March–April): 120–26.

Munro, William Bennett. 1930. *The Makers of the Unwritten Constitution.* New York: Macmillan.

Nardulli, Peter F. 1992. "The Constitution and American Politics: A Developmental Perspective." In Peter F. Nardulli, ed. *The Constitution and American Political Development: An Institutional Perspective.* Urbana: University of Illinois Press.

Nathan, Richard. 1975. *The Plot That Failed: Nixon and the Administrative Presidency.* New York: John Wiley.

———. 1983. *The Administrative Presidency.* New York: John Wiley.

Nelson, Michael. 1982. "A Short, Ironic History of American National Bureaucracy." *Journal of Politics* 44 (2): 747–78.

Nelson, Richard R. 1977. *The Moon and the Ghetto: An Essay on Public Policy Analysis.* New York: W. W. Norton.

Nelson, William E. 1982. *The Roots of American Bureaucracy, 1830–1900.* Cambridge: Harvard University Press.

Okun, Arthur M. 1975. *Equality and Efficiency: The Big Tradeoff.* Washington, D.C.: Brookings Institution.

"Opinion Roundup: The Role of Government." 1987. *Public Opinion* (March–April): 21–29.

Ornstein, Norman J., and Shirley Elder. 1978. *Interest Groups, Lobbying and Policymaking.* Washington, D.C.: Congressional Quarterly Books, CQ Press.

Osborne, David, and Ted Gaebler. 1992. *Reinventing Government.* Reading, Mass.: Addison-Wesley.

Ostrom, Vincent. 1987. *The Political Theory of a Compound Republic: Designing the American Experiment,* 2nd ed. Lincoln: University of Nebraska Press.

Page, Benjamin I., and Robert Y. Shapiro. 1989. "Restraining the Whims and Passions of the Public." In Bernard Grofman and Donald Wittman, eds. *The Federalist Papers and the New Institutionalism.* New York: Agathon Press.

Patterson, James T. 1967. *Congressional Conservatism and the New Deal.* Lexington: University of Kentucky Press.

Pennock, J. Roland. 1962. "The One and the Many: A Note on the Concept." In Carl J. Friedrich, ed. *The Public Interest, Nomos V.* New York: Atherton.

Peters, Charles. 1979. "A Kind Word for the Spoils System." In Charles Peters and Michael Nelson, eds. *The Culture of Bureaucracy.* New York: Holt, Rhinehart, and Winston.

Phillips, Kevin. 1993. *Boiling Point: Republicans, Democrats, and the Decline of Middle-Class Prosperity.* New York: Random House.

Pitkin, Hanna Fenichel. 1967. *The Concept of Representation.* Berkeley: University of California Press.

Pohlenberg, Richard. 1966. *Reorganizing Roosevelt's Government.* Cambridge: Harvard University Press.

Posner, Richard A. 1974. "Theories of Economic Regulation." *Bell Journal of Economics and Management Science* 5 (autumn): 335–58.

"Public Opinion and Demographic Report." 1993. *The Public Perspective* 4 (March–April): 82–104.

Purcell, Edward, Jr. 1967. "Ideas and Interests: Business and the Interstate Commerce Act." *Journal of American History* 54: 561–78.

Register of Debates in Congress. 1848a. 23rd Cong., 2nd sess., part 1. Washington, D.C.: Gales and Seaton.

Register of Debates in Congress. 1848b. 23rd Cong., 2nd sess., part 2. Washington, D.C.: Gales and Seaton.

Reich, Robert B. 1988. "Policy Making in a Democracy." In Robert B. Reich, ed. *The Power of Public Ideas.* Cambridge, Mass.: Ballinger.

Richardson, James D. 1911. *A Compilation of the Messages and Papers of the Presidents.* 11 vols. Washington, D.C.: Bureau of National Literature. (N.B.: 1897 original has 18 vols. paged in one sequence.)

Rogers, Lindsay. 1938. "Reorganization: Post Mortem Notes." *Political Science Quarterly* 53 (June): 161–72.

Rohr, John A. 1986. *To Run a Constitution: The Legitimacy of the Administrative State.* Lawrence: University Press of Kansas.

———. 1989a. "Public Administration, Executive Power, and Constitutional Confusion." *Public Administration Review* 49 (March–April): 108–14.

———. 1989b. *The President and the Public Administration.* Washington, D.C.: American Historical Association.

———. 1989c. *Ethics for Bureaucrats: An Essay on Law and Values,* 2nd ed. New York: Marcel Dekker.

Roosevelt, Franklin D. 1938. *The Public Papers and Addresses of Franklin D. Roosevelt.* Vol. 5. New York: Random House.

Roper, Burns W. 1994. "Democracy in America: How Are We Doing? We're Doing Our Best to Make the Answer 'Badly'." *The Public Perspective* 5 (March–April): 3–5.

Rosenbaum, Walter A. 1995. *Environmental Politics and Policy,* 3rd ed. Washington, D.C.: Congressional Quarterly Books, CQ Press.

Rosenbloom, David H. 1971. *Federal Service and the Constitution: The Development of the Public Employment Relationship.* Ithaca: Cornell University Press.

———. 1992. "Democratic Constitutionalism and the Evolution of Bureaucratic Government: Freedom and Accountability in the Administrative State." In Peter F. Nardulli, ed. *The Constitution and American Political Development: An Institutional Perspective.* Urbana: University of Illinois Press.

Rossiter, Clinton. 1962. *Conservatism in America: The Thankless Persuasion,* 2nd ed., rev'd. New York: Knopf.

Rourke, Francis E. 1984. *Bureaucracy, Politics, and Public Policy.* 3rd ed. Boston: Little, Brown.

———. 1991. "American Bureaucracy in a Changing Political Setting." *Journal of Public Administration Research and Theory,* 1 (2): 111–29.

———. 1992. "American Exceptionalism: Government without Bureaucracy." In Larry B. Hill, ed. *The State of Public Bureaucracy.* Armonk, N.Y.: M. E. Sharpe.

Salamon, Lester M., ed. 1989. *Beyond Privatization: The Tools of Government Action.* Washington, D.C.: Urban Institute Press.

Salant, Jonathan D. 1995. "Senate Passes Spending Bill for Legislative Branch." *Congressional Quarterly Weekly Report* 53 (July 22): 2142–44.

Sandel, Michael J. 1988. "The Political Theory of the Procedural Republic." In Robert B. Reich, ed. *The Power of Public Ideas*. Cambridge, Mass.: Ballinger.

Sanders, Jennings B. 1935. *Evolution of Executive Departments of the Continental Congress 1774–1789*. Chapel Hill: University of North Carolina Press.

Savas, E. S. 1987. *Privatization: The Key to Better Government*. Chatham, N.J.: Chatham House.

Schaefer, David Lewis. 1988. "Theodore Lowi and the Administrative State." *Administration and Society* 19 (February): 371–98.

Schattschneider, E. E. 1960. *The Semi-Sovereign People: A Realist's View of Democracy in America*. New York: Holt, Rhinehart, and Winston.

Schoenbrod, David. 1983. "Goals Statutes or Rules Statutes: The Case of the Clean Air Act." *UCLA Law Review* 30 (April): 740–828.

Schultze, Charles L. 1977. *The Public Use of Private Interest*. Washington, D.C.: Brookings Institution.

Schwartz, Nancy L. 1988. *The Blue Guitar: Political Representation and Community*. Chicago: University of Chicago Press.

Schwartz, Thomas. 1989. "Checks, Balances, and Bureaucratic Usurpation of Congressional Power." In Bernard Grofman and Donald Wittman, eds. *The Federalist Papers and the New Institutionalism*. New York: Agathon Press.

Sedgwick, Jeffrey Leigh. 1987. "Of Centennials and Bicentennials: Reflections on the Foundations of American Public Administration." *Administration and Society* 19 (November): 285–308.

Seidenfeld, Mark. 1992. "A Civic Republican Justification for the Bureaucratic State." *Harvard Law Review* 105: 1512–76.

Seidman, Harold, and Robert Gilmour. 1986. *Politics, Position, and Power: From the Positive to the Regulatory State*, 4th ed. New York: Oxford University Press.

Shapiro, Martin. 1986. "APA: Past, Present, and Future." *Virginia Law Review* 72:460–520.

Short, Lloyd Milton. 1923. *The Development of National Administrative Organization in the United States*. Baltimore: Johns Hopkins Press.

Skowronek, Stephen. 1982. *Building a New American State: The Expansion of Administrative Capacities, 1877–1920*. New York: Cambridge University Press.

Stewart, Richard B. 1975. "The Reformation of Administrative Law." *Harvard Law Review* 88:1669–1813.

Stillman, Richard J. 1991. *Preface to Public Administration: A Search for Themes and Direction*. New York: St. Martin's Press.

Stivers, Camilla M. 1990. "Active Citizenship and Public Administration." In Gary L. Wamsley et al., *Refounding Public Administration*. Newbury Park, Calif.: Sage Publications.

Stone, Clarence N. 1985. "Efficiency versus Social Learning: A Reconsideration of the Implementation Process." *Policy Studies Review* 4 (February): 484–90.

Stone, Deborah A. 1988. *Policy Paradox and Political Reason.* Boston: Scott, Foresman/Little Brown.

Storing, Herbert J. 1980. "American Statesmanship: Old and New." In Robert A. Goldwin, ed. *Bureaucrats, Policy Analysts, Statesmen: Who Leads?* Washington, D.C.: American Enterprise Institute.

———. 1981. *What the Anti-Federalists Were For.* Chicago: University of Chicago Press.

Swift, Elaine K. 1993. "The Making of an American House of Lords: The U.S. Senate in the Constitutional Convention of 1787." *Studies in American Political Development* 7 (fall): 177–224.

Terkel, Studs. 1984. *"The Good War": An Oral History of World War Two.* New York: Pantheon Books.

Terry, Larry D. 1990. "Leadership in the Administrative State: The Concept of Administrative Conservatorship." *Administration and Society* 21 (February): 395–412.

Thach, Charles, C., Jr. 1922. *The Creation of the Presidency, 1775–1789.* Baltimore: Johns Hopkins Press.

Tocqueville, Alexis de. 1945. *Democracy in America.* Translated by Henry Reeve, edited by Phillips Bradley. 1835. Reprint, New York: Vintage Books.

———. 1988. *Democracy in America.* Translated by George Lawrence, edited by J. P. Mayer. New York: Perennial Library.

Tribe, Laurence. 1973. "Technology Assessment and the Fourth Discontinuity." *Southern California Law Review* 46 (June): 617–60.

Truman, David B. 1971. *The Governmental Process: Political Interests and Public Opinion,* 2nd ed. New York: A. A. Knopf.

Tulis, Jeffrey K. 1987. *The Rhetorical Presidency.* Princeton: Princeton University Press.

Van Riper, Paul P. 1958. *History of the United States Civil Service.* Evanston, Ill.: Row, Peterson.

———. 1983. "The American Administrative State: Wilson and the Founders— An Unorthodox View." *Public Administration Review* 43 (November–December): 477–90.

van Wagtendonk, Jan W. 1991. "The Evolution of National Park Service Fire Policy." *Fire Management Notes* 52 (4): 10–15.

Wamsley, Gary L., Robert N. Bacher, Charles T. Goodsell, Philip S. Kronenberg, John A. Rohr, Camilla M. Stivers, Orion F. White, and James F. Wolf. 1990. *Refounding Public Administration.* Newbury Park, Calif.: Sage Publications.

Weaver, R. Kent. 1988. *Automatic Government: The Politics of Indexation.* Washington, D.C.: Brookings Institution.

Weber, Gustavus A. 1919. *Organized Efforts for the Improvement of Methods of Administration in the United States.* New York: D. Appleton.

Wharton, Francis. 1889. *The Revolutionary Diplomatic Correspondence of the United States.* (N.p.)

White, Jay D. 1990. "Images of Administrative Reason and Rationality: The Recovery of Practical Wisdom. In Henry D. Kass and Bayard L. Catron, eds. *Images and Identities in Public Administration.* Newbury Park, Calif.: Sage.

White, Leonard D. 1948. *The Federalists: A Study in Administrative History.* New York: Macmillan.

———. 1951. *The Jeffersonians: A Study in Administrative History.* New York: Macmillan.

———. 1954. *The Jacksonians: A Study in Administrative History.* New York: Macmillan.

Wiebe, Robert H. 1967. *The Search for Order: 1877–1920.* New York: Hill and Wang.

Will, George F. 1991. "If Saddam Survives, He Wins." *Washington Post.* January 27, C7.

Wills, Garry. 1994. "What Makes a Good Leader?" *Atlantic Monthly* 273 (April): 63–80.

Wilson, James Q. 1975. "The Rise of the Bureaucratic State." *The Public Interest* 41 (fall): 77–103.

———. 1980. "The Politics of Regulation." In James Q. Wilson, ed. *The Politics of Regulation.* New York: Basic Books.

———. 1989. *Bureaucracy: What Government Agencies Do and Why They Do It.* New York: Basic Books.

———. 1990. "Juridical Democracy versus American Democracy." *PS: Political Science and Politics* 23 (December): 570–72.

———. 1992. *American Government: Institutions and Policies,* 5th ed. Lexington, Mass.: D. C. Heath.

———. 1994. "Can the Bureaucracy Be Deregulated?" In John J. DiIulio, ed. *Deregulating the Public Service: Can Government Be Improved?* Washington, D.C.: Brookings Institution.

Wilson, Woodrow. 1908. *Constitutional Government in the United States.* New York: Columbia University Press.

———. 1941. "The Study of Administration." 1887. Reprinted in *Political Science Quarterly* 56:481–506.

———. 1981. *Congressional Government: A Study in American Politics.* 1885. Reprint, Baltimore: Johns Hopkins University Press.

Wiltse, Charles M., and David G. Allen, eds. 1977. *The Papers of Daniel Webster: Correspondence.* Vol. 3. Hanover, N.H.: University Press of New England.

Wiltse, Charles M., and Alan R. Berolzheimer, eds. 1988. *The Papers of Daniel*

Webster: Speeches and Formal Writings. Vol. 2. Hanover, N.H.: University Press of New England.

Wood, B. Dan. 1988. "Principals, Bureaucrats, and Responsiveness in Clean Air Enforcements." *American Political Science Review* 82 (March): 213–34.

Wood, Gordon S. 1980. "Democracy and the Constitution." In Robert A. Goldwin and William A. Schambra, eds. *How Democratic Is the Constitution?* Washington, D.C.: American Enterprise Institute.

Yates, Douglas. 1982. *Bureaucratic Democracy: The Search for Democracy and Efficiency in American Government.* Cambridge: Harvard University Press.

Zinsmeister, Karl. 1995a. "Indicators: Revolt against Government." *The American Enterprise* (March–April): 16.

———. 1995b. "Indicators: Do Americans Really Fear Their Government?" *The American Enterprise* (July–August): 16.

Index

Library of Congress Cataloging-in-Publication Data
Cook, Brian J., 1954–
   Bureaucracy and self-government : reconsidering the role of public
administration in American politics / Brian J. Cook.
      p.   cm. — (Interpreting American politics)
   Includes bibliographical references and index.
   ISBN 0-8018-5409-1 (hardcover : alk. paper). — ISBN 0-8018-5410-5
(pbk. : alk. paper)
   1. Bureaucracy—United States—History.   2. Public administration —
representation—United States—History.   4. United States—Politics and
government.   I. Title.   II. Series.
JK411.C66   1997   96-20325
350´ .00973—dc20